Saving the Marin-Sonoma Coast

The Battles for Audubon Canyon Ranch, Point Reyes, and California's Russian River

by L. Martin Griffin, M.D.

FOREWORD BY HAROLD GILLIAM

SWEETWATER SPRINGS PRESS
HEALDSBURG, CALIFORNIA

ISBN 0-9661680-2-X Cloth
ISBN 0-9661680-1-1 Paper
Library of Congress Number 97-062072

Published and distributed by
SWEETWATER SPRINGS PRESS
P.O. Box 66
Healdsburg, CA 95448
(707) 431-1910
(707) 433-8162 FAX

Available from
Audubon Canyon Ranch Bookstore
4900 Shoreline Highway
Stinson Beach, CA 94970
(415) 868-9244
(415) 868-1699 FAX
http://www.egret.org

Designed by Robert Cooney
Composition by Archetype Typography
Logo by Debra Turner
Printed in Canada

Cover photograph by Robert Campbell.
Back cover photographs by Clerin Zumwalt and Julia Macdonald.
Photographic credits can be found on page 274.

To my dear family, and to those in grassroots organizations who are attempting to bring environmental sanity to their counties

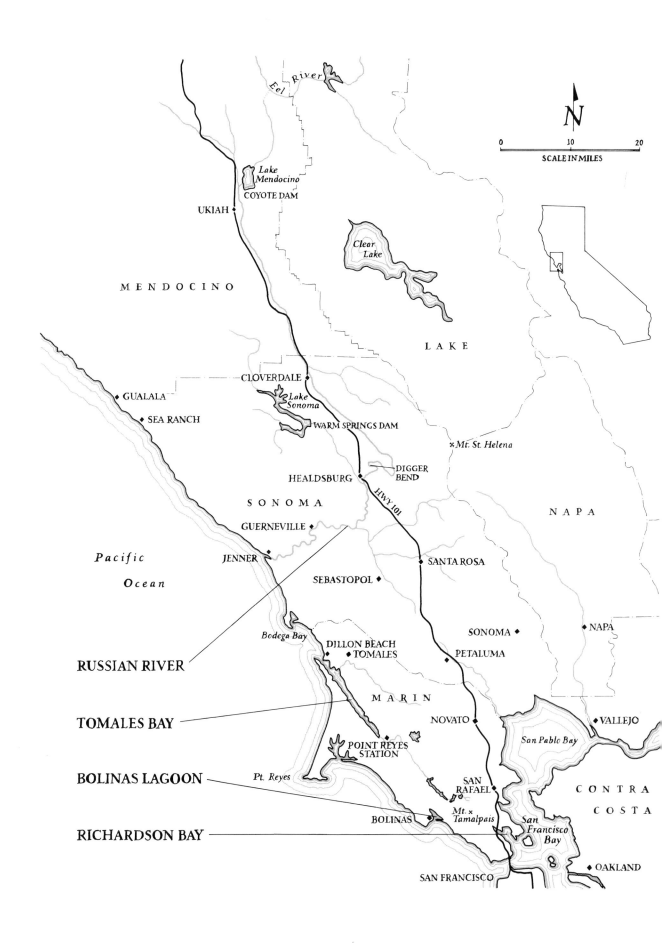

N

0 10 20
SCALE IN MILES

Eel River

Lake Mendocino
COYOTE DAM

UKIAH

M E N D O C I N O

Clear Lake

L A K E

CLOVERDALE

Lake Sonoma
WARM SPRINGS DAM

GUALALA

SEA RANCH

✕ *Mt. St. Helena*

DIGGER BEND

HEALDSBURG

HWY 101

N A P A

S O N O M A

GUERNEVILLE

Pacific Ocean

JENNER

SANTA ROSA

SEBASTOPOL

RUSSIAN RIVER

Bodega Bay

DILLON BEACH
TOMALES

SONOMA

NAPA

PETALUMA

M A R I N

TOMALES BAY

NOVATO

VALLEJO

San Pablo Bay

POINT REYES STATION

Pt. Reyes

SAN RAFAEL

C O N T R A

BOLINAS LAGOON

Mt. ✕ Tamalpais

BOLINAS

C O S T A

San Francisco Bay

RICHARDSON BAY

OAKLAND

SAN FRANCISCO

LIST OF ORIGINAL MAPS

by Dewey Livingston

I was lucky. I had the good fortune to grow up in Los Angeles at a time when we could hike up wooded canyons to waterfalls in the Hollywood Hills, buy fresh produce from farms in the San Fernando Valley, and drive out Foothill Boulevard through mile after mile of orange groves below snow-capped Mount Baldy.

Since that time the hills have been amputated into pads for mansions; the farms in the valley have been replaced by subdivisions, freeways, and shopping malls; the orange groves have given way to besmogged suburbia; and the mountains are seldom visible. Paradise Lost.

When I moved to San Francisco, I gazed with amazement at the open hills and valleys and farmlands of Marin County, and I knew then for a certainty that so much open space immediately adjacent to a densely populated city could not long endure. I envisioned the coming of the bulldozers and the Los Angelizing of the entire region north of the Golden Gate. I was sure that sprawling suburbanization was the inevitable fate of all open land in or near booming metropolitan centers everywhere.

As it turned out, I was wrong. Drastically, happily wrong.

I was wrong because I failed to account for such residents as Dr. Marty Griffin, who had also lived in Los Angeles, had seen what happened there and was determined that it would not happen in Marin. He was undismayed when he was told that you can't fight city hall or the energetic developers with their huge bankrolls and the determination to urbanize everything in sight.

Even in Marin he could see natural areas rapidly vanishing, farmlands sold to speculators, bays and wildlife marshes filled to accommodate an exploding population. His dander was rising steadily. In the face of the ongoing destruction he still held the irrational conviction that it was possible to control the inevitable forces of "progress."

He joined forces with other residents who shared his naive fantasy, and against all odds they succeeded in beating city hall, turning around planning commissions and boards of supervisors, and forcing the bulldozers to grind to a halt time after time.

They didn't do it all at once. They didn't win every battle. But they were undeterred by losses and won enough campaigns to give them the courage to keep going when skeptics scoffed at their prospects. Marshland by marshland, bay by bay, ridge by ridge, over a period of forty years of toil, sweat and tears, they fought the developers to a standstill, expanded north from Marin to Sonoma County and the Russian River, and preserved some of the most idyllic natural sanctuaries—in land and water—in any metropolitan region on this continent.

In a series of Perils-of-Pauline cliffhangers, Griffin tells here how it was done. He describes the players in the drama—as colorful a cast of heroes and villains as you will find anywhere—the strategy, the tactics, the political maneuvers, the techniques of persuasion and pressure, the coordination of grassroots efforts, the struggles with bureaucracy and corporate greed, the defeats and the victories.

Some years back, a national TV network broadcast a documentary on Marin County, picturing it as a place dedicated to hot tubs, peacock feathers, BMWs, and general decadence, an enclave populated exclusively by wealthy sybarites. How blind can you get? Of course there are wealthy people in Marin—and some of them do have hot tubs. There are also low-income groups and a populous middle class brimming with community activists.

The minions of the network totally missed the real story that should have been in front of their eyes: Marin as a county pioneering in grassroots action and innovative techniques to defend its own integrity against the tidal waves of commercialism and urban sprawl. Griffin's story provides a model with tools and techniques that will be invaluable to residents of every metropolitan region who hope to preserve its quality of life in the face of population pressures.

The struggle is ongoing, in Marin and Sonoma as elsewhere. There is much more to be saved, and there are no final victories. But the story told here offers the kind of encouragement that is badly needed in a time when individuals and small groups seem powerless in the face of forces beyond their control.

As a physician, Griffin is convinced that the physical and mental health of the individual is closely related to the health of the environment. Clean air, unpolluted waterways, wildlife preserves, productive farmlands, marshes, woodlands and open hills between communities can make immense contributions to personal health, providing sanctuaries from the stresses and frenzied hyperactivity of urban life, sources of refreshment and renewal for the body and the spirit.

Saving the Marin-Sonoma Coast affirms a message that should be shouted from the housetops: citizens working together have the power to shape the course of events that affect their lives. In a time of cynicism about the workings of democracy, there is no message more urgent.

Threats to the Marin-Sonoma Coast

During the post-war boom in California in 1957, a master politician, Governor-elect Pat Brown, together with his developer friends, set out to fulfill his campaign promises to build one thousand miles of freeways and dam the wild rivers of the North Coast. In the next decade developers descended on Marin and Sonoma counties to urbanize their baylands and coastline spurred by plans for:

- A giant nuclear reactor to produce electricity at Bodega Bay
- A large dredged marina on Bolinas Lagoon
- Two hundred miles of coastal and cross-county freeways
- Warm Springs Dam on the Russian River, with large pipelines to deliver unlimited, subsidized water to any city that would buy it from the pro-growth Sonoma County Water Agency

Eight sprawling new cities were planned that would scar the bays and coast, destroy wildlife habitats, cut off public access, and essentially doom the proposed 53,000-acre Point Reyes National Seashore:

- Reeds Port on Richardson Bay, San Francisco Bay—6,000 people
- Marincello on the Marin Headlands, Marin—25,000 people
- Stinson Beach and the Bolinas Ridge and Mesa, Marin—50,000 people
- Dillon Beach, Oceana Marin—10,000 people
- Point Reyes Peninsula, Limantour Bay, and the east shore of Tomales Bay, Marin—150,000 people
- Bodega Bay, Sonoma —10,000 people
- Jenner and Willow Creek, Sonoma—5,000 people
- Sea Ranch on the Mendocino border, Sonoma—15,000 people

Millions of tons of gravel and sand for concrete and asphalt needed for this construction were to be dredged from the gravel aquifers of the Russian River, imperiling drinking water quality for both counties and killing one of the state's finest steelhead fisheries.

Few Californians realize how narrowly the North Coast counties of Marin and Sonoma escaped becoming tentacles of Southern California and its notorious water schemes. In 1957, fifteen years before voters created the California Coastal Commission, a few conservationists in Marin began plotting a revolution to save its bays, birds, tidelands, and coastline, and to help protect the Point Reyes Peninsula from being suburbanized by the state's aggressive freeway, water, and real estate lobbies.

Their determination led to a citizens revolt against dams and imported water, unprecedented in semi-arid California. Voters shattered Marin's "old boy" politics and transformed its land-use ethic. By "designing with nature" Marin protected its beauty, wildlife, and economy to become one of California's best planned and slowest growing counties.

For years my friends have urged me to tell this story of the creation of the three Audubon Canyon Ranch wildlife preserves in Marin and Sonoma Counties, and the years of struggle to protect California's coastal watersheds and to keep the Russian and Eel Rivers wild. My hope is that this history can serve as a model for other counties where damaging growth is dictated by developers.

As a boy growing up in the sprawling port city of Oakland, I idolized Marin and Sonoma counties across San Francisco Bay. Their salt-scented baylands and coastline supported millions of birds and uncounted species of marine life. Her majesty, Mt. Tamalpais, looming above the fog, guarded the unbridged Golden Gate and California's virgin treasure, the gravel-bedded rivers of the north coast where I had fished for silver salmon and steelhead with my father. These rivers held forty percent of the state's water and, tragically, much of the river gravel coveted for construction.

When I commenced my medical practice in Marin County at the end of the second World War, San Francisco Bay was labeled the "largest open sewer in America." On my rounds, I was angered as I saw the hills of Marin being bulldozed to fill its sparkling bays, while tidelands were ringed with burning garbage dumps. Having been trained in plant and animal ecology as well as medicine, I knew that such a savage assault on the county's environmental health posed an intolerable threat to the health of my patients, my own family, and our communities.

To best tell this story, I have divided it into four parts, each one covering a separate yet often overlapping watershed and wildlife battle. I start with development threatening Richardson Bay, a vital arm of San Francisco Bay, in 1957, then move on to Bolinas Lagoon and Tomales Bay on the coast in the 1960s and 1970s, and end with the Russian River in the 1980s and 1990s.

Lest the public forget and let them erode, I've recorded here the grassroots political victories won in Marin and Sonoma Counties that have profoundly shaped recent California history. Here are the reasons why two-thirds of Marin, including its encircling bays and marshlands and the Point Reyes Peninsula, are permanent open space, wildlife preserves, parks, and farmland; why there are no freeways on the Marin-Sonoma-Mendocino coast; why the salmon rivers of the North Coast (except the Russian) are protected as Wild and Scenic Rivers; why every California river now requires a watershed management plan; why all the state's tidelands are now legally preserved; and why the public has access to much of the eleven-hundred-mile California coast.

This is a proud legacy to leave for future generations—and one that we should protect vigilantly at all costs. For as the late conservationist Peter Behr would remind us, "Conservation victories can be temporary, while the losses are permanent." The battle is never over.

When storyteller Ane Rovetta referred me to Robert Cooney, graphic designer in Point Reyes Station, this memoir sprang to life. Excited, I retraced the course of each land and water battle by foot, canoe, car, photo, my files, and interviews with compatriots and friendly enemies.

I especially want to thank the staff and board of Audubon Canyon Ranch for their help and support. Individuals who read all or part of the manuscript included George Peyton, Clifford Conly, the late Clerin Zumwalt, Skip Schwartz, Tom Baty, Len Blumin, Jack Harper, and biologists Ray Peterson and John Kelly.

The manuscript was reviewed by Pat and Pete Arrigoni, former supervisor, who also researched the Marin County Supervisors minutes from 1967 to 1974 for dates of Marin's astounding land-use revolution, and Harold Gilliam, author of *Island In Time* on the Point Reyes National Seashore, who generously wrote the foreword. The late Senator Peter Behr and former Resource Secretary Ike Livermore offered corrections and lent me their State Oral Histories; Tom Thorner lent me his files for the crucial years he was attorney for the Marin Municipal Water District; and Beverly Bastian, founder of the Landmark Society of Belvedere-Tiburon, provided advice and photos, as did Beth Huning and Dr. David Steinhardt of the Richardson Bay Sanctuary.

Also critiquing the book were former Marin County Planning Director Marge Macris, Joan Bekins of the Elizabeth Terwilliger Foundation, Becky Hayden, Susan Brandt-Hawley, Dick Day, Gail Jonas, Bill Kortum, Peg Ellingson, Don Emblen, Scott Whitaker, and the late Suzanne Lipsett. I am very grateful to Jerry Friedman, Martye Kent, Jane Arnold, Jean Schulz, Max Shaffrath, Frank Keegan, Ida Egli, Peggy Wayburn, Sally Behr, and Tom Roth for their help.

I am indebted to Steve McNamara of the *Pacific Sun,* Beth Ashley and Carol Farrand of the Marin *Independent Journal,* Christine Taccone of the *San Francisco Daily Journal (Legal),* Sonoma journalists Barry Dougan and Dan Stebbins, Juliana Doms of the *Sonoma Environmental Impact Reporter,* Rita Haberman of River Network in Portland, and Malcolm Margolin of Heyday Press. I also thank Gary Snyder for the use of his watershed prose and Gaye LeBaron for her Sonoma County history columns in *The Press Democrat.*

My thanks to Dolores Richards, curator of The Bolinas Museum, for the previewing and videotaping of this history for seventy museum members, and to Jocelyn Moss of the Anne T. Kent Room of the Marin County Library, Sue Baty of the

Inverness Library, Marie Djordjevich of the Healdsburg Museum, the staff of the Healdsburg County Library, and JoAnne Black of Santa Rosa Junior College Library for their help.

I would also like to thank Jerry Edelbrock and the Marin Conservation League for the 1997 Ted Wellman Water Award. Ted got me into the water fight.

This book benefits from the close ties with members of organizations I've been involved with since their start, including Marin Audubon Society, Richardson Bay Sanctuary, Audubon Canyon Ranch and its Docent Council, The Environmental Forum of Marin, the Russian River Environmental Forum, Friends of the Russian River, and the Russian River Task Force.

While this is not a scientific book, it has benefited from my ties with river experts Bob Curry, Aldaron Laird, Matt Kondolf, Laurel Marcus, Philip Williams, and many others.

Finally, I thank designer and editor Robert Cooney, mapmaker and West Marin historian Dewey Livingston, and illustrator Ane Rovetta for their work on this book; Nancy Adess, Helen Blakesly, and Becky Hayden for their editing help; and Julia Macdonald for critique and indexing. I thank my daughters for their constant encouragement, and, above all, my wife Joyce for her untiring help, suggestions, and support.

During my career as a public health officer for the State of California, I consulted in counties where the exploding population growth had severely degraded the natural environment while creating the nation's largest, and most costly, psychiatric, developmental disabilities, and prison systems.

Over the years I've been dismayed by the non-participation of health professionals at countless public hearings where the fate of our life-giving resources—rivers, watersheds, bays, oceans, and even prime farmlands—was decided by developers, by co-opted, or too often corrupt, county supervisors, and by empire-building water and sewer agency chiefs.

Many people, I fear, have too narrow a view of health, unaware of the importance and benefits of *Land Use Planning*. This is a powerful tool which, skillfully employed, can preserve the true foundation of health: the ecological integrity of each county's natural resources.

This key to sustainable health is not to be found in medical textbooks, but in reports like Marin's battle-tested Countywide Plan. If its lessons on environmental quality and economic opportunity were taught in grade schools, colleges, and medical schools, I believe that within a generation our counties could be transformed into Edens, providing a pride of place in our dissatisfied, overly mobile society.

Therefore, this book is intended as an urgent wakeup call in a state that is overburdened with a half million new people each year. It is a call to mobilize our patients, colleagues, and neighbors as we in Marin did, to return to our roots as naturalists, to help elect the right county supervisors, and to support and create grassroots organizations that will defend, conserve, and restore the counties where we practice.

Summary of Audubon Canyon Ranch Land Acquisitions

The land battles recounted in this book were the result of four National Audubon Society Chapters banding together to buy up waterfront acreage whose development threatened to surround the Point Reyes National Seashore with sprawl.

Led by myself and Stan Picher, some thirty strategic parcels of tidelands and uplands, totaling more than 1,600 acres, were acquired by purchase and gift at a cost of about one and one-half million dollars in private donations. Most parcels are now owned and managed by Audubon Canyon Ranch as wildlife preserves. The Marin County Open Space District manages Bolinas Lagoon and Kent Island.

To acquire and manage these lands, and train supporters, these groups were started: the Audubon Canyon Ranch Project, Audubon Canyon Ranch Inc., the Audubon Canyon Ranch Volunteer Council and the Docent Training Program, the Kent Island Fund Drive, the Environmental Studies of Bolinas Lagoon and Tomales Bay, and The Environmental Forum of Marin.

Bolinas Lagoon Preserve

1. Audubon Canyon Ranch (headquarters) — 503 acres, 1961
2. Kent Island, Gift from Alice and Roger Kent — 9.6 acres, 1961
3. Kent Island Park, with Marin Conservation League and The Nature Conservancy (now owned by the County Open Space District) — 111 acres, 1967
4. Galloway Ranch — 278 acres, 1968 and 1971
5. Thompson Ranch (now Volunteer Canyon) — 234 acres, 1968
6. State tideland lease (now Open Space District) — 1,200 acres, 1969
7. Assorted Bolinas Lagoon tideland parcels — 40 acres
8. Monarch Butterfly Groves at Bolinas and Muir Beach (Terwilliger Grove)

Tomales Bay Preserve

1. Shields Marsh near Inverness—4 acres, 1970
2. Johannson shoreline parcels along 4 miles of bay front—32 acres, 1970
3. Cypress Grove (headquarters), Gift from Clifford Conly, Jr.—10 acres, 1971
4. Livermore Marsh adjoining Cypress Grove—26 acres, 1971
5. Cerini Ranch Parcel—57 acres, 1972
6. Hall Ranch Parcel—40 acres, 1972
7. Marshall Creek Delta—14 acres, 1972
8. Hog and Duck Islands—8 acres, 1972
9. Delta of Walker Creek—97 acres, 1972
10. Olema Freshwater Marsh—42.5 acres, 1972
11. Toms Point, Gift of Margaret Quigley—70 acres, 1985

See Ane Rovetta's Map on pages 130-131.

Bouverie Audubon Preserve

Bouverie Audubon Preserve (Sonoma County), Gift from David Bouverie—570 acres, 1979 and 1994

Additional Key Gifts of Land

Richardson Bay Rosie Verrall Sanctuary (Marin County), Gift of 4 acres from Harry Marshall to the National Audubon Society, 1968

Griffin Russian River Riparian Preserve (Sonoma County), Gift of 100-acre conservation easement from Joyce and Martin Griffin to the Sonoma Land Trust, 1991 and 1998

A watershed is a marvelous thing to consider: this process of rain falling, streams flowing, and oceans evaporating causes every molecule of water on earth to make the complete trip once every two million years. The surface is carved into watersheds—a kind of familial branching, a chart of relationship, and a definition of place. The watershed is the first and last nation whose boundaries, though subtly shifting, are unarguable. . . . But we who live in terms of centuries rather than millions of years must hold the watershed and its communities together, so our children might enjoy the clear water and fresh life of this landscape we have chosen.

Gary Snyder, *A Place in Space*

Awakening to Danger

By the laws of Nature these things are common to all mankind—
the air, running water, the sea and the shores of the sea.

—The Justinian Code, 533 AD

My love of untamed rivers and bays started in my parents' cabin overhanging the banks of the Ogden River in a wild Wasatch Mountain canyon in Utah. I was born in that cabin in 1920. At age three I recall being intoxicated by the cool desert canyon scent of trout, willow and sage while my father's mandolin and the murmuring river waters put me to sleep.

By the time I was four, my parents Frances and Loyal had me fly fishing with a little bamboo pole and hand-tied fly. By then a pre-Depression bank failure in Ogden had forced them to sell their home and dairy supply business and to relocate in Portland, Oregon. This move pleased my father, an accomplished fly fisherman; within a two-hour drive over washboard roads were a half-dozen of the finest steelhead and salmon fishing streams in the west.

On weekends between 1924 and 1926 we explored and camped on wild timber-lined streams in southern Washington and Oregon while my father patiently taught my brother and me camping and fishing lore. This was still Indian country, but the Indian wars had ended and the Indian women were barely getting by selling gooseberries, which my mother bought for her pies.

Near Battleground Lake in western Washington, on a tributary of the then-undammed Columbia River called Tum Tum Mountain Creek, I beheld a sight I have never forgotten. I crawled to the edge of a rocky bank and looked down into a crystal clear pool beneath a waterfall to see a number of ocean-reared steelhead trout, most twenty inches long, charging their gills with oxygen-laden water, preparing to ascend a series of falls in a crescendo of runs and tail-twisting leaps.

Thirty-five years later, I brought my four daughters to that same

A Great Egret soars up from its nest near the Bolinas Lagoon. The beauty and grace of these birds was a key to winning popular support to save the Lagoon from development.

Here, in this cabin in the wilds of the Wasatch Mountains in Utah, my brother Bob and I were born. The Ogden River gurgled under the porch where we all slept outside most of the year to be "closer to nature," as my mother said.

waterfall. The waters were choked with logging debris and silt, and the Columbia River dams had ended forever the runs of anadromous fish — steelhead and salmon — up this stream and a thousand similar tributaries.

America had sacrificed this great fishery for surplus electricity and irrigation water. This was my awakening to the dangers facing the waterways of the west.

The Land Grab Begins

I began learning of California's dangerous growth before the Great Depression when my dad lost his job in 1927 and we moved from Portland to Los Angeles. The roads we drove along were lined with thousands of men streaming down from the played-out mines, logging towns, and fisheries of the northwest looking for work. I could see the desperate look in their faces as they huddled by campfires along the road.

Our family was part of a great human migration. At that time California had about four million people; today it has thirty-two million, far more than its ill-equipped counties can manage. The thirst for land has opened the Golden State to reckless real estate development, with nearly everyone hoping to get rich by speculating in ranches, forests, deserts, marshes, and even underwater lots in tidelands. The on-going California land grab has degraded the world's richest trove of ecosystems and plant and animal species into millions of assessor's parcels.

My parents enrolled me in the Eighth Street Grammar School in downtown Los Angeles, where the clear view of palm trees in the foreground and snow-covered peaks behind was that of a Mediterranean paradise. I cringe at the sprawl and pollution there today. Ironically, we lived with an uncle who designed concrete channels for the city's rivers.

My mother gave me training in self-reliance at the age of seven. We lived near Westlake Park where an opulent movie theater had been completed. "If you don't earn some money, no movies," she said, so I got a route selling *Liberty* magazines at five cents each. If I didn't sell enough to buy my movie ticket she said, "Go back and try again." I've always admired my mother's persistence. She was reared on the plains of Nebraska and never complained about life's hardships, even when she lost her vision from glaucoma at age forty-five. At age ninety-five she still held more than twenty-five phone numbers and the family genealogy in her head. We celebrated her 102nd birthday in 1997.

In 1928 we moved to Oakland, where my dad thought he had finally found a good job. We lived for a few months with an aunt who owned the Fenton Creamery, which was famous for its toasted almond sundaes. In my aunt's home my future association with Marin County began, although I didn't know it at the time. I met my aunt's son-in-law, Sam Gardiner, who later became an attorney and Superior Court judge in Marin where our paths forcefully collided.

Just home from serving in France at the end of World War I, my father Loyal took his new bride Frances camping and fishing in Utah in 1919. The white stripes are rice thrown as they departed on their honeymoon.

The End of the Wild, Wild West

During our boyhood summers, my mother drove my brother Bob and me to visit our grandparents, George and Emma Stoddard, in Rochester, Nevada, a silver-mining town deep in a desert canyon pungent with sagebrush. Pop Stoddard was the Justice of Peace, electrician for a power company, and had the only good well in town. Here I learned to value that precious gift—safe, pure, natural drinking water. Before setting out to explore the desert, we carefully filled canvas canteens with delicious water and strapped them to the sides of his Model T pickup to stay cool. In the soft, starlit evenings we gathered around his well, passing the dipper around while we thrilled to his yarns about extending the railroad telegraph lines from Utah into Idaho.

Pop died at age ninety-three with me, his doctor, at his side at his farm east of Sacramento. He's buried in a pioneer cemetery that I can hardly bear to visit. His farm and the cemetery are engulfed in the post-war urban sprawl. The nearby American River is dammed, the salmon are gone, the farms and orchards of the foothills and great Sacramento Valley are being paved over. It's the end of Pop Stoddard's wild, wild west.

"I Love You, California"

As a Boy Scout in Oakland I worked as an assistant to Brighton "Bugs" Cain, a superb naturalist who taught me the wonders of plants and animals, and the geology of the Sierras and the coast. He advised me to go to medical school.

Oakland in the 1930s was an exciting place to grow up. The schools were excellent. My teacher at Piedmont Grammar School, Miss Olin, insisted the entire class stand up and sing "I Love You, California" each morning after the "Pledge of Allegiance to the United States of America." As a Boy Scout I was inspired by the spell-binding naturalist, Brighton "Bugs" Cain, an accomplished whistler and storyteller, who excited hundreds of boys with his love for the out-of-doors. A Stanford-trained entomologist, he urged me to prepare for medical school at his alma mater by taking courses in botany and zoology.

As Bugs softly whistled their calls, we stalked birds at dawn in the Scout's Camp Dimond in the Oakland foothills. We explored the gravel roads along the rugged Big Sur coast in the Scout Council's fat yellow bus with Bugs at the wheel, binoculars at the ready. In a high Sierra camp we ran through fields of blue and gold wildflowers as we searched for his favorite plant, the stately green gentian. At Yosemite Valley, we stood with Bugs in awestruck silence straining to hear the cry of "Let the fire fall!" from Glacier Point three thousand feet above the valley floor before the moon rose over Half Dome.

In 1937 the Golden Gate Bridge was built, connecting the city of San Francisco with the fertile valleys of Marin and Sonoma counties. That same year I enrolled as a pre-med student at the world-renowned University of California campus at Berkeley, with a tuition of just twenty-five dollars a semester.

In 1940, during a birding course (not a pre-med course) taught by Alden Miller, a famous ornithologist of his day, we visited the egret heronry on Bolinas Lagoon that is now part of Audubon Canyon Ranch. The Lagoon was a welcome contrast to the stench of the purulent tideflats and garbage dumps of the East Bay shoreline.

I first learned of the word "ecology" in 1938 from a book I have carried with me to nearly every rich botanical region of the state, *The Flowering*

Plants of California, by the famous University of California botanist Willis Linn Jepson for whom the Jepson Bishop Pine Preserve at Tomales Bay State Park is named. I have sat on mountain tops and by the sides of marshes fascinated by his descriptions of the more than 1,400 native species found only in California.

Ecology then was a brand-new field; the interdependence of the tidal marshes and aquatic and bird life was only dimly perceived by biologists and not at all by the general public.

In the summers of 1940 and 1941, I was introduced to the grandeur of the forests and the salmon rivers on the fog-bound redwood coast north of Marin County. I joined five rugged UC class members, all Sonoma County farm boys, in a logging camp venture on the Navarro River in Mendocino County. We spent more time exploring and fishing the heavily forested Eel, Trinity, and Klamath rivers than we did splitting fence posts and railroad ties, but we made enough money to enroll for another semester at UC.

I was a young and rather naive physician in Marin County at the end of World War II. My grandfather, Pop Stoddard, predicted I'd either be a preacher or a doctor, or both.

We didn't know then that our camp was the last gasp of the benign era of hand saws and selective logging, or that within a few years the magnificent old-growth forests would be plundered with machine logging and clear cutting for the war effort and for the endless demands of California's postwar growth.

Trained as a Medical Sleuth

In 1941 I enrolled in Stanford Medical School in an Army Specialized Training Program. After three years I interned at the old Stanford Hospital in San Francisco under the prestigious Dr. Arthur Bloomfield, an expert diagnostician. After graduation I spent two years as a Captain in the US Army Medical Corps, honing my skills in psychiatric diagnosis at a large receiving hospital where my task was to get patients back to their home states as quickly as possible.

After the war, I watched as tens of thousands of soldiers returning from the war never made it home. First landing in seductive California, they stayed, adding to the state's crushing post-war population growth.

After leaving the Army I returned to Stanford Hospital for another year of training as Dr. Bloomfield's special resident in internal medicine. "The

Chief," as we called him, trained us to be medical sleuths. I used this training later to diagnose and treat environmental ills. For example, I'd take a careful history of a tideland dredging project, make a thorough inspection of the site, talk with people it affected, read everything available, study maps, visit the agencies in charge, and come up with a diagnosis and a plan of attack for that particular problem. Then I'd predict the outcome, or prognosis.

Dr. Bloomfield introduced me to many of the old-time families, some would call them elite, of Marin County. Among these longtime residents were a few who were already working to protect Marin from rampant growth. But there were many more ready to exploit Marin's potential for development. By the end of the war, all the efficient electric railroad lines in Marin had been ripped up to make way for freeways and autos. By 1946 Marin was already at risk of being Los Angelized.

Welcome to Marin

Right after the war ended, my wife Mimi and I settled in Sausalito, a charming backwater on Richardson Bay, an arm of the San Francisco Bay just north of the Golden Gate. We had met as classmates in medical school and had four daughters: Linda, Anne, Carol, and Joan.

A young orthopedist, Calvin Terwilliger, and his wife Elizabeth were our neighbors. One day she phoned and said, "Marty, I want you to come right over to the Valhalla Restaurant. I'm meeting the City Council there and

Elizabeth Terwilliger, a neighbor in Sausalito, led tours to instruct both young and old about the wonders of salt marshes and tidelands. Thirty years later she taught President Reagan how to flap his arms like a duck, a vulture, and a gull on national television.

we're going to walk them through the town and show them there's not a single decent playground for our children. I've also found a vacant lot that would be ideal and we simply must persuade the City Council to buy it and equip it!" I went, overwhelmed by her enormous energy. Needless to say, the Council bought and equipped the little park. For years Mimi and I remained the Terwilliger family physicians.

This was my first step into the conservation politics of Marin. A busy family and professional life intervened for many years before I took another.

During the fifties my medical practice, with frequent house calls, put me in touch with all parts of Marin County, where the population was starting to increase dramatically. I watched with growing anxiety as the extensive salt marshes of Richardson Bay, Corte Madera Bay, and San Rafael Bay were slowly filled and turned into housing and shopping developments. One day I noticed that the beautiful marsh where the Corte Madera Town Shopping Center now stands was for sale for only $200 per acre. "Suitable for Filling," the sign said. I was heartsick because I knew the large egret heronry high in a Larkspur redwood grove just to the west depended on this marsh for its food supply.

A friend was part of an investment group that was operating a garbage dump on the tidelands of San Rafael Bay which had been purchased from the state some years before. "It's the greatest investment in the world!" he said. "We get paid to take the garbage and we are given a depletion allowance tax break on the tidelands as they are filled in."

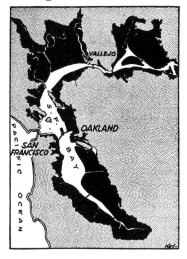

Bay or River?

The white area, according to an Army Engineer's study, shows what would be left if all shallow parts were filled.

Tidelands on San Francisco Bay were being filled at an alarming rate as this 1960 map suggests.

Terminally Ill, Prognosis Hopeless

To me, Richardson Bay appeared to be terminally ill. I jotted down my diagnoses: tidal arms severed by roads and railroad tracks, poisoned by the dumping of mash from a whiskey distillery, smothered with sewage sludge dumped in cover of darkness by the developers who ran the sanitary districts, and dying from toxic wastes dumped during four years of war effort. In 1957, Richardson Bay faced extinction from filling by one of my own medical colleagues who was also a developer. It looked hopeless for the bay and, by extension, for all of Marin County.

Owners of this garbage dump on San Rafael Bay got a tax writeoff in 1952 as they filled in the rich marshlands. Marin Municipal Water District annexed these and other San Francisco Bay tidelands to supply water for the anticipated development. Offshore are the Marin Islands, home of the Bay Area's largest colony of Great Egrets and Snowy Egrets.

In 1957 I received an urgent call from Elizabeth Terwilliger. "Marty," she said, "Mrs. Livermore and I have started the Marin Audubon Society to try to save Richardson Bay from being filled for housing. We'd like you to be on the Board of Directors. I won't take 'no' for an answer." I jumped at the opportunity of learning from these two dedicated women who were the heart and soul of the conservation movement in Marin.

My reputation as a physician had preceded me. "We've all heard of your medical accomplishments," Caroline Livermore said when we met. "But don't you think it's equally important for people's health that we save the marshes and bays and establish parks and open space?" I agreed heartily with this wise woman.

Thus began my long association with Caroline Livermore, which lasted until she died in 1968. I literally apprenticed myself to her. I recognized that she and her "ladies," as she called them, had the vision, connections, and clout to be effective; and I eagerly mobilized my medical practice and colleagues to join them in helping save the bays and lagoons of Marin County.

♦ LARKSPUR

✳ *Mt. Tamalpais*
ELEV. 2571

♦ CORTE MADERA

♦ MILL VALLEY

Tiburon

ROSIE'S
11 ACRES

Strawberry Point

Peninsula

Richardson Bay

TIBURON ♦

Mt Livermore
×
Angel Island

SAUSALITO ♦

MARIN   COUNTY

San

Francisco

Bay

Pacific

Ocean

Golden   Gate

SAN FRANCISCO

N

0   1   2
SCALE IN MILES

PART ONE

RICHARDSON BAY

The small Richardson Bay watershed drains the steep southern slope of Mt. Tamalpais, where small streams still hold spawning salmon. The watershed is part of the San Francisco Bay Delta and the Sacramento-San Joaquin river system that drains nearly half of California. Tidal currents sweep through the Golden Gate, nourishing the shallow tidelands of Richardson Bay and creating fierce cross currents around the deep channels of Angel Island, where river and ocean collide. Note Mt. Livermore on Angel Island, and Rosie's bluff overlooking Richardson Bay on the Tiburon Peninsula. Here is where the first major battle to rescue the tidelands and marshes of San Francisco Bay from landfilling developers was fought.

CHAPTER ONE

The Saving of Richardson Bay

In all planning decisions, it is critical to respect the genius of place.

—Rene Jules Dubos, U.C. Albright Lecture 1970

Noth of the Golden Gate in coastal Marin County there are three marvelous watersheds which are part of Mt. Tamalpais and whose tumbling waterways drain into saltwater estuaries that are part of the Pacific Ocean—Richardson Bay to the east and Bolinas Lagoon and Tomales Bay to the west. These watersheds, and the nearby Russian River watershed in Sonoma County, are but four of many northern California watersheds that once supported extravagant populations of salmon.

These watersheds' brackish estuaries are essential for the physiological changes that salmon undergo as they migrate from the salty Pacific into the freshwater tributaries where they spawn and die and from which the juveniles drift back to the ocean.

The swift tidal currents of San Francisco Bay are fed by the waters of the Sacramento–San Joaquin river system that drains the spectacular watersheds of the Sierra Nevada through the Central Valley. The tragic saga of the damming and diversion of this great river system, and the decimation of the state's once-abundant salmon populations in my lifetime, is told in *The California Water Atlas* by the State of California. This is the tale of Richardson Bay, my boot camp for battles in the years to come.

Who Owns the Bay?

Today, to ask, "Who owns San Francisco Bay, or Bolinas Lagoon, or Tomales Bay?" would be like asking, "Who owns the sky?" Surely most people would answer, "The bays and rivers of California belong to the public." But forty-five years ago, when I started practicing medicine in Marin

Marin County lies north of the Golden Gate Bridge with extensive frontage on San Francisco Bay and the ocean (left)—but with very little fresh water. The plan after World War II was to construct freeways, fill in tidelands, bring in water from the Russian River, and build cities for nearly one million people. Filling in Richardson Bay (center) for a two thousand home marina was but one of several ominous development plans.

With Mt. Tamalpais, in the background, a lone egret is reflected in Richardson Bay where 800 acres were to have been filled in to create the Reeds Port marina. The night before Belvedere voted to buy part of the bay in 1957, a seaplane dropped floating flares to show the public what they would lose.

County, large parts of these bays were owned by developers. Some of them—physicians, patients, and lawyers—were friends of mine.

Here was the tragedy. Ever since 1850 when California became a state, it had held title to its bay tidelands, submerged lands, and navigable rivers. Under the Doctrine of Public Trust, these priceless bodies of water were to be protected and preserved for public use, for navigation, and as wildlife habitats. This doctrine dates back nearly two thousand years to the sea-faring Romans. So these lands belonged to the public, yes, but frontier California betrayed this trust and from the 1850s sold tidelands at auction to developers.

In 1957 Caroline Livermore, and later the Audubon Society branches, were forced to buy back tidelands of San Francisco Bay, Bolinas Lagoon, and Tomales Bay in West Marin that the state should never have sold. It didn't matter to the politicians who sold off parts of San Francisco Bay that it was a busy shipping harbor with great naval bases, or that these three tidal areas formed the largest and richest tidal wildlife habitats on California's 1,100-mile coastline.

"If we keep filling the bay," Wallace Stegner wrote about San Francisco Bay in 1963, "we will turn it into a fuming mudflat, with a sewer running down the center." Stegner was correct. Within a century after statehood, the bay and its tidelands had been reduced from seven hundred square miles to fewer than four hundred, and the famous, active port of San Francisco had become but a shadow of its former self.

A Waterfowl Spectacle

At the start of World War II, the return of wintering waterfowl and shorebirds to the Central Valley and Marin's marshes still presented one of the nation's greatest wildlife spectacles. In Marin overlapping flying V-formations, some a mile wide, formed an undulating, twinkling necklace around blue-green Mt. Tamalpais, their migration landmark. The Bay was also teeming with life. At night in certain seasons, I saw Richardson Bay glitter like a tropical sea with billions of phosphorescent organisms. It was still clean.

The Lady of Marin, Mt. Tamalpais, holds a special place in the hearts of those who have fought to preserve its ridges and saltwater bays. Another Lady of Marin, Caroline Livermore, founded the Marin Conservation League before the Golden Gate Bridge was completed.

Flights of millions of birds such as pintail, mallard, Canada geese, snowgeese, bufflehead and goldeneye came sailing down the Pacific Flyway from Canada and Alaska. For thousands of years more than half the birds that used the Pacific Flyway depended on California's tidelands, bays, and thousands of acres of wetlands (now many of them rice fields) in the Central Valley as their winter home. But each year they looked down on more diked-off salt marshes, drained wetlands, and tideland garbage dumps. Each year there was less of San Francisco Bay and more urban sprawl.

One of the world's greatest ecological and economic tragedies was underway on the public's land without the public's knowledge. Around the perimeter of San Francisco Bay were vast saltwater marshes nearly level as a pancake, made up of pickleweed and cordgrass and fed by the strong tidal currents that surged through the Golden Gate. Here avocets, rail, curlew, willets, and the harvest mouse searched for food. These marshes were photosynthetic factories that produced huge volumes of oxygen and cleared the air and water of pollutants. They were being diked off—ten thousand acres at a crack—for salt works or pasture.

No one seemed to know or care that the cordgrass as it decayed provided the nutritious plankton soup that was the start of the food web. Further up this web in silvery billions were tasty bay shrimp, clams, oysters (hangtown fries), succulent Dungeness crab, herring, anchovies, sardines, salmon, striped bass, and sturgeon laden with roe (caviar). Until the tidelands were smothered before the turn of the century under layers of silt unleashed by hydraulic gold mining into the Sacramento River, these organisms were a bonanza that provided abundant food for both wildlife and humans. Many of these species recovered only to be hit again by toxic wastes dumped into the bay by oil refineries.

As the filling of San Francisco Bay accelerated, irate citizens acted to preserve wetlands and wildlife. In 1965 the San Francisco Bay Conservation and Development Commission was created by the state legislature to manage the bay.

Betraying the Public Trust

The State Lands Commission, created by the State Legislature in 1938, regarded these marshes and tidelands as merely real estate rather than great natural resources to be safeguarded. Thousands of acres in the Bay Area had been divided into parcels by the state and auctioned off for as little as one dollar an acre and, according to hearings to form a Bay Conservation and Development Commission in 1964, many of these sales were of questionable legality.

By then, twenty percent of San Francisco Bay was in private ownership and another twenty-five percent was owned by cities and counties that sought to fill it. In Marin County developers had already planned streets for a filled-in Richardson Bay. There were four hundred privately owned tideland parcels in Marin County—the third-highest in the Bay Area. Making matters worse, the Marin Municipal Water District was encouraging development by annexing submerged lands that they hoped would be filled so they could supply water. My relative, Sam Gardiner, was the attorney for that agency. Ironically, with the growing affluence of the well-educated families that were attracted to Marin by its beauty and the short commute across the Golden Gate Bridge, these garbage-filled tidelands became extremely valuable for waterfront homes and businesses, although their foundations often sank.

In the 1950s the Army Corps of Engineers built Coyote Dam on the Russian River in Sonoma County to store water diverted from the Eel River. This potential cheap source of drinking water set off a wave of land speculation in rapidly growing Marin. The lands that were often cheapest to develop, and to lay with sewage and water pipelines, were the remaining shallow pickleweed marshes and tidelands of Richardson, Corte Madera, San Rafael, and San Pablo bays.

Finally, the battle began.

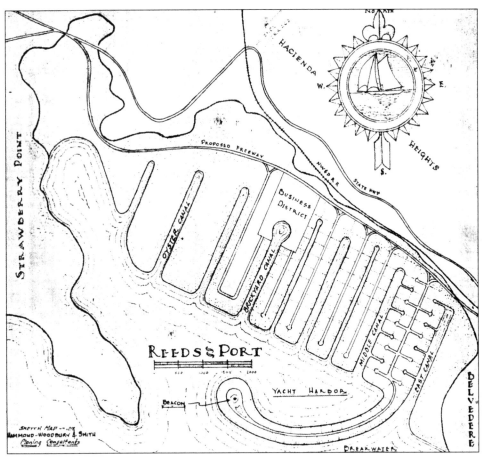

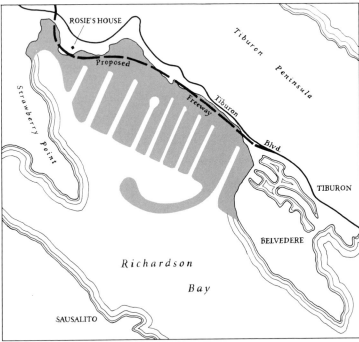

The official plan for Reeds Port (above) showcased its canals, yacht harbor, and waterfront homesites in 1957. The grand scale of the development is better shown at left, where the gray area indicates the 800 acres of Richardson Bay to be filled in with tons of dirt bulldozed from a nearby mountain. A freeway would cut through Rosie Verrall's property.

The Struggle for Richardson Bay Starts

Dr. David Steinhardt, a young Marin County surgeon who lived with his family on the unspoiled eastern arm of Richardson Bay, was the first in 1955 to raise the alarm when he saw a gigantic dredger moving along the bay toward his house. He quickly bought a tidal lot that was for sale for $3,000 and blocked the path of the dredge. Then he alerted the National Audubon Society and the Marin Conservation League, which brought Caroline Livermore, a patrician lady from Ross, on board. She formed the Richardson Bay Foundation made up of prominent citizens.

Rose da Fonta, as an attractive young woman, captivated John Reed, an ailing landowner. Before he died, Reed willed Rosie the beautiful eleven-acre bluff overlooking Richardson Bay where she had lived since childhood.

David and Caroline decided in 1957 that the only way to save Richardson Bay was to buy it from its owners. This glorious bay arches the foot of Mt. Tamalpais between the wooded Sausalito hills, Strawberry Point, Belvedere, and the bluffs off the Tiburon Peninsula. A prominent pathologist at Marin General Hospital, Dr. Warren Bostick, his brother Benton, a divinity student at the seminary in San Anselmo, and the Utah Construction Company planned to bulldoze a five-hundred-acre Tiburon mountain and fill eight hundred acres of Richardson Bay for two thousand lagoon homes and a marina named Reeds Port, after an early pioneer. "To fill Richardson Bay would be like filling the reflecting pools of the Taj Mahal," I told Benton, a patient of mine.

Caroline Livermore was no novice. In 1935 she and her friends had started the Marin Conservation League to cope with population pressures created by the easy access to Marin provided by the Golden Gate Bridge. Later, she convinced county supervisors to hire their first full-time professional county planning director, Mrs. Mary Summers, one of whose first acts as director was to shock the State Lands Commission, who controlled the tidelands, by standing up at a meeting and telling its director to "get out of the real estate business."

Known as the Grand Lady, Caroline Livermore was a tall woman of extraordinary energy with remarkable persuasive powers and a commanding presence. Those who knew her watched in awe as she enlisted the bureaucrats of the state highway system, Belvedere's city government, Howard and David Allen, whose father had developed Belvedere, other tideland owners, the county supervisors, the National Audubon Society—not to mention her own group, the Marin Conservation League, and her own influential sons—to raise the money needed to purchase and save Richardson Bay.

Rose da Fonta Verrall became the Goat Lady of Tiburon in her later years. With the help of Caroline Livermore, and my nurses at the Ross Valley Medical Clinic, she went through a remarkable change.

The Saga of Rosie and the Marin Audubon Society

Caroline Livermore's motto was "Flash the cash to let them know you mean business." Her other gem was "Fortune favors the bold." If she needed a new support organization, she simply started one. In 1957 a group of bird watchers, including Elizabeth Terwilliger, joined her for lunch at Sam's Cafe in Tiburon, and before they finished the cracked crab they had formed the Marin Audubon Society with Dr. David Steinhardt as president and Dr. Herman Schwartz, another physician, as treasurer. In 1960 I was elected president and Stan Picher of Belvedere treasurer. Elizabeth Terwilliger, by that time known as the Bird Lady, was vice president. We had learned by then that Caroline and David needed us in their plan to save Richardson Bay; without a local Marin chapter, the National Audubon Society wouldn't help them.

For many years Caroline was the center of a network of her friends dedicated to conserving Marin's natural treasures. Another of Caroline's friends, Rosie Verrall, born Rose Rodrigues da Fonta in the Azores, was affectionately known as the Goat Lady because for years she tethered goats on the road to Tiburon. As a young woman, Rosie met John Paul Reed, a pioneer Tiburon peninsula landowner, who owned the choice eleven-acre

In 1957 Caroline Livermore persuaded Crowley Marine to barge the abandoned Lyford Mansion, where Rosie had met John Reed, from Strawberry Point over to Rosie's bluff on Richardson Bay.

promontory on the east shore of Richardson Bay where Rosie had lived in a small shack with her parents since childhood. They became lovers and shortly before his early death Reed willed that land to Rosie. She later sold off four bayside acres. Rosie was in her seventies when Caroline persuaded her to deed those seven remaining acres to the Marin Conservation League in exchange for cash, the right to stay there, lifetime care, and a personal physician—me. That's how I became known as the Goat Lady's doctor.

By 1958, the Richardson Bay Foundation had arranged for seven hundred acres of Richardson Bay to be purchased by the county and two hundred acres by the city of Belvedere. They, in turn, leased the 900 acres to the National Audubon Society for fifty years to operate the Richardson Bay Wildlife Sanctuary. The developers —Utah Construction, which had recently filled four hundred acres of tidelands off Alameda—wisely backed off before dredging commenced, and the Bosticks were paid $230,000 by the Foundation for their title to the bay. Reeds Port, named after Rosie's benefactor and lover, was dead in the water. The Bosticks went on to other real estate ventures.

Rosie Becomes Presentable

With Rosie's parcel forming the centerpiece to her plan for Richardson Bay, Caroline Livermore decided to move the abandoned, once-elegant Lyford house by barge from nearby Strawberry Point to Rosie's bluff to serve as National Audubon Society headquarters. The house had been obtained by David Steinhardt as a gift from its owners, who planned to bulldoze it. Caroline persuaded the Crowley Marine Company to move the four-story Victorian mansion by barge for free, which was accomplished with great fanfare on December 4, 1957.

More and more women from the Ross, Piedmont, and San Mateo garden clubs wanted to arrange tours and picnics to the bluff to "see what Caroline was up to now," and how she planned to restore the derelict mansion with funds donated by her friend, Mrs. Donald Dickey. The trouble was that when Caroline was ready to lead these tours, Rosie Verrall wasn't in very good shape to greet guests. She was tending her goats, who were tethered on long chains so they could wander the property and keep down the grass, and she was sleeping in an old car body on newspapers of ancient vintage because her little cabin was piled high with keepsakes. Something had to be done.

With offers of new clothes and a new house, Caroline tried frantically to make Rosie presentable. Rosie would have none of it. She ran when anyone approached. She would walk all the way to Mill Valley each day for a bag of chocolates and arrive back tired and sweaty. She slept in her long stockings, which seemed glued to her legs. In desperation, Caroline summoned Bill Goodall, National Audubon Society representative, and me. "Dr. Griffin," she commanded, "You are the Goat Lady's doctor. It's your responsibility to get Rosie into first-class condition so she can greet my friends with me."

I enlisted the help of my clinic nurse, Rebecca Harkins, another powerful woman. We tried gentle persuasion—no luck. Together the three of us ran Rosie all over her pasture and finally cornered her. Although tiny and bent, she was as fleet and wiry as her goats. We carried her to a couch, and Rebecca washed her from head to foot. When Rebecca cut off her stockings with surgical scissors, she discovered Rosie had been in pain from leg sores that had made it impossible for her to remove her stockings. She had been too proud to tell Caroline.

Rebecca put bright new clothes and shoes on Rosie and combed and braided her hair. Meanwhile, Rosie's cabin was cleaned out. She was given a new bed, a new bathroom, and a whole new life. Caroline encouraged Rosie to keep her goats, which were as familiar a sight on Tiburon Boulevard as Blackie the horse, who has since been commemorated with a statue and a park named after him.

When Rosie greeted Caroline Livermore (left) and her elegant friends, her favorite goat was often at her side while the others wandered on chains to keep down the grass.

A Different Life for Rosie

As Rosie's leg pains subsided, she put her trust in me and allowed me to drive her twice a week to the Ross Valley Clinic in Kentfield, where Rebecca bathed her, dressed her leg ulcers, and redressed her in an outfit from the regal wardrobe Caroline chose for her. We had to see her during the lunch hour and then allow the clinic to air out from the lingering odor of goats before seeing patients in the afternoon.

The glorious setting of the restored Lyford Victorian on Rosie's bluff overlooking Richardson Bay (above) is often used for fundraising events like this to support the National Audubon Society's Wildlife Education Program. A new bench (right) dedicated to Caroline Livermore was envied by Rosie, so another bench overlooking the bay was built nearby for her before she died in 1964 at age eighty.

A remarkable change took place. Rosie, the Goat Lady—who was now in her mid-seventies, about the same age as Caroline—began to smile, sing, do little dances, and recount her past. Caroline presented her to her friends as "the lady who saved Richardson Bay." Rosie loved it. Caroline, Rosie, and Elizabeth Terwilliger would stand graciously side by side in receiving lines at the Audubon headquarters. Rosie even became somewhat competitive and was determined to outlive Caroline.

Later, after a lovely bench had been built in honor of Caroline Livermore on the bluff overlooking Richardson Bay, I saw Rosie Verrall slip onto it at dusk and stare off. Was she dreaming of her lover, John Paul Reed, who had given her this special spot on Earth and then died at fifty-four? His gift to Rosie, and her gift to Caroline and the Audubon Society, had become a permanent treasure for the people of Marin.

The beautiful Richardson Bay Sanctuary of the National Audubon Society has numerous trails, springtime flower displays, and a wide variety of marine and upland habitats.

Saving Rosie's Four Acres

In 1968, after Caroline and Rosie had died, I worried that condominiums would be built on the valuable four acres overlooking San Francisco Bay that Rosie had sold much earlier. The National Audubon Society hadn't tried to buy it because of the expense, so out of the blue I phoned the owner, Harry Marshall, and arranged to visit him in Chicago. He toured me around Chicago for two days, enjoying my stories about Caroline and Rosie. He didn't want Rosie's bluff defaced and the sanctuary ruined either. To my delight he offered to donate his spectacular four acres to National Audubon, and asked me to present them with the gift (see Chapter Five). The original eleven-acre gift of land to Rosie was again intact—a tribute to the efforts of the grassroots groups that had saved Richardson Bay.

Today, Richardson Bay is one of Marin County's loveliest wildlife preserves. Marine life is slowly returning to its tidelands and great flights of ducks, geese, cormorants, and shorebirds winter in its waters, which are again clean enough to swim in. Power boats are forbidden. Thousands of children visit the Richardson Bay Sanctuary annually and enjoy the restored Victorian headquarters of the National Audubon Society in Marin County, where its dedicated manager, Beth Huning, has fought for years to save the bay from many new threats.

Caroline Livermore's Example

Caroline Livermore in her garden, with Mt. Tamalpais in the distance.

Caroline Livermore has become a powerful symbol of how citizens of each county can promote sound ecological county planning and education, elect honest supervisors, and demand absolute protection for a county's water, wildlife, and scenic resources. She played a part in the creation of many of the great state parks of Marin County, including Samuel P. Taylor, Tomales Bay, Mt. Tamalpais, Stinson Beach, and Angel Island. She also founded the Marin Art and Garden Center in Ross. The influential Marin Conservation League, that she and friends started, has grown into an organization that helps establish both county and state environmental policy.

Caroline Livermore was born in Galveston, Texas, in 1885 and died in Marin in 1968. She and her family moved to Marin County in 1930. Her husband served on the board of the Marin Municipal Water District and was a chairman of the California Academy of Sciences. They had five sons, all prominent. One of her sons, Norman B. (Ike) Livermore, served as Secretary of Resources from 1967-1974 under Governor Ronald Reagan.

Honoring her posthumously in 1990 for her environmental work, a display in the Marin Women's Hall of Fame at the Anne T. Kent History Room of the Marin County Library states, "Caroline came from a family of wealth and prestige. She could have lived a life of ease. Yet she decided to use her time, influence and resources on behalf of the people of Marin, the Bay Area and beyond. She did not spare herself from decades of constant, grueling effort to achieve her goals."

Caroline also was the driving force that turned 640-acre Angel Island, a Civil War Army post and immigration center, into a state park in the heart of busy San Francisco Bay. Its cannon emplacements are aimed straight out the Golden Gate. From the crest, named Mt. Caroline Livermore, one can look down on Richardson Bay, a nine hundred acre open-space preserve. Both Angel Island and Richardson Bay are skirted with foot and bicycle trails with her majesty, Mt. Tamalpais, reflected in the bay.

Finally, in 1965 Caroline's work helped in the formation of the San Francisco Bay Conservation and Development Commission, whose role became preservation of the bay. That commission, however, had no power to help in the brewing battle to preserve the tidelands and wildlife of Bolinas Lagoon and Tomales Bay on the far side of Mt. Tamalpais.

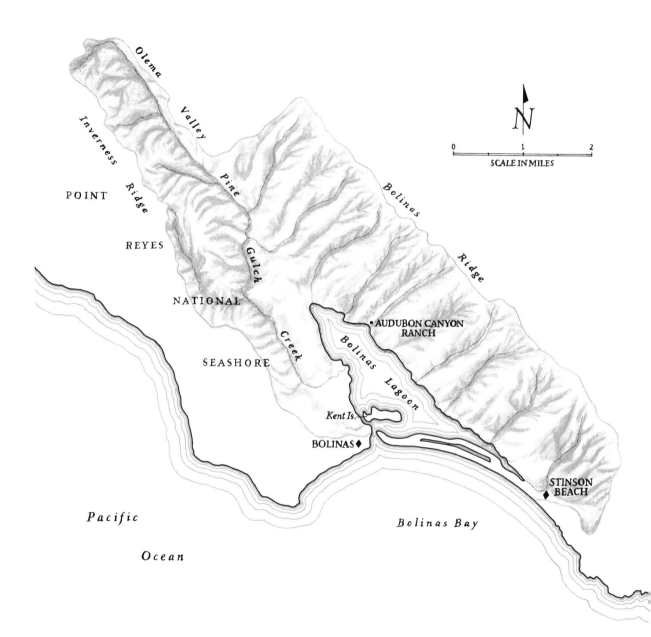

Olema Valley

Inverness Ridge

POINT

REYES

NATIONAL

SEASHORE

Pine

Gulch

Creek

Bolinas Ridge

N

0   1   2
SCALE IN MILES

AUDUBON CANYON
RANCH

Bolinas Lagoon

Kent Is.

BOLINAS ◆

Pacific

Ocean

Bolinas Bay

STINSON
BEACH ◆

PART TWO

BOLINAS LAGOON

The Bolinas Lagoon watershed lies northwest of the Golden Gate, formed by the mighty Bolinas Ridge on the west side of Mt. Tamalpais. Salmon still spawn in its creeks, whose outlet to the Pacific Ocean is the mouth of Bolinas Lagoon. This small watershed was the site of the first revolt against freeways on the North Coast and the battle to save the southern gateway to the Point Reyes National Seashore. Two towns, Bolinas and Stinson Beach, are separated by the San Andreas Fault, which created the "earthquake bays" of Bolinas Lagoon, Tomales Bay, and Bodega Bay to the north. Bolinas' drinking water comes from Arroyo Hondo and from Pine Gulch Creek, whose headwaters are in the National Seashore. Stinson Beach's water comes from small springs. Note Audubon Canyon Ranch headquarters, home of a large colony of egrets, on the east shore of Bolinas Lagoon.

CHAPTER TWO

"Flashing the Cash" for Audubon Canyon Ranch

If you want to know the answer, you have to ask the question.

—L. M. Griffin, Sr., Sales Manager, Griffin Supplies

Inspired by the success of grassroots organizations in preserving Richardson Bay, I decided in 1961 to see if the same approach could be used to help save the wildlife of Bolinas Lagoon in West Marin from a proposed freeway. This small saltwater lagoon lies on the ocean side of Marin at the foot of the Bolinas Ridge and, with its twin to the north, Tomales Bay, flanks the Point Reyes Peninsula. It was incomprehensible that the federal government had no plan to preserve them; they were the unspoiled gateways to the proposed 53,000-acre Point Reyes National Seashore, soon to be authorized by the US Congress.

Moreover, considering Marin's pro-growth political climate, it seemed that the National Seashore was a mirage. The county supervisors opposed it. At a raucous meeting I attended, they voted to cut the size of the National Seashore by more than half and to rush construction of the freeway that would open the unprotected coast to sprawl.

As president of the Marin Chapter of the National Audubon Society in 1961, my plan was this: if we could purchase the ranch containing a large colony of nesting egrets and herons that lay directly in the path of the freeway, it might be the handle we needed to stop the freeway, preserve the lagoon, and build local support for the wounded National Seashore. It was worth a try.

Leaders of the effort to create the National Seashore, Congressman Clem Miller and Dr. Edgar Wayburn (one of my former medical school instructors), informed me that there was no financial help to be had from the federal government to buy lands on Bolinas Lagoon. In fact, if funding could be found for the Seashore, it would be a miracle.

The town of Bolinas is on the lower left and Bolinas Lagoon is on the lower right in this aerial view of West Marin looking north up the San Andreas Fault (center) toward Tomales Bay and Sonoma County. The wild lands on either side of the Fault were threatened by development in 1960. Forty miles distant—on the Fault—a nuclear power plant was to be built by PG&E. Over the Bolinas Ridge (right) is the watershed of the Marin Municipal Water District, which we feared would be sold to developers if cheap Russian River water became available.

So the only group available to try to save these two wildlife-rich bays, which were in turn crucial to the success of the Point Reyes National Seashore, was our tiny band of bird watchers—and I hadn't talked to them as yet.

My First View of Bolinas Lagoon

The story of Audubon Canyon Ranch really began for me in 1932 when I joined Boy Scout Troop 51, which met at the old Plymouth Church on Piedmont Avenue in Oakland. For years, scouts rode their bikes to Camp Dimond in the Oakland foothills to explore a beautiful oak-lined canyon and creek alive with birds and wildlife. Here, its naturalist for twenty-six years, Brighton "Bugs" Cain, an entomologist, molded generations of boys to respect and defend wild places and wildlife, even rattlesnakes. The anguish we all felt when the Oakland Boy Scout Council sold Camp Dimond in 1951 for development has shaped my entire life.

Bugs' heart was broken; he was given a desk job, then resigned, and later took his own life. However, my training as Bugs Cain's assistant and the experiences I had with Troop 51 would help atone for the loss.

One of my most memorable adventures as a Boy Scout was an overnight trip we took the year I was thirteen to Steep Ravine on Mt. Tamalpais overlooking the Bolinas Lagoon and the Pacific Ocean. Some fifteen scouts with bedrolls and cooking cans dangling took the speedy yellow Key Route Train to the Oakland Mole, then caught the ferry to San Francisco. There we transferred to the Sausalito ferry and boarded the electrified train to cross the tidelands of Richardson Bay to Mill Valley. We struggled up the thousand steps to Panoramic Highway, then up the road on the shoulder of Mt. Tamalpais and down the Steep Ravine trail about two miles. By flashlight, we descended a log ladder over a little waterfall and dropped, exhausted, in a redwood grove at midnight in a drizzling rain. The next morning, ignoring our blisters, we hiked along the Dipsea Trail and came out on a most glorious sight: the sparkling Bolinas Lagoon, dotted with white birds, with fog-bound Point Reyes beyond. Behind the lagoon, thirty-mile-long Bolinas Ridge, an arm of Mt. Tamalpais, loomed in the mist. The smell of salt from the crashing surf at Stinson Beach, combined with the aroma of coastal sage after a rain, was unforgettable.

In the 1930s, our Boy Scout troop rode on ferries such as The Klamath to get to Marin County from Oakland. The ferry trip was fast and thrilling, with wind in our faces and gulls overhead.

Little did I dream at thirteen that saving the white birds and their lagoon home would become the passionate goal of my life and that, some twenty-eight years later, I would make my home on this lovely coastal expanse.

My next exposure to the Bolinas Lagoon came seven years later, in 1940, just before World War II. As a zoology and pre-med student at UC Berkeley, I hiked with my ornithology class up through the tangled poison oak on a dairy ranch at the lagoon's north end to see the nesting egrets and herons. This ranch, called Canyon Ranch, extended along the northern end of the lagoon and nearly to the top of the Bolinas Ridge. It was a superb lesson in the new concept of ecology.

Even then, there were danger signs that angered me. The dairy ranches around the lagoon were flushing all their manure into its waters, and the tiny resort towns of Bolinas and Stinson Beach were dumping their garbage and flushing untreated sewage directly into it too. This fragile, life-filled lagoon was not only home to the large colony of egrets and herons, but it was also the wintering and feeding grounds for birds coming down from the Arctic Circle and Alaska. Was it destined to be just another stinking dump for garbage, like the thousands of acres of tidal flats on San Francisco Bay?

Great flocks of Dunlin migrate along the coast from Alaska to Baja California. They depend on Tomales Bay and Bolinas Lagoon for resting and food. Tomales Bay consistently tallies one of the nation's highest Christmas bird counts.

The Battle for West Marin Begins

The year 1957 spelled doom for Bolinas Lagoon: development was encroaching from every side. The Army Corps was building the first dam of its Russian River Project, the Coyote Dam. George Leonard, an astute developer, purchased eighteen hundred acres of the Bolinas Ridge that year. This purchase encompassed small creeks, the meager water source for Stinson Beach, and two miles bordering Highway 1 on Bolinas Lagoon. At the same time the State Lands Commission, still in the real estate business, leased twelve hundred acres of the lagoon to the Bolinas Harbor District, which had plans to dredge a harbor and build a marina.

In 1958 Pat Brown, the new Governor, started building the one thousand miles of freeways he had promised. By coincidence perhaps, his chief of advance freeway planning for the state was Harold Summers, whose wife, Mary, headed the Marin County Planning Department. Hearings began on transforming rural Highway 1 into a freeway, eventually connecting it to both the Golden Gate and Richmond bridges, and running it up the

Great Egrets have made their nests high in the redwood trees of Canyon Ranch for generations. In 1961 their home and feeding grounds were threatened by the freeway and harbor development plans. For thirty years, ACR Research Associate Helen Pratt has scientifically studied and published the nesting successes of the heronry. In 1990 there were ten Great Blue Heron nests, eighty-six Great Egret nests (above), and four Snowy Egret nests.

coastline through Sonoma County. If the freeway project had gone through, it would have made huge cuts and fills on the border of Bolinas Lagoon and urbanized the area around the entrances to the proposed National Seashore.

By 1961 nearly the entire southern Bolinas Ridge, and the lagoon itself, were in the hands of experienced developers. However, they did have one problem: they had no water supply. Even so, that year they prodded Mary Summers and the supervisors into adopting a frightening Bolinas-Stinson Beach Master Plan, which showed a freeway along the lagoon and a "parkway" along the ridge. There were also home sites and service roads on the steep, unstable ridge. At that time there were no zoning restrictions to prevent cutting up much of the rural land in both Marin and Sonoma counties into two-acre parcels.

Marin Audubon strongly protested the plan, but Mary Summers called it a "done deal" engineered by the pro-growth supervisors. And it was probably true that the general population still favored growth and freeways.

Our dream of saving the Bolinas Lagoon seemed impossible. Treasurer Stan Picher and I, representing the Marin Audubon Society, had spoken with other groups against the plan at state freeway hearings, but no one else was speaking on behalf of leaving the lagoon alone. Quite the contrary: there was considerable amusement at the idea that the lagoon's tire-studded mud flats and burning garbage dumps might have any value whatsoever except for landfill. Some of the residents favored a large harbor development, or even a racetrack, because of the jobs they would bring.

With Caroline Livermore's training behind me, it was all too clear that to preserve the lagoon, we had to do exactly what the developers had done: flash the cash and buy strategic land—and soon. I visited the State Lands

This proposed free-way route would have crossed over a ridge of Mt. Tamalpais from Highway 101 at Mill Valley to Muir Beach and headed north through Stinson Beach, cutting through the mountain ridges and filling in the valleys and shoreline.

Commission in Sacramento and, closer to home, talked to the directors of the Bolinas Harbor District.

My grand strategy was to convince the Marin Audubon Society, first, to purchase land bordering the lagoon, preferably on both sides of Highway 1, as a deterrent to the freeway and, second, to work to change the five-man elected board of the Bolinas Harbor District from a group of developers into a group of bird lovers who would help us preserve the lagoon as a wildlife sanctuary.

I Make My Move

In January 1961, about twenty years after my first climb up to the Canyon Ranch heronry, I put in a call to realtor Gene McDaniel, president of the Bolinas Harbor District, to let him know I was interested in buying land bordering the lagoon. He phoned my medical office in Kentfield a few days later with startling news.

"Dr. Griffin," said McDaniel, "I thought I'd tell you that the Canyon Ranch is going to be subdivided and you can pick up a parcel. If you're

The steep 503-acre Canyon Ranch on Bolinas Lagoon was to be cut into parcels in 1961 by William Tevis, a speculator. The redwood grove in the center canyon where egrets nest was to be logged. The lagoon where they feed was to be dredged and freeways were to be built along both the ridge and shoreline.

interested, go directly to Bill Tevis." He explained that the owners of the ranch were now William Tevis and Madame Suzanne de Tessand, owner of a large San Francisco department store. My heart sank. I had thought that the ranch was still in the hands of the Galloway family, conservation-minded landowners in West Marin. In fact, Alan Galloway had been a president of the California Academy of Sciences.

I realized that subdividing the Canyon Ranch would mean the end of the egret and heron colony. McDaniel went on to tell me about his own plans to build a marina and motel and to dredge the lagoon. And, he said, a pipeline was coming from Sonoma County to provide water for subdivisions, answering the need for water development.

I put in a call to Mary Galloway. "Yes, indeed," she said, "we sold 503 acres four years ago, including the egret heronry, to Mr. Tevis for some eighty thousand dollars and kept the remaining 274 acres at the north end of the lagoon." She said that they had bought the ranch in 1941 and at that time the heronry was well established. Then I called Tevis, who was visiting the other ranch he owned within the proposed National Seashore. I made an appointment for the next day.

William Tevis was born in California into a family that controlled the Kern County Land Company with huge land holdings in Southern California. His method, it seemed, was to buy a piece of land, take as much of the timber and minerals as he could, and then resell the land at a profit.

My meeting with Tevis took place on his private polo field at his two-thousand-acre Lake Ranch overlooking the Pacific at the south end of the Point Reyes Peninsula. A polo match was in progress, with Tevis and a younger man riding superbly. They were dressed in full polo regalia. They kept me waiting for about an hour, but I was entertained by this scene of landed nobility cavorting in West Marin.

Then Tevis sat down and we discussed the Canyon Ranch. He was a formal older man, athletic and handsome. "I represent Marin Audubon Society as president," I said, although I hadn't spoken to them about the purchase. "My concern is to save the heronry, which is one of the largest on the Pacific coast."

Tevis said emphatically, "I plan to subdivide into twenty-acre parcels and the birds can move elsewhere. I'm unloading because Mrs. de Tessand is impatient and needs money for her department store."

"What would you take for the entire ranch?" I ventured.

He did some figuring. "Eight hundred dollars per acre, about $400,000," he stated without hesitation.

I weighed the figure and then jumped in with both feet. "We'll never get another chance. I'd better take it now."

Tevis said he might lower the price in exchange for a substantial tax

Canyon Ranch hasn't changed much since 1961 when I obtained an option from Tevis and persuaded the Marin Audubon Society to buy it. Behind the 1875 Peter Bourne Victorian is the heronry that I had visited as a UC student in 1940. We changed the name to Audubon Canyon Ranch in 1961.

write-off to a nonprofit organization. "If we can work out favorable terms," I said, "I think I can persuade Marin Audubon to buy it. We'll start a fund drive to raise the money." Tevis was amused by my presumption, but he accepted a personal check for one thousand dollars to option the deal. Then he called his land broker, Pardow Hooper, in San Francisco, filled him in, and made an appointment for me to see him.

Picher and Griffin On the Hook

The next day Stan Picher agreed to walk over the property with me. As Audubon treasurer, he was thrilled with the idea of buying the heronry but appalled at the price. I had to sell him on the idea that the ranch had great strategic value in protecting the entire area. The 503-acre parcel contained about a mile of frontage on Bolinas Lagoon on both sides of the proposed freeway (Highway 1), and went nearly to the top of the Bolinas Ridge. There it was separated from the then eighteen thousand acre watershed of the Marin Municipal Water District by a two hundred acre dry parcel owned by Bolinas real estate broker Hurford Sharon. By owning a little of the ridge, we would hold a key to stopping the proposed high-speed freeway that was planned to cut across Mt. Tamalpais to the coast.

Great Egrets, with wingspans of nearly six feet, were poached nearly to extinction for their splendid feathers, called aigrettes, worn on ladies' hats. The National Audubon Society was created to protect them and their habitat.

Stan was convinced that if we presented the wild idea of buying the ranch to the board of Marin Audubon Society we'd be laughed out of the room. "Marty," he said, "as treasurer, the largest check I have ever written for the society was $125 to send a ranger to National Audubon's summer camp." The thought of a huge fund drive didn't exactly thrill him. Still, knowing California land values, we both felt that in five years the eight hundred dollars per acre price would seem like a great bargain.

Later that day I called on Caroline Livermore. I found her in her study dictating her daily correspondence to a secretary. She advised me to "get a written agreement signed by Tevis to sell his ranch. I'll pledge two thousand dollars if you get one."

Next came a cordial meeting in San Francisco with Pardow Hooper, Tevis' real estate broker. He was a dapper man, always dressed in pressed khakis with a jaunty hat and tie. Hooper specialized in buying and selling ranches for his wealthy clients. Hooper was highly professional and scrupulously honest. We were to become lifelong friends, and he would handle many of our future purchases in West Marin. Everyone trusted him. Without his help we could never have completed the many complicated purchases

The large Audubon Canyon Ranch heronry is located high in redwood trees overlooking Bolinas Lagoon where the birds feed. Some nests can be seen in the left mid-photo where their tree-top nests offer protection from predators.

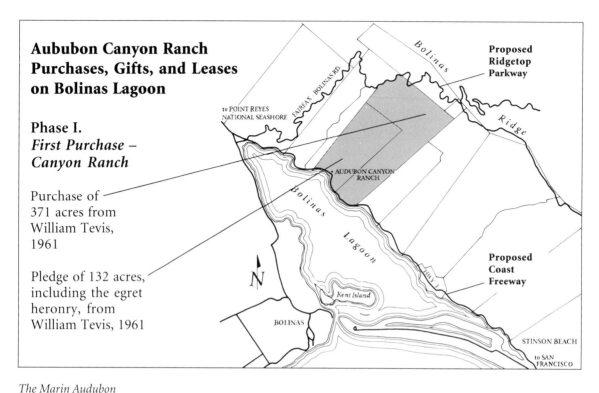

Aububon Canyon Ranch Purchases, Gifts, and Leases on Bolinas Lagoon

Phase I.
First Purchase – Canyon Ranch

Purchase of 371 acres from William Tevis, 1961

Pledge of 132 acres, including the egret heronry, from William Tevis, 1961

Within map:
to POINT REYES NATIONAL SEASHORE
FAIRFAX-BOLINAS RD.
Bolinas
Proposed Ridgetop Parkway
Ridge
AUDUBON CANYON RANCH
Bolinas Lagoon
N
Proposed Coast Freeway
Kent Island
BOLINAS
STINSON BEACH
to SAN FRANCISCO

The Marin Audubon Society agreed to purchase 371 acres of Canyon Ranch from William Tevis in 1961, who then donated 132 acres, including the heronry, for the tax benefit. But before the escrow closed, he stripped the topsoil in a canyon and sold it for land-fill.

of the next dozen years.

At that first meeting, Hooper told us Tevis' final price for 371 acres was firm: $335,000 at six percent interest spread over ten years. The 132-acre heronry canyon was to be a gift to Marin Audubon Society from Tevis, to be made when it best suited him for a tax write-off. We were given thirty days to raise a one-thousand-dollar down payment, then ninety days to raise nine thousand dollars, then nine months to raise ninety thousand. We had nine years to raise the balance. Later Stan and I agreed that we would personally refund all donations we received from our contributors if we had to default on the property and lose their down payment money. This was a frightening prospect to both of us, but a powerful incentive to make our project succeed.

Little Marin Audubon Agrees

On April 6, 1961, Stan Picher and I met with the directors of the Marin Audubon Society at the National Audubon's local headquarters on Richardson Bay, where I outlined the plan. The directors, including the Bird Lady, Elizabeth Terwilliger, were astounded at the idea of buying the Tevis ranch but, to their credit, they agreed to go ahead, with the understanding that Stan and I would be responsible for the project. For fear that someone might make Tevis a better offer, we pledged the board to secrecy. We had our board attorney, Larry Jordan of Mill Valley, draw up agreements with Hooper. Then we had the papers signed and the deal put in escrow. For some reason, Tevis insisted that the escrow be put in my name.

Not until then did we find out about the man we were buying from. Tevis had sold thousands of cubic yards of the topsoil in the north canyon (now The Garden Clubs of America Canyon) that was to be part of his tax-reducing gift to Marin Audubon. The buyer of the topsoil had it bulldozed into trucks and then hauled it to a site across the lagoon near the Bolinas grammar school to be used for fill. This little deal on the side turned the stream bed into a barren gully and caused floods for the next *twenty years*. Two forlorn oaks were left standing on hummocks by the creek but they later died. A few years later Tevis sold his Lake Ranch to loggers who began cutting while the Point Reyes National Seashore was still attempting to negotiate its purchase.

As soon as we heard about the sale of topsoil, Stan Picher and I rushed to the ranch. The deed was half done. We phoned Hooper, who was furious with Tevis and called him to protest. Tevis responded calmly, "Let Audubon drop the deal if they don't like it." Our lawyer ruled out litigation in favor of negotiation. Our great fear was that he would log the heronry canyon before it was deeded over, as he had bulldozed a road to the ridge two years before.

William Tevis (right) accepts a check for $90,000 as the first major payment on his ranch in 1962 from Aileen Pierson and Stan Picher, co-founders with me of the Ranch. Aileen was a Mills College and UC graduate, an expert in state administrative law, and a president of Golden Gate Audubon Society. She served on the ACR board for twenty-five years.

Raising Half a Million

In spite of this setback, the down payment money came in without a hitch. We decided to bring in as many donors as possible to enlarge our base of public support. Ten phone calls to ten people brought one hundred dollars each. One of the donors was Mrs. Gwin (Bunny) Follis, birding friend of Elizabeth Terwilliger. We soon found that she would be a powerful ally. Her husband was president of Standard Oil of California, and he volunteered the services of his public relations firm for our fund drive. He also introduced us to attorney Dick Madden of the venerable San Francisco law firm Pillsbury, Madison and Sutro. For years after that, Madden handled several of our leases and gifts of lands *pro bono* and served on our board.

Later in 1961, Stan succeeded me as president of Marin Audubon

Society, and I was named chairman of the Audubon Canyon Ranch Project to pursue our purchases. I enlisted the help of many Marin doctors and their wives, including Nancy Barbour and Debbie Ablin, who served on the Ranch Board for many years. Our first Audubon Canyon Ranch letterhead looked like a "Who's Who" of San Francisco and Marin County. Stan and I led groups of prospective donors, as well as the board of the Golden Gate Audubon Chapter, through the marshes, over the mud flats and up the steep trail to the overlook.

Laurel Reynolds and Mindy Willis were two well known wildlife photographers who donated a fundraising film for the Ranch. Laurel's husband, Dr. Rick Reynolds, was a president of the Golden Gate Audubon Society, which became a Ranch sponsor in 1962. Marin and Golden Gate are chapters of the National Audubon Society.

Expanding Our Support Base

Our next step, in 1962, was to expand the fundraising base of the Marin Audubon Society by joining forces with the Golden Gate Audubon Society to form Audubon Canyon Ranch, Inc. The Golden Gate Society had two thousand members in the East Bay and San Francisco. They were led by their president, Aileen Pierson, a state Public Welfare executive, who became a co-founder of the Ranch and served on its board for twenty-five years. Sequoia Audubon Society of San Mateo and Madrone Audubon Society of Sonoma County joined us later. Our appreciation for the splendor of the canyons, heronry, and lagoon was contagious.

Next we hit on the scheme of asking donors to pledge eight hundred dollars, the cost of one acre, with the promise that their name would be permanently displayed at the ranch. Some two hundred donors became sponsors, including Stan and his brother, my family, and my parents. One acre was purchased by Bugs Cain's friends in his memory and in memory of his wild Camp Dimond canyon. In the process of attracting donors, our little Marin Audubon Society, which had begun with twenty members in 1957, rapidly grew to one thousand members. We now had a powerful constituency throughout Marin and the Bay Area.

At the Ross Valley Clinic, my secretary doubled as an Audubon volunteer, typing hundreds of fundraising letters and lining up many of my well-to-do patients as sponsors. There was a standing joke that a visit cost ten dollars for Dr. Griffin and eight hundred dollars for Audubon Canyon Ranch.

After five years of fundraising, which reached statewide proportions under Stan Picher's leadership, the entire ranch was paid off. I personally delivered a Ranch check for sixty-one thousand dollars in 1966 to close the purchase, take title, and make absolutely sure this debt with my name on it was paid off. Picher and I were at last off the hook—and ready to buy more land to save Bolinas Lagoon and rescue the gateway to the National Seashore, which was still only partly purchased four years after it was authorized.

The Miracle

In the sixty-four years since I first laid eyes on the egrets and herons of the Bolinas Lagoon, there has been a steady improvement in their habitat. Each spring is a celebration of the miracle of their survival through the eras of plume hunters, logging, fires, oil spills, pesticide poisoning, predators, and bay filling. And each spring I hike with my grandchildren up to the Ranch's Henderson Overlook, where we gaze awestruck at the noisy nesting and feeding behavior of these birds in the Schwarz Redwood Grove below. These sites were named for generous donors who helped us during the early years.

Keeping track of the birds' nesting successes is a task of great scientific value. It is an exquisitely accurate indicator of the health of the birds' habitat. Since 1961, biologist Helen Pratt has counted each nesting bird pair and each of their eggs and chicks. The average number of nesting egrets has remained fairly constant at one hundred pairs, while the number of great blue heron nests has been declining for reasons unknown.

Still, the greatest thrill is the look of wonder on the faces of schoolchildren, teachers, docent trainees, and visitors from all over the world. This unspoiled wildlife scene, devoid of commercial overtones, cannot be duplicated anywhere by man. It can only, at best, be preserved and shared.

For Stan Picher and me, the creation of Audubon Canyon Ranch and its wildlife preserves was the best thing we could ever have done for future generations. I am proud that the heronry canyon was named Picher Canyon by the Ranch Board in honor of him, and that the Martin Griffin Trail, which winds around it, was named for me some thirty years ago.

On several occasions I have overheard visitors wonder if that trail leads to my burial site, and I have thought, if I were to die today, my life would be complete knowing that the heronry and the Bolinas Lagoon are safe—permanently.

I'm proud of this trail sign (where visitors think I'm buried) placed by the Ranch board in 1966. It reads, "This trail was named in honor of Loyal Martin Griffin Jr., MD, president of Marin Audubon Society in 1961, whose vision and action created the Canyon Ranch project." The circular three-mile trail loops around Picher Canyon and the Aileen Pierson Marsh.

How the Bolinas Heronry Was Saved

Before World War II there were dozens of colonies of so-called common egrets nesting in the tops of trees around San Francisco Bay. They and their cousins, the Great Blue Herons, are the largest of California's wading birds, with six-foot wing spans. However, they were considered a noisy nuisance by many, and they gradually disappeared as their trees were cut down and their tideland feeding grounds filled. The Bolinas Lagoon heronry, one of the largest on the coast, survived fires, logging, and poaching until 1960 only by its isolation.

To save this heronry from a freeway in 1961 required a disciplined, well-thought-out campaign with a simple goal: Save the Bolinas Lagoon. Next we needed to build a growing constituency of citizens: members of our local Audubon Chapters, school children, voters, and organizations to help us raise funds and manage the preserves. We knew from the start that our battle was largely political, and that to win it we needed to educate the public and convince the supervisors. As a non-profit organization, we had to tread a fine line between education and political action.

In 1961, the Marin Audubon Society chose the name Audubon Canyon Ranch for its project as a way to link ourselves to the National Audubon Society, which gave its approval. Next we took the liberty of changing the name "common egret" to the more appropriate Great American Egret. An artist drew this stately bird, wings extended, as our symbol, and this logo appears on every letterhead and publication along with our list of officers, directors, board, and advisory board members.

This stunning image of a Great Egret became the logo for all Audubon Canyon Ranch Preserves.

To raise public awareness, our naturalist, Clerin Zumwalt, supplied his photos to the media and to schools. One picture, we confirmed, is worth a thousand words. Few could ignore the images of the birds in their stunning breeding display, courting, preening, their squabbling antics, the feeding of their young, or their graceful descent like white parachutes into the lagoon feeding grounds.

We trained classes of docents to teach in schools, on the trails, and at the heronry overlook. There they explained to children and adults why the secluded heronry nests are located by the parents in a steep wooded canyon, fairly safe from the wind and marauding Golden Eagles, ravens, and raccoons. Through telescopes, visitors counted two to four eggs in the six-foot nests, saw the young fed by regurgitation, and heard docents and naturalists describe the birds' habits.

Visitors marveled at the redwood groves with more than one hundred nests, the Great Egrets and Great Blue Herons and tiny Snowy Egrets contrasting against the brilliant green forest of wind-sculpted bays, oaks, madrones, and buckeyes. Docents, Ranch Guides, and trained hosts explained the geology and how the active San Andreas Fault is still forming the Bolinas Lagoon and its twin, Tomales Bay. Above this beautiful and astounding geography floats a cacophony of raucous sounds from the heronry as the famished young call to their parents feasting in the lagoon below.

Gradually, the public's perception of these beautiful birds changed and word spread that the birds' habitat should be preserved. By the time we ended our land purchases after thirteen years, Audubon Canyon Ranch was well known in the Bay Area and thousands of people had contributed to its preservation work.

Now, twenty thousand adults and school children come each year to witness this scene and to realize that, in the end, it was the birds who saved themselves—with a helping hand from Audubon Canyon Ranch.

The colony of approximately a hundred pairs of nesting egrets and herons is among the largest on the Pacific Coast. Our strategy was to educate the public and the press that the heronry and the Bolinas Lagoon were far too valuable to be sacrificed for development.

CHAPTER THREE

The Picher-Griffin Team

It is important to have bold initiatives, not simply to play defense.

—General Dwight D. Eisenhower

T here were years starting in 1961 when neither Stan Picher nor I dared show our faces at Smiley's Saloon in Bolinas, or the Two Ball Inn (a railroad term) in Point Reyes Station. The truth is that for the next thirteen years we weren't too popular with landowners who favored development in West Marin. We'd already wasted months at fruitless freeway hearings playing defense. Now we simply decided to ignore their plans, not to seek consensus, and to outmaneuver them wherever we could. Stan and I therefore decided on a bold initiative for Audubon Canyon Ranch: a campaign of strategic land purchases and organization building.

During the campaign to save West Marin, we had the enthusiastic support of many of our neighbors and friends "over the hill" in the more urbanized eastern parts of the county. Kentfield was filled with conservationists such as members of the Kent family, who later would be willing to lie down in front of bulldozers and get hauled off to jail to save Tamalpais Creek. Nor did my medical practice suffer, even though our clinic had many real estate people and developers for patients; in fact, several of their family members eventually took our docent training courses at Audubon Canyon Ranch. All in all, the Ranch became a very popular project that no politician or developer in Marin County could ignore.

Although several physicians were land speculators in West Marin, the close-knit Marin Medical Society became one of our strongest supporters. Dr. John Lee formed an Environmental Health Committee, which took out newspaper ads opposing any subdivisions along Tomales Bay as a threat to public health.

During those thirteen years, my wife complained about the personal checks I wrote for options, and my name could be found on page after page in the county recorder's office. But Stan Picher had exceptional fundraising

Low tide on Bolinas Lagoon brings out walkers who share the tidelands with the millions of mud holes, home to numerous unstudied species of invertebrates that make up ninety-five percent of the animal species on earth.

Stan Picher, speaking at the dedication of Audubon Canyon Ranch as a National Historic Landmark in 1969, announces the start of our docent education program. In the foreground is William Kent Jr., a grandson of Congressman William Kent and developer of the Seadrift subdivision in Stinson Beach.

and organizational talents, which made each of our land options and purchases succeed. Together with our board members, we turned the four Bay Area Audubon Chapters that sponsored the Audubon Canyon Ranch into an efficient land-buying organization, backed by a splendid training program for hundreds of docents in wildlife education and advocacy. We had built a winning team.

A Leader in the Art World

Stan Picher and I had vast differences in lifestyle and interests, but we worked well together. My contribution was a knowledge of wildlife, county politics, water supplies, and real estate, plus a large family and an influential medical practice with many patients throughout Marin.

Stan was articulate, charming, and financially astute. He had a passion for art collecting, and had run a successful bookstore and art gallery in Chicago before he retired to Marin in 1955 at the age of forty. He was among the leaders of the art world in San Francisco and New York.

We often held our meetings at the three-tiered home of Stan and his companion, Wally Goodman, which they had built on a steep, wooded Belvedere lot teeming with birds and overlooking the Golden Gate. "I didn't know one bird from another," Stan told me, "that's why I joined Audubon." He also served on the board of the De Young Museum, once as president.

You could tell us apart by our shoes. Mine were always muddy from tramping through marshes and climbing hillsides while Stan's were spotless and shiny.

Jewels Worthy of Preservation

Fortunately for Marin County, Stan Picher considered the canyons, marshes, and the egret heronry of West Marin to be "jewels worthy of collection and preservation." He used this metaphor, borrowed from his efforts in the art world, to raise funds from wealthy donors whom he graciously entertained at his home or at the Ranch. Stan Picher was one of those rare people to whom others love to give money for worthy causes. He said, "It's easier to raise one hundred thousand dollars from one donor than ten thousand donations of ten dollars." However, he also established a box for donations by Ranch visitors. Two Brownie troops collected Blue Chip Stamps and raised eight hundred dollars each for the Ranch.

Raising $337,000 wasn't easy in 1962, so we were out raising money for years. Here a check for $800, the cost of one acre, is being presented to me by Steve Lato, President of the Marin Rod and Gun Club. A large gift came from The Garden Clubs of America in 1964 and a canyon is named in their honor.

Stan had the ability to ask for sizable donations both to the Audubon Canyon Ranch and the De Young Museum practically in the same breath. Few donors could resist his twin passions for wildlife and art. We once accompanied Mrs. Alma Brooks Walker in her limousine to the Ranch for a simple farm luncheon. It was preceded by a properly chilled martini, prepared by me under Stan's direction, in her own silver-handled cup. Mrs. Brooks Walker later donated twenty-five thousand dollars to repair the original ranch house, at that time called the Bourne House but now named in her honor.

An astute businessman who never allowed any donations to be used for frills, Stan used nearly every cent collected to pay off land purchases. He hated to pay salaries, and for years our employees, secretary Edris Cole and naturalist Clerin Zumwalt, were practically volunteers. To cover Ranch expenses, Stan started a successful nature bookstore on the premises. All the rest of our workers were volunteers, with Stan and me running the day-to-day operations until 1967.

Hardly a day went by that we didn't meet or talk, and the board put their trust in our decisions. Even on our vacations we kept in touch by long distance. We took turns speaking at public hearings. We met with county supervisors, the governor, legislators, and agency chiefs. We handed out press releases and made ourselves available for newspaper interviews and photo opportunities. We had stunning slide and film shows. I even invested in the liberal new weekly, the *Pacific Sun,* started by Steve McNamara, so the county would gain an alternative viewpoint from that of the conservative Marin *Independent Journal,* which had been our constant critic.

Stan and I controlled the Audubon Canyon Ranch during its first years as either president or vice president, so we could seize the now-or-never chance to buy a ranch or shoreline parcel and keep land purchase our primary goal. Stan had free time; mine was borrowed from my practice and family life. This balancing act caused a drain on my sleep and health, especially during the formation of the ranch from 1961 to 1963, and in 1967 when Stan was in Europe and the purchase and fund drive for Kent Island fell into my lap.

Stan was a quick-witted, twitchy type who tapped his foot rapidly when meetings dragged. His favorite put-down was, "I've known people less vague." He was authoritarian and couldn't abide indecision. At first he was reticent about speaking at public hearings, but he overcame this in a dramatic presentation to the Board of Supervisors in 1967. First he described a half dozen parcels the Ranch owned encircling the Bolinas Lagoon. Then he handed their deeds to Pierre Joske of County Parks, as the start of a County Shoreline Park. Finally, he topped off his talk by handing a Ranch check for eight thousand dollars to Joske to buy another parcel. This brought prolonged applause, and from then on Stan was irrepressible.

Learning How to Buy Land

Friends have asked how I learned to obtain land options that ultimately led to purchases. Fortunately I had helped my medical partner, Dr. John Siemens, purchase and develop land for the Ross Valley Medical Clinic, Ross Hospital, Ross Psychiatric Hospital, and the Tamalpais Retirement Center. From John I learned how to work with title companies, banks, and lawyers.

I also found that people won't sell their lands to committees, but will sell it to one person whom they trust. When I approached someone to ask for an option or a gift of land, I always went alone. The Ranch had an excellent reputation that preceded my visits or phone calls. Part of my success, I think, was my sincere dedication to wildlife and my reputation as a physician. Often I was able to secure options on parcels with only a handshake or a modest personal check. However, our offers were always based on careful research, appraisals, and legal review, and as much cash down as possible.

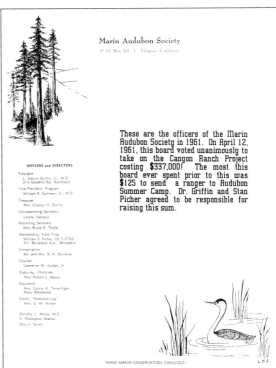

These are the officers of the Marin Audubon Society in 1961. On April 12, 1961, this board voted unanimously to take on the Canyon Ranch Project costing $337,000! The most this board ever spent prior to this was $125 to send a ranger to Audubon Summer Camp. Dr. Griffin and Stan Picher agreed to be responsible for raising this sum.

Marin Audubon Society
P. O. Box 441 · Tiburon, California

OFFICERS and DIRECTORS

President
  L. Martin Griffin, Jr., M.D.
  313 Goodhill Rd., Kentfield
Vice-President, Program
  William R. Eastman, Jr., M.D.
Treasurer
  Mrs. Charles H. Durrie
Corresponding Secretary
  Loreta Pacheco
Recording Secretary
  Mrs. Bruce R. Towle
Membership, Field Trips
  William S. Picher, GE 5-0766
  401 Belvedere Ave., Belvedere
Conservation
  Mr. and Mrs. B. K. Dunshee
Counsel
  Lawrence W. Jordan, Jr.
Publicity, Historian
  Mrs. Robert L. Mayer
Education
  Mrs. Calvin K. Terwilliger
  Mary Westwood
Editor, "Redwood Log"
  Mrs. G. M. Milner

Dorothy L. Morse, M.D.
S. Thompson Walker
Otis H. Smith

"MAKE MARIN CONSERVATION CONSCIOUS"

Sometimes we purchased large ranches with hardly a dime in the bank. A banker new to our board was shocked when we told him we always bought the ranches first and then raised the cash. We told him that if we had waited, there would have been no Audubon Canyon Ranch. One other point: I knew from my research and studying maps just which parcels we needed, and I called on the owners repeatedly asking that they let me know when they were ready to sell. That's how we got the Thompson Ranch (Volunteer Canyon), the Galloway Ranch, Kent Island, and numerous parcels along Bolinas Lagoon and Tomales Bay. I always pledged the owners to secrecy so no one would trump me with a better offer until each parcel was safely in escrow. Jack Mason, West Marin historian, complained in one of his books that we were buying ranches so fast he couldn't keep track.

Amazingly, during those thirteen years, when more than 1.5 million dollars changed hands in numerous escrows, we were never served with a subpoena or received a threatening call from an attorney. I attribute our success to honesty on our part and dealing only with trusted title companies, brokers, and especially our Ranch attorney of thirty years, George Peyton. Stan and I took some enormous personal financial risks, but they faded away as each fund drive succeeded.

Left: The influential Marin Medical Society opposed sprawl in West Marin as a threat to the county's environmental health. Here I am flanked by Jack Manwaring, MD (left), president of the Society, and Ike Livermore (right), Resource Secretary under Governor Reagan, who spoke to Society members in 1969 against dams on north coast rivers. Right: This simple stationery has served the Marin Audubon Society well since 1957.

Setting a Relentless Pace

Board meetings were often at my home in Kentfield or at Alice Kent's home nearby. We always served food and drink to make the meetings as enjoyable as possible. Later we met at Stan's new apartment in Pacific Heights, where Wally cooked hamburgers for the board. Because our board meetings were fun and cozy, our attendance was phenomenal. At these super-organized meetings, which moved at high speed, Stan reveled in his financial reports. He had a high sense of drama, and each of his reports contained some new surprise that evoked applause and cheers—a ranch paid off, an unrestricted fifty thousand dollar gift, a donation of oil rights in Fresno County. Stan was also generous in his own donations to the Ranch. To my amazement, he even persuaded my parents to donate their home in Citrus Heights near Sacramento to an endowment fund for the Ranch, which was set up with the San Francisco Foundation.

Our four daughters were a constant reminder of our responsibility to future generations. Left to right are Linda, Anne, Joan, and Carol in 1964.

Stan was meticulous in his correspondence. He answered every letter warmly and eloquently. Every donor received a personal, typed note, and he kept a card file with cryptic notations to personalize future letters of thanks. But the push, push, push took its toll. It was as if he and I were courted by the same demon. We drove ourselves and each other. Several of our valuable volunteers in the early years dropped out from our relentless pressure. In 1963, after two years of fundraising, I took a year leave of absence from the Ross Valley Clinic and moved to Italy with my family to regain my perspective.

The greatest fear of the Picher-Griffin team was that some future Ranch board might sell these hard-won lands, paid for by thousands of donors, to raise funds to pay salaries, or for extravagant education programs. It was for this reason that we wrote the reverter clauses into our deeds: if someone tried to sell the land or misuse it, it would revert to the National Audubon Society or the County Open Space District. We didn't want any of our lands to meet the fate of my Oakland Boy Scout camp.

Our mission from the start was to preserve these lands permanently for wildlife habitat, as buffers to the National Seashore, and to help protect, restore, and maintain the watersheds of Bolinas Lagoon and Tomales Bay. Today the Ranch has active research, educational, property, and development committees to achieve these ends.

Remembering Stan Picher

Stan Picher's greatest achievement for Audubon Canyon Ranch and for Marin and Sonoma counties was his ability to build a large and successful organization embracing four National Audubon Chapters with six thousand members, thousands of donors large and small, boards, committees, and training courses for volunteers and docents. He established endowment funds that grew under his direction, and he made sure that all land purchases were promptly paid off.

His fundraising abilities were legendary, attracting not just funds but actual gifts of land for new wildlife preserves. In addition, he gave his full support to able young activists who showed promise of developing a leadership role in the battle for West Marin. He enthusiastically helped raise the funds for scientific studies, for public education programs, and for employing outstanding naturalists.

William Stanton Picher was renowned throughout the Bay Area for his expertise in Asian art and for his dedication to Audubon Canyon Ranch. Stan was a Missouri native, held a Master's Degree in Art from Harvard, and served in the US Army Intelligence Corps during World War II.

A talented writer and lecturer, Stan wrote fundraiser letters and brochures that were classics of brevity and succinctness. He attracted people from all walks of life to support the Ranch, helping to create a warm and loving Audubon Canyon Ranch family.

Stan suffered an untimely death from a brain tumor in 1981. A memorial service in San Francisco overflowed with his friends, including many from Audubon Canyon Ranch and the De Young Museum, to which he also donated his time, talents, and financial support.

Shortly before Stan's death, the board of Audubon Canyon Ranch honored him by naming the main canyon the Picher Canyon. The plaque at the Ranch headquarters reads, "His fundraising abilities and inspired leadership were there when the Ranch needed them."

CHAPTER FOUR

Saving Bolinas Lagoon

*Parts of Bolinas Lagoon produce seven thousand pounds per acre
of protein annually. It is one of the richest habitats in terms of food
production on the face of the Earth.*

—Clerin Zumwalt, Soil Scientist, 1968

For a dozen years, Kent Island in Bolinas Lagoon was Marin County's most bitterly contested and costliest tideland battle. The struggle divided the tiny coastal town of Bolinas, the entire county, and the state legislature into two opposing camps: wildlife versus marina. To look at sleepy Bolinas and peaceful Kent Island today, you'd wonder what all the uproar was about.

Kent Island is only partly an island and, because of tides and wind, not a place where you'd want to spend the night. It lies close to the quaint old smuggling town of Bolinas, separated by a tidal channel. At low tide you can walk across to Kent Island from Smiley's Saloon at the edge of town; at high tide most of the island is submerged.

This is important to remember: the tidelands of Kent Island, like all state tidelands, rightfully belong to the people of California—not to the Pepper family who originally owned it, nor to the Kents. Years earlier, the state had improvidentially sold its ownership to this and a few dozen other public tidelands. We at Audubon Canyon Ranch felt it essential to buy back all these tidelands, which were so necessary to wildlife habitat, and to secure them permanently. But the Ranch had an even wider purpose: our owner-ship of the 120-acre Kent Island could be the key to preserving the twelve-hundred-acre Bolinas Lagoon, and indeed the entire watershed, as the gateway to the Point Reyes National Seashore. Also, with defeat of the large marina planned for the island, there would be less support for the proposed ridgetop parkway and coast freeway.

To make this prediction come true, I devoted seven years to the Kent Island battle and took one of the bigger gambles of my life.

Wading egrets feed in Bolinas Lagoon before returning to their nests high above the Ranch house. A four-lane freeway was planned to be built between the heronry and the lagoon.

A Wildlife-Rich Island

Looking west toward the Pacific at low tide, Bolinas Lagoon lies in the foreground with Kent Island on the left. Marin citizens challenged the state for disposing of these public tidelands for commercial real estate development.

Kent Island contains a few scattered pines on sand dunes and a half-dozen roosting squawkers, Black-crowned Night-Herons, which sleep there after their nightly food forays in the tideflats. Shorebirds such as willets, sandpipers, and curlews feed busily around the island's edges. Harbor seals haul out on its sandy beaches and pelicans, terns, and osprey crashdive around it for fish. Behind the island lies the mighty Bolinas Ridge and the Audubon Canyon Ranch heronry, where the Great Egrets and Great Blue Herons return after feeding in the shallow lagoon. To the south, across the narrow inlet from the ocean, is an exclusive enclave of homes called Seadrift, with locked gates, on the Stinson Beach sand spit, where the battle of who owns the state beaches is still being fought in the courts. Tragically, dredging along the edge of the sandspit to create Seadrift Lagoon has impaired the tidal circulation of the adjacent Bolinas Lagoon.

Early in the history of Marin County, U.S. Congressman William Kent, a friend of Teddy Roosevelt and John Muir, recognized the value of Marin real estate and bought up large tracts of land. These extended from his home estate near Kentfield across Mt. Tamalpais to Steep Ravine and to the ocean hot springs at Stinson Beach and to Bolinas Lagoon. At one time a rider on horseback could ride entirely on Kent land from Kentfield to Stinson. Kent once planned a large resort at Bolinas to be served by a railroad that would descend Steep Ravine to the ocean.

Eventually, over a thousand acres of the Kent estate on the eastern side of the county were subdivided and dubbed Kent Woodlands, which soon sported expensive homes. In 1912, Kent assembled thousands of acres of forested watershed lands on the rainy north slope of Mt. Tamalpais to help start the Marin Municipal Water District. Parts of Mt. Tamalpais State Park are former Kent lands donated by the congressman. He named Muir Woods, the first National Monument, for his friend and gave it to the nation; and at one time his heirs offered the whole of the Stinson Beach sandspit to the state as a park, but the state turned it down. Just hours before his death in 1928 he donated the 204 acres of Steep Ravine where I camped as a Boy Scout to the state park system. Kent's pioneering work in preserving large parts of Mt. Tamalpais as state and national parks laid the groundwork for the purchase of the Point Reyes National Seashore and the Golden Gate National Recreation Area some forty years later.

When William Kent died, his two sons inherited Kent Island in the heart of the Bolinas Lagoon. Roger Kent and his wife Alice received nine and one-half acres. Thomas Kent and his wife Anne inherited 111 acres. Alice and Roger were our neighbors in Kent Woodlands, and Alice knew Stan Picher through the Asian Art Museum. Roger was a well-known attorney and chairman of the State Central Democratic Committee. Unforeseen by the congressman, the battle for this low-lying island—really just a shifting sand-bar—was to determine the future of the Bolinas watershed and the National Seashore.

This one-meter frame was laid on the "worth-less" muddy sand in Bolinas Lagoon and the organisms within were dug up and counted. Ranch naturalist Clerin Zumwalt, or Zumie, estimated that parts of the lagoon produce seven thousand pounds of protein per acre per year, while good pasture land only produces about eight hundred pounds of beef per acre.

Dredging the Egrets' Food Basket

The controversy started quietly in 1957 when the California State Lands Commission leased twelve hundred acres of tidelands adjacent to Kent Island in Bolinas Lagoon to the Bolinas Harbor District. The District, as established by the Bolinas voters, had been allotted ten years by the state to dredge a harbor in the lagoon and make "other improvements," meaning a large marina, a motel, and parking lots on the filled-in Kent Island tidelands. Over the next decade the district spent $317,843, mostly for studies and

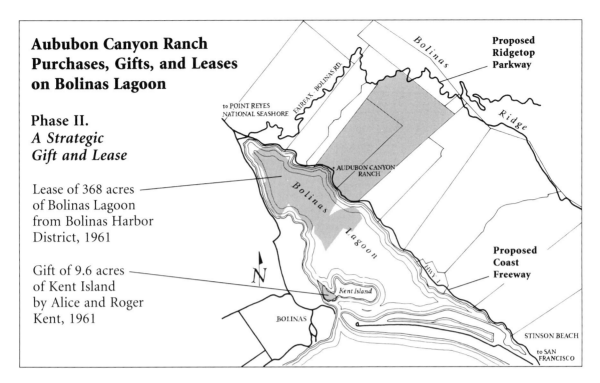

**Aububon Canyon Ranch
Purchases, Gifts, and Leases
on Bolinas Lagoon**

Phase II.
*A Strategic
Gift and Lease*

Lease of 368 acres
of Bolinas Lagoon
from Bolinas Harbor
District, 1961

Gift of 9.6 acres
of Kent Island
by Alice and Roger
Kent, 1961

*In 1961 we obtained a
lease of 368 acres of the
lagoon for one dollar a
year from the Harbor
District, and we received
a key parcel from Alice
and Roger Kent—9.6
acres of Kent Island.*

expenses, but didn't move a single shovelful of mud.

When the Marin Audubon Society bought the Canyon Ranch in 1961, Alice Kent became the chapter's first new board member. To help deter dredging, Alice and Roger donated their nine-and-one-half-acre portion of Kent Island in 1961 to the Marin Audubon Society as a wildlife preserve. This gift proved to be a gigantic thorn in the side of the Bolinas Harbor District, which needed that portion for its marina.

With the Kent's deed as leverage, Stan and I met with Gene McDaniel, chairman of the Harbor District. Gene was happy to see us when we told him that our purpose was to lease an old 368-acre oyster farm at the north end of the lagoon that was a feeding ground for the birds of the heronry at the Canyon Ranch. Gene said he would give us a fifty-year lease, but insisted on a one-year cancellation clause. The lease would be canceled, he said, "if we need to dredge that end for a turning basin for motor boats."

Gene consulted with the district's board, and it demanded a rent of ten thousand dollars per year. "That's ridiculous," we said. We held firm at our offer of one dollar per year and finally they agreed. The Marin Audubon Society carefully sent one dollar per year by registered mail until the lease was abruptly canceled on January 27, 1967.

This turned out to be one hell of a bargain. The Ranch played this ten-

uous year-to-year lease to the hilt for the next six years, educating thousands of visitors and schoolchildren to the value of the tidelands as the herons' and egrets' primary feeding grounds. We taught everyone that the birds could die if their mudflat food basket was dredged or filled. Fortunately, the birds didn't know of the one-year cancellation clause or they might have moved on. For one dollar a year, we bought the egrets and herons six years of safety while we waited out the threat that the heronry might be ruined.

Some Unwanted Bedfellows

Our lease granted us forty percent of the tidelands of Bolinas Lagoon. As lessee, Audubon Canyon Ranch had a legitimate interest in the lagoon's other tenants. Our first bedfellow was the Army Corps of Engineers, whose plans were to dredge the mouth of the lagoon and build a jetty out into the sea. In the sixties, the Corps was known as a killer of wetlands, marshes, lagoons, and rivers. It did its dirty work at the request of local developers and chambers of commerce. But Audubon was able to wear the Corps down with biological studies of the "worthless" lagoon mud which, it turned out, was teeming with mudworms and ghost shrimp essential to the food chain. The Corps finally folded its tents and left.

To see what might have happened to Bolinas Lagoon, take a look at

Zumie counted about six hundred egrets feeding in Bolinas Lagoon one day. By proving that the lagoon is essential habitat for the hundreds of species using it, the Ranch hoped to preserve the watershed ecosystem intact. But despite the scientific data, the Harbor District forged ahead with plans to dredge the lagoon for a marina.

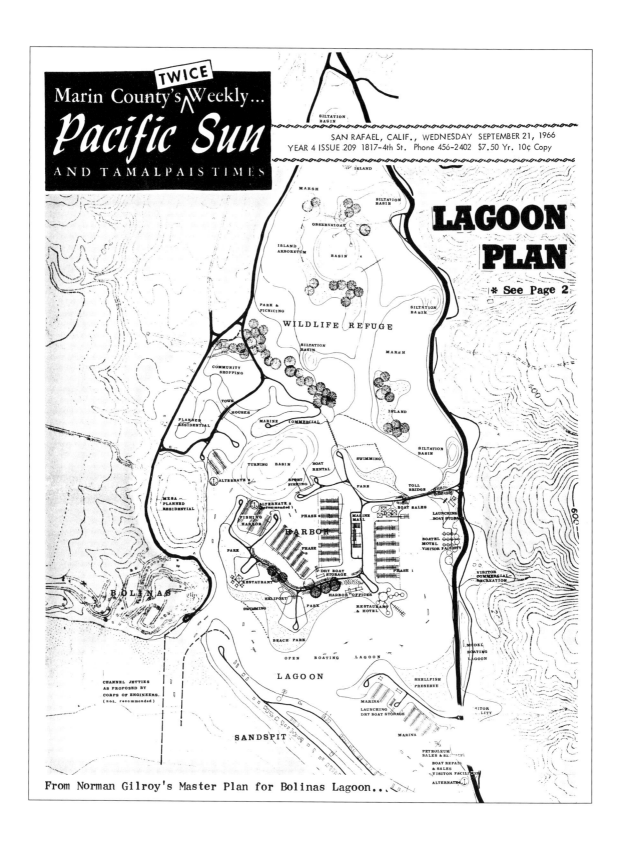

Marin County's Weekly... TWICE

Pacific Sun

AND TAMALPAIS TIMES

SAN RAFAEL, CALIF., WEDNESDAY SEPTEMBER 21, 1966
YEAR 4 ISSUE 209 1817-4th St. Phone 456-2402 $7.50 Yr. 10¢ Copy

LAGOON PLAN

✳ See Page 2

From Norman Gilroy's Master Plan for Bolinas Lagoon...

Morro Bay just north of Santa Barbara which was once similar in its wild beauty. Its hills are now covered with tract houses and a freeway, and its heronries and wildlife habitats decimated. The Corps blasted part of Morro Rock, a historic rock beacon for sailing ships, to build a six-thousand-foot rock channel. Then it dredged part of the bay for motor boats, disturbing the ghost shrimp and mudworms. Though damaged, Morro Bay is still a major link along the Pacific Flyway for migratory waterfowl.

Our second bedfellow was Dr. Knox Finley, a professor of surgery at Stanford Medical School, and his brother, Malcolm. I knew Knox from medical school. Like the Bostick brothers, whom we had overcome on Richardson Bay, the Finley brothers were developers of major subdivisions and marinas in Marin and southern California. In 1965 the Bolinas Harbor District gave them a fifty-year lease, with no cancellation clause, to build a boat ramp from their eight-hundred-acre ranch on Highway 1 to Sand Island in Bolinas Lagoon, famous for its pelican rest and seal haulout. Their future subdivision was to be called Bahia Baulinas, a lovely name for a misplaced project.

In a progress report to the State Lands Commission, the district cited our tideland lease, the Corps' feasibility studies for a jetty, and Finley's proposed boat ramp as evidence of lagoon development. This report was generated by a Sacramento lobby for marina developers that we called the "sneaky, crafty harbor lobby." Nevertheless, the Finley threat never materialized. In February 1968 the Marin *Independent Journal* reported that the Finley's Bahia and Marina, a 1,300-lot tideland subdivision on nine hundred acres near Novato, a town in north Marin, had gone bankrupt. The Finleys gave up their Bolinas projects and later sold their ranch to the Golden Gate National Recreation Area.

The Gilroy Plan—A Fatal Mistake

The only bedfellow whose work we actually encouraged in the lagoon was Norman T. Gilroy, a Mill Valley architect and planner for the Bolinas Harbor District. We thought that after several years of discouraging feasibility studies for a marina, he would recommend to the district that the best thing they could do was leave the lagoon and island alone.

We were wrong. In October 1966, just one year before their lease from State Lands expired, the district released to the press the ten-million-dollar "Gilroy Plan" with much fanfare.

The Gilroy Plan made a theme park out of the egret and heron feeding

The Gilroy Plan, released with great fanfare in 1966, called for a heliport and busy marina on Kent Island and a freeway all along Bolinas Lagoon. This huge, misguided development plan threatened both the heronry and the not-yet-purchased Point Reyes National Seashore. I was able to obtain an option to purchase 111-acres of Kent Island in 1967, leading to "The Kent Island Coup."

grounds and Kent Island. It proposed to build an arboretum and observatory and to dredge the north end of the lagoon to make a turning basin for motorboats. Kent Island was to be raised several feet above sea level with dredged materials to accommodate a heliport, harbor police headquarters, district offices, parking lots, restaurants, a hotel, and fourteen hundred boat slips. A final flourish, a toll bridge, would cross the entire lagoon to Knox Finley's Bahia Baulinas on Highway 1.

While on leave from my medical practice, I researched land for Audubon Canyon Ranch to purchase, trying to outwit the developers. Here I'm inspecting Kent Island in my canoe in 1967.

The five Harbor District directors were completely sold on the plan. They liked the money it would generate for the district and the sumptuous 360-degree-view offices they would occupy.

The plan did one good thing: it polarized most of West Marin against the Harbor District. So much opposition rose up against the proposal that Norman Gilroy vowed to "eat the Gilroy Plan in public" if people would just leave him alone. But that didn't stop the District.

There was just one hitch in their ten-million-dollar plan—the Harbor District didn't own Kent Island, so the five Harbor District members decided to take bold action. Quietly (they thought), they decided to cancel our lease and take legal steps to acquire all of Kent Island through condemnation. They would let the courts decide the price, but their first step was to file a *lis pendens,* which freezes a piece of property pending a legal action.

Smiley's Saloon

After their meetings, the Harbor District board often adjourned to Smiley's Saloon in downtown Bolinas, a famous if somewhat raunchy watering hole since 1856. Greg Hewlett, a regular patron and an avowed enemy of progress, monitored their loud conversations. He became renowned for removing State Highway signs pointing to Bolinas in order to keep out the hated tourists. He heartily approved of Audubon's do-nothing plan for the Bolinas Lagoon. In January 1967, Hewlett woke me with a late-night phone call. "Tom Barfield, the District's attorney, is going to cancel Audubon's lease and then condemn Kent Island," he told me.

Hewlett's intelligence was accurate. The district sent us a letter by registered mail canceling our lease. We sent it to the newspapers and the story made headlines. The article tipped us that the district's appraisal for the 111-acre Kent Island parcel that we did not own was $54,000. The county assessor valued it as $85,000 and Mrs. Anne Kent was asking twice that.

It was incomprehensible that the Bolinas Harbor District had spent hundreds of thousands of tax dollars on studies of Kent Island and on salaries for Gilroy and others, when they didn't own this crucial part of the puzzle, the island itself. Acting as if they did was a fatal mistake.

The ball was now in the Ranch's court. It was our turn for bold action.

A Risky Offer

Stan Picher was out of town and would be away for several months. Caroline Livermore's "flash the cash" motto was etched in my mind. George Peyton, city attorney for Piedmont and a member of the Ranch's board, offered me his proxy and suggested that we buy the island on the chance that the District would fold up and go away. Knowing Tom Barfield, their feisty attorney and local historian who wanted a place in history, I didn't think we could pull that off. It was a risk either way.

Paul Newell, our title company expert, said that he thought he could insure title even though the island was mostly submerged and possibly owned by the state. He provided me with a deposit receipt for Anne Kent to sign if I decided to act.

I visited Anne Kent in her lovely home, New Haven, in Kent Woodlands and sat down with her and her two daughters, Nancy and Martye, and her sons-in-law, Bob Danielson, a commercial real estate developer, and Clinton Jones, a banker. "On behalf of the Ranch," I said, "I'm here to make a formal offer for Kent Island. Our offer is firm: $85,000 with $10,000 down and the balance over ten years at six percent interest." The family discussed the offer and they all accepted, saying they were relieved that Audubon would get the property. We signed the deposit receipt, and they accepted my personal check for two thousand dollars. I pledged them to secrecy.

My next call was to Huey Johnson, head of the western branch of The Nature Conservancy, an effective organization that buys wildlife habitat for preservation. One of Caroline Livermore's sons, Putnam, was the Conservancy's attorney. Huey lived in Mill Valley and later served as State Secretary of Resources under Governor Jerry Brown. Huey committed the Conservancy to loan $10,000 to the purchase and recommended that we give Kent

Wading birds such as these egrets depend on the shallow tidelands for food. Fossil evidence indicates that birds are descended from reptiles. Feathers are unique to birds and are an evolutionary advance on scales. Ranch visitors find that observing wildlife in the field with trained naturalists and docents is a thrilling experience.

Independent Journal
SERVING ALL OF MARIN COUNTY
10c PER COPY   SAN RAFAEL, CALIFORNIA, TUESDAY, FEBRUARY 14, 1967

ift Of Bolinas Island May Nip Harbor Plans

Supervisors Accept Bird Refuge Property

Kent Island, in the center of Bolinas Lagoon, was sented to Marin County as a wildlife refuge today, unanimously accepted by the county board of ervisors.

The action will reduce significantly the extent marina development in the lagoon.

ature Conservancy, a national servation organization, was d the isand for $90,000 morning by Mrs. Thomas D. Kent of Kentfield. Huey D.

work toward arranging the purchase.

Kettenhofen said he wanted a public hearing before the county accepted the property, since it would affect the Bolinas Harbor District's plan for development. However, he backed off from this condition on learning that the island could revert to Nature Conservancy if the county breaks the restrictions on its use.

Acceptance by the county makes the land public and presumably exempt from condemnation by the harbor district for harbor use.

The district's master plan developed by architect Norman T.

Supervisor Thomas T. Stor said the gift of the island v have "tremendous impact" the harbor district plans. tenhofen suggested putting acceptance of the deed un meeting at 3 p.m. today district directors on the plan, but Supervisor Pe Behr said this would be filing of a condemnati ment of the gift and then accepted the gift

Supervisors agreed extensive harbor would still be possi

Johnson said Will er of Belvedere wo on the A

RNIA, THURSDAY, MARCH 16, 1967 $2.00 A MONTH BY CARRIE

Kent Island Gift Strings Revealed: Ranch Mortgage

By ROBERT STREBEIGH

The much-publicized gift of Kent Island in Bolinas Lagoon to Marin County is more dream than fact and may take years to become reality, the Independent-Journal learned today.

Last month Nature Conservancy, a national conservation organization, announced it had purchased the land from Mrs. Thomas T. Kent Jr. for $85,000 and deeded it to the county for preservation as a wildlife refuge.

The only money that has been paid, however, is a $10,000 down payment to Mrs. Kent by the Marin Audubon Society, which has also pledged itself to raise an additional $50,000 and has given a mortgage yon Ranch for that amount to Huey D. Johnson, western direcvancy, confirmed.

has been put in escrow by the ague, which has pledged itself d the purchase.

y is legally obligated to pay d said, but is relying on other ome up with the money. He ortgage on Audubon Canyon future directors in line over come less inclined than the e money.

property.

Asst. County Counsel Thomas Hendricks today said the county will not accept the island until is unencumbered and its title lear.

Johnson said Nature Conservancy would normally have completed the transaction without all this uncertain fund-raising activity, but that "Nature did not have $85,000 in its loan fund." In fact, he said, his organization has pledged $10,000, but "will have to raise it."

He said the Sierra Club has offered to join the fund-raising and expressed certainty of success. "As conservationists, we are in this thing together," he declared.

The surprise announcement of the "gift" on Feb. 14 by Johnson, a resident of Mill Valley, brought charges that the plan had been hurriedly put together to block a Bolinas Harbor District plan for development of the island along lines proposed by Mill Valley architect Norman T. Gilroy.

Gilroy raised the question of whether the county would "in effect assume obligation if the subscriptions (by conservationists) aren't forthcoming."

The board of supervisors on Feb. 14, unanimously accepted the "gift" of the island, overriding a suggestion by Supervisor Ernest N. Kettenhofen that a public hearing be held since it would affect the Bolinas Harbor District plan.

Though the money will be

TUESDAY, MARCH 28, 1967   Independent-Journal

Board, Jury Exchange Slaps On Kent Island

Behr Cries Politics; Foreman Hits Haste

By RICHARD LYTTLE

The Marin County Grand Jury today took a slap at county supervisors for their handling of the gift of Kent Island, and got slapped right back.

In an interim report, the grand jury recommended that no county funds be expended on development of the island until a $75,000 deed of trust on the property has been paid off and until the 55-year term of a reversionary clause has expired.

Grand Jury Foreman Clifford S. Lund read the interim report to supervisors at the start of today's meeting.

Supervisors accused Lund and the grand jury of getting into politics. Lund countered that there had been several requests for an investigation and conflicting reports in the press, but supervisors were decidedly unhappy.

"When the grand jury wants to enter politics," said Supervisor Peter H. Behr, "it should run for election. This is not a proper and fair report. It is an attempt to justify what you did not find. It reflects on the unanimous policy of the board."

DOESN'T AGREE

Supervisor Ernest N. Kettenhofen did not agree with Behr and said the grand jury had the right to investigate and criticize where it wished, but other board members were generally symathetic with Behr's view

Chairman Thomas T. Storer said he was incensed that the report and opined that all members of the board should have been recalled had they not accepted the gift of Kent Island.

The 110-acre island was given to the county Feb. 14 with the deed transferred the same day. The presentation was by Nature Conservancy, which put up $10,000 for the $85,000 purchase and gave a $75,000 deed of trust to owner Anne Thompson Kent.

OUTLINES TERMS

Today's report outlined the terms of the deed of trust, calling for interest of 5 per cent for the first three years, 6 per cent for the next three years, and 7 per cent thereafter. Principal installments shall be at least

Eugene A. Ostaggi, chairman of the grand jury county offices committee which made the investigation, said this may have been so but there was no note about it filed with the county documents until the second week of this month.

The grand jury concluded that although no apparent risk or liability is assumed by the county, excepting the possible loss of substantial property taxes from the ultimate development of a proposed yacht basin, we believe that the board did not allow sufficient time between presentation and acceptance of conveyance to adequately evaluate the proposal."

The grand jury also concluded that "as this proposal was presented by a group with a singleness of purpose, far more caution should have been exercised to assure the board that the terms of the transaction provided necessary safeguards in order to protect any possible expenditure of public funds."

The jury also said that "the opposition and the general public was not afforded an opportunity to challenge the transaction and was denied the opportunity to agree or disagree in a normal democratic process."

Lund said the report was adopted at a meeting last Wednesday and that he since showed it to County Counsel Douglas J. Maloney. He said Maloney explained that the county must spend some money to establish use of the island as a legal condition. He said $1,500

keep the lagoon from silting in, but their development proposals stirred a controversy.

Conservationists said the board thought only in terms of a major harbor facility, and their plans would ruin the natural beauty of the lagoon.

District supporters argued that retaining the district would provide local control and tended that the county h constructive suggestions f future of the lagoon.

At the campaign's c district opponents charge the district had spent $ including $67,518 to p consultant, Norman T. without correcting any problems.

There also had been c of the harbor commi plan to dredge 60,000 cu of mud from Bolinas and a channel past Ke

IJ 3/12/69

Voters Dump Harbor Area

Dissolution of the Bolinas Harbor District, formed in 1957, was voted yesterday 313 to 266 as nearly 86 per cent of the district's 698 registered voters went to the polls in the hotly contested election.

Dissolution was favored in Bolinas by a 166 to 156 vote, in Stinson Beach by 137 to 102 and by absentee voters 10 to 8, reported Peter C. Meyer, Marin County elections officer.

The election was called by the Marin County Board of Supervisors after two years of controversy about the district's plans for development of the Bolinas Lagoon, which were vigorously opposed by conservation groups.

Proponents of dissolution wanted Marin County to take over administration of the lagoon. State action will be re-

quired to give the county jurisdiction since the harbor district got administration from the state Lands Commission.

As proposed, Marin County also would absorb the liabilities of the district, not to exceed $125,536, which stem from district purchases of property and state loans for lagoon studies. Any other liabilities would remain the responsibility of the property owners in the district, supervisors agreed.

The state granted the district the lagoon in 1959 on condition that it be "substantially improved" within 10 years, and last year the Legislature extended the deadline to 1971.

Harbor district board members proposed development of the lagoon to finance dredging which they said was needed to

See BOLINAS, page 4

Island to the county as a gift for a new county park right away. That way, he reasoned, the Harbor District would be unable to condemn it from the more powerful county government.

That made sense to me. Huey and I agreed to meet at Paul Newell's office the next day to work out a strategy. My next call was to Grace and Ted Wellman. Grace was president of the Marin Conservation League. She and her husband were known as "Mrs. and Mr. Conservation." The Wellmans were thrilled to help save Bolinas Lagoon for wildlife. They pledged that the League would raise twenty-five thousand dollars toward purchase of the island whether Marin County accepted the gift or not. Again, secrecy.

Nello Kearney of The Nature Conservancy and Admiral Bransom-Cooke of the Marin Conservation League present me (left), as chairman, with a report on the 1967 Kent Island Fund Drive. Looking on is Mrs. Anne Kent, daughter-in-law of Congressman William Kent, who sold us Kent Island for $85,000.

The Kent Island Coup

Huey Johnson, Bob Danielson, and I met with Paul Newell on Friday morning. I handed over my signed deposit receipt for the island I'd bought on behalf of the Ranch to Newell. We decided that the island should be owned by The Nature Conservancy. Newell then drew up a deed showing that Anne Kent had sold Kent Island to The Nature Conservancy, with Audubon Canyon Ranch guaranteeing the price. Now came the hard part, the political part: convincing the Marin County supervisors to accept the gift of Kent Island.

Luckily, I was able to arrange a visit to "Kett" Kettenhofen, chairman of the Board of Supervisors, at his office in San Rafael on Friday afternoon. He was a real estate developer, with extensive holdings in Sausalito and West Marin. We had been friends for a number of years, and his wife and daughter later became Audubon Canyon Ranch docents. He was running for re-election soon, and he wanted my support.

I was forthright. "Kett, Audubon Canyon Ranch and The Nature Conservancy now own the entire Kent Island in two parcels, nine and one-half and 111 acres. We want to give the 111 acres to the county for a wildlife park with no strings attached." He was astonished. He said that he admired the fact that we had put our money where our mouths were, and that he would help us. He advised me to have Huey Johnson present the deed to the board early Tuesday morning.

Kett remarked that this gift would double the acreage of county parks in Marin and would help in his re-election. The entire board might even go for

Newspapers were full of "The Kent Island Coup." With the option to buy Kent Island in 1967, we outmaneuvered the Harbor District by giving Kent Island to the county for a park. This killed the marina, but threatened a Grand Jury investigation for mortgaging Audubon Canyon Ranch to make the purchase.

it, he speculated, since none of the supervisors had been pleased with the Harbor District performance. Kett advised me not even to tip Supervisors Peter Behr and Tom Storer, two of my close friends on the board, and reassured me that he would handle Byron Lydecker and Bill Gnoss.

At nine o'clock on Tuesday morning, February 14, 1967, Huey presented the deed to the Marin County supervisors as an off-agenda item. The board voted unanimously to accept the $85,000 gift providing there was no cost to the taxpayers. Kent Island was safe. Afterwards, Behr and Storer told me that our political savvy in pulling this off absolutely astounded them. We raised the money for the purchase of Kent Island from three sources: Audubon Canyon Ranch placed a mortgage on the Ranch property that committed itself to raising fifty thousand dollars, the Marin Conservation League committed itself to raising twenty-five thousand dollars, and The Nature Conservancy agreed to loan ten thousand dollars to the escrow.

At the news that the supervisors had accepted the gift of the island park, there was genuine excitement throughout the Bay Area. We had beaten developers and the most powerful state agencies at their own game. In editorials and cartoons, San Francisco newspapers called our action "The Kent Island Coup." Meanwhile, the Bolinas Harbor District was planning to file a *lis pendens* the next day to block the sale.

But by then it was too late.

When the Marin *Independent Journal* learned that Audubon Canyon Ranch had mortgaged its property, headlines triggered a Grand Jury investigation. They were after blood. It never happened. The Grand Jury was satisfied with our thoroughly prepared documents. We withstood the political blustering. My boyhood dream was achieved, and the Bolinas Lagoon was saved. I never in my life felt so relieved of a burden. Today, when I look at the birds in their lofty heronry or feeding in their tideflats around pristine Kent Island, a chill goes through me and tears come to my eyes. We came so close to losing it all.

Back then, however, there was a sizable problem left: raising the eighty-five thousand dollars.

The Joint Fund Drive

I was afraid that Stan Picher would be annoyed with the mortgage on the Ranch, and I was right. He was pleased that Kent Island was safe, but said, "Marty, you've gotten yourself into this arrangement, and you'll have to lead the fund drive." Gleefully, he added, "I'll be out of town."

My first move was to retire from the Ross Valley Medical Clinic and devote more time to land purchases. Besides, I was dead tired from my medical practice with its many night calls. This was the time to make the break.

Next, we recruited co-chairs from each group: Admiral Bransom-Cooke from the Conservation League, Nello Kearney and Huey Johnson from The Nature Conservancy, and Erline Hevel, Bertha Underhill and Rhoda Boyd from Audubon Canyon Ranch. Anne Kent was named honorary chair of the fundraising group and generously reduced the mortgage by two thousand dollars. Then we sent out a large fundraising mailing to members of our three organizations. We also made phone calls for larger donations. The response was enthusiastic. In the mailer we used the *San Francisco Chronicle* cartoon showing a large heron (conservationists) catching a frog (developers). Within a few months, the entire amount had been raised, all loans had been repaid, the mortgage on the ranch was removed, and Kent Island had become the largest park in the county park system—at no cost to the taxpayers. I received a routine certificate of thanks for my work from the supervisors with no mention of the lagoon or Kent Island.

Our big gamble had paid off and Stan Picher was again speaking to me. To relax I went to work on a short-term basis for Huey Johnson on The Nature Conservancy purchase of the Kipahulu Preserve on Maui.

The San Francisco Chronicle *published this editorial cartoon by Robert Bastian after our successful fund drive to purchase Kent Island. We felt emboldened to oppose the even more extensive commercial development planned for Tomales Bay.*

There was still one more problem: the Bolinas Harbor District held a lease from State Lands for 1,200 acres in the Bolinas Lagoon. As long as the district held this lease, the lagoon was not safe. Harold Gregg, dynamic director of the Marin Conservation League, handled the legislative chore in Sacramento to end this dangerous lease and Frances Stewart, a Bolinas conservation leader, was elected to the Harbor District board to convince them to end the lease. In 1969 the voters dissolved the Harbor District and the State transferred title to the County of Marin. In 1988 the lagoon and the Ranch's donated parcels were turned over to the 10,700-acre Marin County Open Space District. The voters established this district, and former Supervisor Pete Arrigoni was its first chairman.

A Well-Managed Lagoon

Today, Bolinas Lagoon is also protected under the flags of the Gulf of the Farallones National Marine Sanctuary, Point Reyes National Seashore, the Golden Gate National Recreation Area, and the Central California Coast Biosphere Preserve.

Although often forgotten, the lagoon is also part of Audubon Canyon Ranch, which still owns part of Kent Island as insurance that the lagoon's protection will be permanent. Without the grassroots efforts many years ago, these agencies might not exist today. The lagoon might instead be a giant marina, surrounded by housing tracts and hamburger stands spoiling the entrance to a much smaller National Seashore.

But with preservation comes problems, and the most threatening is siltation. The Bolinas Lagoon Management Plan of 1968 is currently being updated, with Burr Heneman, Ranch board member, and others in charge. The tidal prism—the volume of water exchanged—has been reduced by twenty-five percent since then, and controversial corrective dredging may be required to prevent the lagoon from turning into a salt marsh.

But in the 1960s we feared a far greater erosion problem in the plan to carve out four-lane freeways along the coast, which would have inevitably led to the filling in of Bolinas Lagoon. The egrets and herons, in their tall redwoods, had no idea they had a formidable enemy still threatening them: the bulldozers of the California State Highway Commission.

The Bolinas Solution

The Bolinas sewage ponds are a splendid example of designing with nature. For decades, the town of Bolinas had a stinky sewage problem, labeled the worst in the state, and was under repeated abatement orders. Raw sewage flushed directly into the Lagoon entrance on Wharf Road, supposedly on the outgoing tide, but the flap didn't work and sewage backed up in the manholes, flooding the streets, polluting the Lagoon, and contaminating shellfish. A huge joint powers sewage treatment plant for both Stinson Beach and Bolinas was proposed, with an ocean outfall near Duxbury Reef, but it would have allowed unlimited growth.

The Bolinas Public Utilities District solved this problem with an innovative, self-contained lagoon ponding system installed on the mesa. I had studied this method under Professor William J. Oswald while a student in Public Health at Berkeley. The town sewage of Bolinas is lifted by pump and aerated in a series of ponds where the sewage nutrients are consumed by small plants called *spirulina*. These are suctioned off, dried, and used for animal feed or food supplements for humans, while the pond water—now relatively clean—is used for irrigation.

The Bolinas system offers an environmentally friendly alternative to the costly, over-engineered works that rely on dumping wastewater into our rivers, estuaries, and oceans. It is a method that appealed to the "slow-growthers" of Bolinas because it limited population growth to the capacity of the system. It also attracts birds and other wildlife. The system deserves to be used widely in other parts of the state.

Four large ponds dominate the modern, environmentally sensitive Bolinas Septic System. For years Bolinas dumped its untreated waste at the mouth of the Lagoon where it was washed back in with the tides. The public was warned not to eat the clams.

CHAPTER FIVE

Rescuing the Gateway to the National Seashore

The proposed Point Reyes National Seashore is a miserable hodge-podge of conflicting ownerships. I don't know if we can save it.

—Peter Behr, Chairman, "Save Our Seashore" 1969

Without realizing he would set off a speculative land boom, President John F. Kennedy in 1962 signed both the Point Reyes National Seashore and the Warm Springs Dam bills. We predicted then that cheap Russian River water would open the arid Marin-Sonoma coast, including the National Seashore, to urban sprawl.

By 1967 Audubon Canyon Ranch's purchases and the Kent Island coup had helped secure the Bolinas Lagoon as a wild and unspoiled southern gateway to the still incomplete National Seashore. The huge Bolinas marina and Mary Summer's Master Plan were dead; nevertheless, Stan Picher and I felt that the Ranch should quickly purchase as much as possible of the Bolinas Ridge to also guard the seashore entrance from development and help assure its completion. There were still the threats of shoreline and ridgeline freeways—and the importation of water.

The Galloway Ranch—Key to the Puzzle

Two wild and beautiful ranches flanked the Audubon Canyon Ranch, the Galloway Ranch to the north and the Thompson Ranch to the south. Both had frontage on the lagoon and both extended nearly to the top of the Bolinas Ridge. The Galloway Ranch also held part of the Bolinas-Fairfax Road, which was planned by the state to be turned into a steep connecting freeway between the shoreline and ridgeline freeways.

I knew both owners, but would they sell, and could we afford the prices?

The Galloway Ranch (also known as Pikes Gulch) figured in the county's

By 1962 Audubon Canyon Ranch's Bolinas Lagoon Preserve was established with headquarters in the center canyon, giving us leverage against the planned ridgetop and shoreline freeways. Our next step was to purchase the canyons on either side, plus much of the shoreline.

This map, obtained at state freeway hearings in 1960, shows the route north of the proposed coast freeway along the Bolinas Lagoon towards Point Reyes Station. The freeway would have increased already rampant land speculation, hastened development, and prevented the purchase of the National Seashore (left) and the Golden Gate National Recreation Area (right) in 1972.

early plan that would have carved the Bolinas Ridge into ranchettes with views of Point Reyes and the Farallones Islands.

Since 1941, the Galloways had owned the Bolinas Ridge from the Bolinas-Fairfax Road south to and including the Canyon Ranch, which they later sold to Tevis. Allen Galloway, a noted geologist, created the exhibit on the San Andreas Fault in the Ranch's display hall. His wife Mary was a descendent of an old Marin family.

With Harold Summer's expansive freeway network on the Bolinas Ridge burning in my brain, I called on Mary Galloway. As a result of that first meeting, she and Allen sold us their tidelands, recognizing their importance in preserving the lagoon. Later the Ranch donated them to the county as the first units in a Shoreline Park. Next, we persuaded the Galloways to split their ranch from top to bottom, from ridge to lagoon, selling us sixty-seven acres of the southern half, which gave us more road frontage on state Highway 1. We insisted at the time of that sale that the Galloways agree to give the

The proposed freeway through Stinson Beach would have sliced through the heronry as it crossed the bluffs of Bolinas Lagoon. An expanded freeway headed south to development in the Marin Headlands past Green Gulch. The rapid growth of both counties was needed to pay for Warm Springs Dam, authorized in 1962, and PG&E's nuclear power plant in Bodega Bay.

Audubon Canyon Ranch the right of first refusal to purchase the rest of their ranch, about two hundred acres, which included part of the connector between the ridge and shoreline freeway, the Bolinas-Fairfax Road.

On a rainy Saturday morning in 1967, Stan, our architect, Jack Hermann, a surveyor, and I struggled up the steep hillside covered with poison oak and chaparral to set the stakes with the Galloways that would split the parcel into two parcels. We argued like school children back and forth over every rock, tree and promontory, and finally, to the profound dismay of our surveyor, agreed on a very crooked line. We paid for the sixty-seven acres with an amazing gift of forty thousand dollars from the estate of Max Lewis and Elizabeth Sprang. These were benefactors who had heard about the Ranch's work. Their will included the following wisdom:

> To preserve in a wild state various and sundry places so that the present and future generations of Americans and visitors may enjoy, in part at least, nature unharnessed by man for use and profit. Such "living

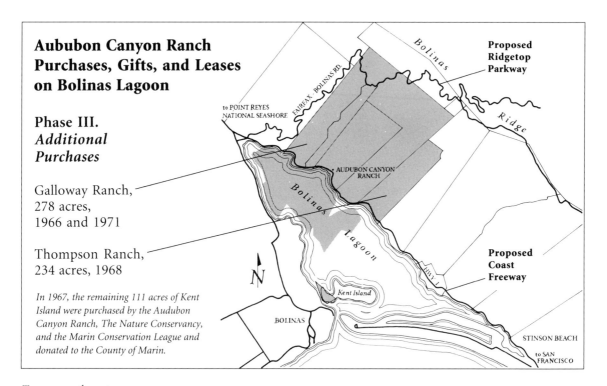

Aububon Canyon Ranch Purchases, Gifts, and Leases on Bolinas Lagoon

Phase III.
Additional Purchases

Galloway Ranch, 278 acres, 1966 and 1971

Thompson Ranch, 234 acres, 1968

In 1967, the remaining 111 acres of Kent Island were purchased by the Audubon Canyon Ranch, The Nature Conservancy, and the Marin Conservation League and donated to the County of Marin.

To preserve the gateway to the proposed Point Reyes National Seashore and give us more frontage on Highway 1, the Ranch purchased the Galloway Ranch adjacent to the north and the Thompson Ranch to the south. By 1971, the Ranch had grown to 1,017 strategic acres, ending the threat of freeways, subdivisions, and marinas in the Bolinas watershed. We renamed the Thompson Ranch Volunteer Canyon after the 1971 oil spill, and named the canyon to the north of the heronry in honor of The Garden Clubs of America.

museums" are precious and irreplaceable for their scientific, educational and aesthetic values. They frequently afford the only home for a multitude of living things that might otherwise vanish from the earth, destroyed by civilization.

Pardow Hooper put the sale in escrow, and only then did Stan and I breathe easily. A short time later the Galloways moved to San Francisco and sold us the rest of their land for $210,000 under the terms of our agreement. Now their wilderness ranch, where cougar sightings were common, was safe.

With our acquisition of the Galloway ranch and the Tevis ranch, the pieces of the gigantic Bolinas Ridge puzzle were beginning to lock into place. The freeway threat was fading away. The state would be foolish to attempt to condemn lands for freeways from four publicly powerful Audubon Chapters. Audubon Canyon Ranch now controlled the southern portal to the Point Reyes National Seashore.

For years now, the Audubon Canyon Ranch has leased the Galloway ranch house to the Point Reyes Bird Observatory for just one dollar per year. The Observatory carries out bird research on the Farallones Islands and many other parts of the world. Our board has deemed this a worthwhile use of the buildings, but the rest of the land remains wild.

Strange Suitors for Enid's Ranch

The Enid Thompson Ranch (the old Weeks Ranch), now Volunteer Canyon just south of the Audubon Canyon Ranch on Highway 1, was next on my agenda. It was steeply forested, had a small creek running through it, and contained a lush meadow dotted with ancient apple trees. A large grove of alders in a bog blocked the view of the land from Highway 1. A trail connected to the Griffin Trail on the Canyon Ranch and passed perhaps the largest buckeye tree in the Bolinas watershed. The Thompsons had restored the Victorian house, with windows looking out on coveys of quail and herds of deer feeding in the meadow. The land was rich in chaparral habitat and deserved to be preserved.

If it hadn't been for two elderly patients of mine from Bolinas, the Audubon Canyon Ranch would never have gotten the chance to purchase Enid Thompson's ranch. Enid was a Christian Scientist who, in the late sixties, chauffeured her two friends "over the hill" in her limousine from Bolinas to my office. We became friends, and she would occasionally ask my medical advice, rewarding me with a crate of apples from the ancient trees that thrive to this day in her meadow.

But Enid was a closer friend of Hurford Sharon, the head of the local Christian Science Church, who had a real estate office in downtown Bolinas. He lived right in town on Brighton Avenue, where he was widely known as the man who had cut down "the squawkers' trees," a row of ancient cypresses near the tennis courts where a large colony of noisy Black-crowned Night-Herons had roosted after their nightly forage in the lagoon.

Stately birds such as this Great Egret migrate throughout the Bay Area. For the birds' protection, ACR volunteers monitor colonies of Great Egrets, Great Blue Herons, Snowy Egrets, and Black-crowned Night-Herons in seven Bay Area counties, supervised by biologist John Kelly.

Enid said that Sharon wanted her to sell her ranch, retire modestly, and donate part of the proceeds to the church building fund. But she began to switch sides after we bought the Tevis ranch in 1961.

I believe I may have wrecked Sharon's plans for Enid's ranch, which we feared would be subdivided. For five years I told Enid that her bountiful canyon and chaparral-covered hills, with the steep redwood and fir forests beyond, should be protected as a living cathedral. It didn't hurt that we promised to pay cash that would enable her to get out of foggy Bolinas and retire to Pebble Beach, where she had many friends. Still, we never really dreamed we would be able to afford her ranch.

On October 28, 1968, during my tenure as land acquisitions chair of Audubon Canyon Ranch, Enid called me at my medical office. As soon as I

If Audubon Canyon Ranch had not acted in 1961, a decade before the federal government, these rolling hills on Bolinas Lagoon could have been covered with two-acre ranchettes all the way north to the Sonoma-Mendocino border, urbanizing the north coast of California like much of Southern California.

got on the phone she turned me over to her lawyer, Aaron Cohen. "Mrs. Thompson is anxious to move to a warmer climate. She says she will offer the ranch to Audubon first. She will give you a week to see if you can swing it. She doesn't want Mr. Sharon to know until the deal is finished." This sounded great until Cohen told me her price: $300,000 for 132 acres! That was three times as much per acre as we had paid for the 503 Tevis acres just four years before.

But the ranch was such a prize, we knew someone would buy it the minute it hit the market. I consulted with Stan Picher, Marin Audubon Society president Howie Allen, and George Peyton, our attorney; we decided to have Pardow Hooper give us an appraisal and make Enid an offer.

Paul Newell, my friend of many years at the title company, said he would handle the escrow at half price; Hooper, our real estate expert, ordered a survey of the property. To our amazement he found that the steep wooded valley and ridge was 234 acres, not 132. Fudging acreage on tax bills was not an uncommon practice to reduce property taxes in wicked old Marin.

Pardow then did a careful appraisal and came up with a price of $210,000. We authorized him to make Enid a firm offer and on November 22, 1968, she accepted. The one condition she insisted on was that the ranch be kept intact, used only by Audubon for wildlife protection and education, and never sold or subdivided. We agreed.

Volunteer Canyon Named

The prized canyon finally belonged to the Ranch and Enid moved south. Then began a frenzy of planning and fundraising. To accommodate overnight wildlife education programs, architect Clifford Conly remodeled the Thompson farmhouse to create a reference library, a meeting and film room, a large kitchen, and a rustic bunkhouse on the meadow's edge. To pay the costs, Stan Picher and Jack Harper obtained a matching $50,000 grant from the Whittell Estate through the National Audubon Society.

The canyon was later renamed from Weeks Gulch to Volunteer Canyon in honor of those who helped clean up Bolinas Lagoon and its birds after the huge Standard Oil tanker spill off the Coast in 1971. Zumi helped in the dramatic bird rescue which involved blocking the Lagoon's entrance with roped-together bales of hay. Mimi's and my house on Wharf Road at the Lagoon's mouth was used as headquarters for the oil cleanup.

Stan and I set out together to raise the $210,000 as quickly as possible. We didn't want the purchase price hanging over our heads. Stan sent out a letter, brief and to the point, to our supporters and friends. After the oil spill, Standard Oil donated twenty-five thousand dollars toward the purchase for mitigation and sent a college classmate of mine to deliver it.

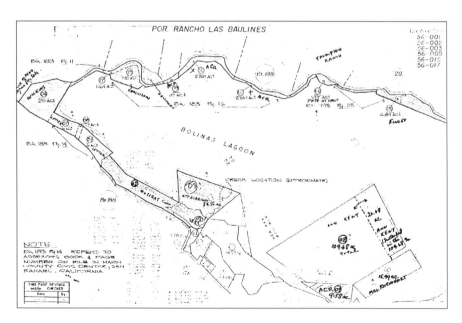

The Ranch used this assessor's parcel map in 1961 to purchase available tideland lots around the periphery of the Lagoon for wildlife habitat. To prevent their condemnation by the Harbor District we donated them to County Parks, now the Open Space District. The Ranch still owns a ten-acre parcel on Kent Island (lower right).

Before that I pulled off a financial feat that left Stan gasping. As described in Chapter One, at just about this time I had obtained a gift of four acres of Rosie's Bluff and tidelands on Richardson Bay after a visit with the owner, Harry Marshall, in Chicago. Armed with this valuable gift, I phoned Charles Callison, president of National Audubon Society, to tell him this gift was for his organization. He was overwhelmed. Then I asked the big question, "Would National Audubon make a fifteen thousand dollar gift to our Canyon Ranch education fund and extend to us a $100,000 low-interest loan for the Thompson purchase?" He said, "Yes!" on the spot. With both deals concluded, a bench was named for Marshall's wife and placed on the Richardson Bay bluff, Enid got her money sooner, and Pardow got his commission of twelve thousand dollars (we figured he had saved us more than $150,000). Marshall flew out for the bench dedication.

Celebrating Pardow's Skills

Pardow Hooper, our real estate broker, then helped us acquire two small but vital parcels on Highway 1 that had once been part of the Thompson ranch. The first was an acre with a small house on it that was owned by Mrs. Sylvia Crimmins, a tiny, eccentric elderly lady who wore a beanie with a propeller on top. She sold the property to us when she moved to Texas. With a gift from Eleanor Evans Crum, a close friend of Stan Picher, the house was moved back from the highway for use as naturalist housing.

Today rural Highway 1 is still a two-lane winding road rather than a four-lane freeway with a bridge across Bolinas Lagoon to a marina on Kent Island.

Second, to our astonishment, Pardow researched a parcel that bordered a large bend in the old county road parallel to Highway 1. The Thompsons had sold this property years before to the State Highway Department with a condition that if the highway was moved the parcel would revert to them. The bureaucrats were dismayed when Pardow proved from old deeds that this parcel had now reverted to Audubon Canyon Ranch. The parcel gave us more strategic frontage on Highway 1 to fight the freeway, plus room for a beautiful parking lot lined with alder. We celebrated Pardow's skills at a large party in his honor.

The Ranch now owned four of the eight canyons on the southern Bolinas Ridge, all bordering Highway 1. The only remaining threats to the ridge were the Knox Finley and Leonard ranches. But without water, sewer,

freeway or marina, subdivisions there were impossible. Eventually the Golden Gate National Recreation Area acquired these parcels and today the Bolinas basin, lagoon, marshlands, and ridge are secure. I often wonder what the area would look like today if the Audubon Canyon Ranch had never been created.

The Ranch's land purchases and the defeat of the Harbor District made possible the scientific management plan for the Bolinas watershed from ridgetop to ridgetop that was developed by the Conservation Foundation of Washington D.C. in 1968. This study is still being used as the basis for watershed management plans for the Bolinas Basin.

However, there were a few other serious threats that needed attention in this part of West Marin. The shooting of eagles and hawks and logging on the Bolinas Ridge had to be stopped. The continued dumping of raw sewage into the Bolinas Lagoon was intolerable, as was the senseless cutting of peely madrones for firewood.

Stopping the dumping of garbage into Bolinas Lagoon took many years. Finally, in 1994 the remnants of the Stinson Beach dump were removed and the channel dredged with great community fanfare, reflecting a profound change in the environmental ethic of West Marin in the years since Audubon Canyon Ranch was purchased and the southern gateway to the Point Reyes National Seashore was secured.

The National Audubon Society has grown from a small group of bird guardians to an effective national advocate of ecosystem preservation with chapters in many states and counties. Its participation was critical in saving Mono Lake. Recently it created Audubon–California to preserve large wildlife corridors including the 12,000 acre Mayacamas Mountain Sanctuary in the Russian River headwaters.

CHAPTER SIX

Zumie–The Sage of Audubon Canyon Ranch

The people most likely to make a success of saving the planet will not be found in large international bodies, but in small grassroots organizations caring for their own lands and water.

—Barbara Crossette, *The New York Times,* 1992 Rio Conference

It's amazing that I wasn't drummed out of the Marin Medical Society for proselytizing my patients to work for, donate funds to, or serve on the board of Audubon Canyon Ranch. Everyone who came through my office was assessed for their potential to "help save Bolinas Lagoon." Clerin Zumwalt was my greatest success. *Zumwalt* means "to the forest," and Zumie fit his name: compact build, tanned face, capable hands, reliable. Zumie reminded one of an articulate oak. Moreover, he was a forester.

When I first met Zumie, he was a Western Regional Chief of the US Forest Service in charge of range analysis for the California region, and stuck in an office in downtown San Francisco. Every work day he was subjected to the daily grind of commuting, with thousands of others, from his home in the suburban tracts of Greenbrae. He told me then that he longed to work again in the wide open spaces of Utah or Colorado, or even California. Besides being an expert naturalist, wildlife photographer and raconteur, Zumie, I learned, was one of the nation's experts in soil science, forest, grassland, and wildlife management. He had spent twenty-three years with the US Soil Conservation Service.

What good fortune! When we bought Audubon Canyon Ranch, it was a soil scientist's dream—or nightmare. It sat on an unstable, eroding ridge on a moving fault. The forests had been overcut, the meadows overgrazed, and the creeks were sliding into the lagoon. Once Zumie visited he was hooked; he saw his life's work cut out for him.

His wife Alis was also a patient of mine, and I had a consultation with

This peaceful inlet of Bolinas Lagoon barely escaped plans by the Army Corps of Engineers to dredge it for a marina and build a rock jetty into the Pacific Ocean. This would have eliminated the sandspit where the rare Snowy Plover lays its eggs.

them together. "Zumie," I said, "is having some chest pain, and it would be best if he didn't commute any more. If he must, perhaps he could stop somewhere and relax until the traffic has cleared." Alis, a beautiful, flaxen-haired, exuberant woman was alarmed. "Never in your life!" Then I made my point. I suggested that Zumie take early retirement at age fifty-two and come to work for the Ranch as our first paid naturalist.

Thus began Zumie's association with Audubon Canyon Ranch, which lasted for more than three decades. During this time Zumie also served as land manager for the Marin Municipal Water District, expert witness for the Ranch, teacher, photographer, historian, and consultant for land-use studies of both Bolinas Lagoon and Tomales Bay. He served on the Ranch board for more than twenty years. And after he took the Ranch job in 1965, thousands of people enriched their lives by walking along the Bolinas Ridge and Bolinas Lagoon with Zumie, a man carved by wind, sun, and the morning fog. What Zumie gave them was a love of

Snowy Egrets, and one Great Egret, feed in this fifteen-acre marsh by Redwood High School. It was one of the few marshes to survive the bulldozers in eastern Marin.

nature so pure, so cultivated, so filled with humor and wisdom that he himself became a treasure. He trained hundreds of docents to be valuable teachers and leaders in wildlife protection.

But when Zumie first came to work at the Ranch, there were pressing problems to resolve: eagle shooting, logging, erosion, and the cutting of peely madrones. Taking advantage of his talents, I immediately engaged Zumie in three skirmishes on the Bolinas Ridge that I had for years wanted to confront head-on.

The Last Great Eagle Shoot

Dead eagles and hawks nailed up on fences with their wings outspread were a common sight in West Marin when we purchased the Canyon Ranch. Some of the ranchers, especially those who raised sheep, considered these birds lamb predators and shot them on sight.

The Bolinas Ridge and the headlands overlooking the Golden Gate are on one of the great raptor routes of California. In the fall, thousands of birds of prey migrate south along this route and cross San Francisco Bay near its narrow mouth. Sharp-shinned, cooper, and redtail hawks go by in great numbers, as does the occasional Golden Eagle.

In the late sixties, the Bald Eagle, our national symbol, was threatened with extinction. In the United States they were down to four hundred pairs, and the federal government listed them as an endangered species. At statehood a century earlier they had nested along the water courses of Marin County, but loggers and farmers cut down most of their ancestral nesting trees or shot the birds on sight.

In 1965, Leroy Martinelli had the dubious honor of shooting two eagles, one apparently the last Bald Eagle reported in Marin. This shooting occurred on his father's sheep ranch, high on the Bolinas Ridge on the east shore of Tomales Bay. Leroy was hauled into federal court for shooting the national emblem without a permit but was acquitted with the help of lawyers from the powerful Wool Growers Association. Two years later, he again spotted several eagles feeding on a lamb carcass. He called Loren Parcher of the US Fish & Wildlife Service, who obliged and gave him a permit to shoot three. Leroy promptly shot one bird with a six-foot wingspread and called the newspaper. His photo with the dead Golden Eagle, wings outspread, appeared on the front page.

The outraged public demanded a permanent stop to eagle killing, but there was no action. Incredibly, no one had inspected Martinelli's ranch to see why it attracted so many Golden Eagles, which migrate south from the Eel River each winter looking for food. These great birds, with golden headfeathers glistening in the

Clerin Zumwalt, a soil scientist, was our much-loved Ranch naturalist and sage for thirty years. Hundreds of inner-city schoolchildren who had never been in the wild before were transformed by rambling with Zumi along the trails of Audubon Canyon Ranch.

sun, search the land below for rabbits and ground squirrels. They are in fact the farmer's best friends for keeping rodents under control.

On December 23, 1967, I persuaded Clerin Zumwalt to visit the Martinelli ranch with me to inspect the pasture there. At the time, I was chairman of the Environmental Health Committee for Marin County. Martinelli's father, whom I had met at an inspection of his landfill dump the year before after a complaint of pollution in Tomales Bay, agreed to let me inspect. I reminded him that his cousin Rod was our attorney at the Ross Hospital.

Without knowing what he was getting into, Zumie agreed to go. Being plucky but not foolish, we asked Constable McLean of the small town of Point Reyes Station to go with us. We found Leroy in his pickup truck with a rifle in the back window. We met his father on the top of a hill behind the dump. Sheep were everywhere.

Zumie discovered that Leroy had the impossible task of looking after four thousand steep acres and eighteen hundred ewes, and seldom could go on the range where lambing took place. Instead, he had been checking his lambs by long-distance from the road. On further questioning, Zumie learned that the nine hundred ewes on the adjoining ranch were losing many

Rancher Leroy Martinelli displays a Golden Eagle shot on his father's ranch on Tomales Bay. When this photograph appeared in the local paper, the public outcry marked a turning point in county sentiment. The shooting stopped and some of the ranchers' wives later became Ranch docents.

of their lambs because their owner had only been showing up once a week during the lambing season. Zumie deduced that dogs and inadequate feed, not the eagles, were the main killers of both the adult sheep and the lambs. All the delectable carcasses littering the two ranches were attracting goldens as well as vultures, he concluded.

Zumie also noted that the condition of the range was less than ideal; he saw overgrazing and erosion. He pointed this out tactfully to the elder Martinelli, who said, "Look, we're getting out of the sheep business in a year or two. And I promise you that no more eagles will be shot on this ranch."

"How about hawks?"

"No hawks either!"

All of us, including Leroy, shook hands. This proved to be a turning point for ranchers in the area, since the Martinellis and McLean were well known.

In case they reneged, Zumie and I then formed a committee to "Protect the Soaring Birds of West Marin." We held three or four meetings, received a lot of publicity, and then disbanded since the killing had stopped. Two years later, to our joy, a Bald Eagle was spotted flying over Tomales Bay.

Today, there are probably no Bald Eagles breeding in Marin County. However, the nationwide count in 1993 was 4,016 pairs, along with several thousand juveniles. Many more eagles than that live in Alaska. With this comeback, the Bald Eagle is being reclassified not as endangered but as threatened, a less serious category, so the 1973 Endangered Species Act has worked for Bald Eagles as it has for gray whales along the Pacific Coast.

Golden Eagles were never on the endangered list. Occasionally, an individual bird has marauded the egret heronry and killed the young there, sending the heronry into decline.

When Zumie and I were running around the county trying to save eagles, madrone trees, and salt marshes, the Pacific Sun *labeled me the "nature doctor." Here Zumie (left) and I are explaining to Frank Miller (center), Trustee for the Tamalpais School District, why this marsh should be cleaned up and saved for the Red-wood High School students' biology classes.*

Illegal Logging on the Bolinas Ridge

To protect the Bolinas Lagoon watershed from erosion, we had to stop the logging that was planned for Dr. Ethel Righetti's ranch on the Bolinas Ridge in 1969. This bitter fight came just two years after we had given Kent Island and its perimeter to the county as a park. Because the county now controlled the lagoon, all five county supervisors, led by Peter Arrigoni, came into this battle with guns blazing. They assigned Doug Maloney, our astute county counsel, and county planner Sol Silver, to lead the battle against ridgetop logging. Their work led to a new Logging and Quarrying Ordinance for all of Marin County, one of the first of its kind in the state and a regulation that became a model for other counties.

Dr. Righetti's heavily timbered property sat above the Olema Valley, which was created by the unstable San Andreas fault. Because the ranch straddled the valley's divide, half of it drained southward into Bolinas Lagoon three miles away and the other half drained northward to Tomales Bay, seven miles away. If the logging weren't stopped, silt from erosion could partly fill the two bays we were fighting to save. Clerin Zumwalt and Howie Allen, Ranch chairman, were assigned to represent the Ranch.

For $500,000, Dr. Righetti had quietly sold the logging rights on her ranch to the Matthews Walker Timber Company of Coos Bay, Oregon. In April 1969, that company set up two portable sawmills and started cutting furiously, planning to take ten million board feet from the property. They did a sloppy job and started a fire. Sol Silver nailed them because they had no permit for a sawmill, and the supervisors promptly enacted a ninety-day freeze so they could write a new ordinance. Before this, however, two hundred West Mariners held a funeral march for the trees. Some lay down, blocking Highway 1, and several, including Planning Commissioner Mel Harris's son, went to jail.

The logging firm fought back. They hired Dr. Paul Zinke of the University of California Department of Forestry, who stated, "This is one of the *best* logging operations I've ever seen." The county retained Bob Burge, also a UC forester, who stated, "This is one of the *worst* logging operations I've ever seen."

Arrigoni asked Zinke, "Won't all the churned-up soil go into the Bolinas Lagoon?"

"Sure," said Zinke, "And so will all of Mr. Tamalpais and the Bolinas Ridge. It's natural for the lagoon to fill up with silt."

Arrigoni countered, "Well, let's not accelerate it."

Finally, the case went to trial in Alameda, where Dr. Righetti lived. Maloney, noted for his jugular approach, filed criminal charges against Dr.

Tenacious women, young and old, are why Marin County has preserved its open space, bay lands and farm lands. The old milking barn, now Zumwalt Gallery, displays the history of West Marin and Audubon Canyon Ranch.

Righetti and the loggers. The most important expert testimony on the soil erosion question was that of Clerin Zumwalt, who, according to Maloney, won the decision for Marin County.

In his best Kansas drawl, Zumie told about the men who had cleared these forests for logs and firewood a century before, and about the Irish potato farmers who had plowed the land straight up and down. He showed photos of land slides from previous logging operations. His story, entirely scientific, was so entertaining that the court was spellbound, and the judge ruled for the county.

Later, Maloney took the logging battle to the state and got it to change the "outrageous" logging rules that had been made by owners of timberlands themselves. Commercial logging never resumed in Marin County.

Anarchy in Fairfax

Fairfax lies on the eastern side of the Bolinas Ridge and is reached from the west by a steep road starting at the Canyon Ranch. It is a rustic town with steep narrow streets and spectacular views of Mt. Tamalpais and its tree-covered ridges. Today its citizens are outspoken environmentalists, but that was not so twenty-five years ago. News of our success in stopping eagle shooting spread, and a year later I dragged Zumie into another confrontation. Frank Egger, a Fairfax councilman, had called to tell me that Fairfax Mayor Sousa had marked forty-two madrones in the Fairfax City Park for felling because they had "peely bark." This is a natural condition, but County Agricultural Commissioner Allan Ballard had pronounced the trees "dead or dying." Egger also told me that the trees were to be cut by relatives of the mayor for firewood.

Nothing raises my blood pressure like the cutting of a ruddy bark madrone, one of California's most beautiful native trees and essential for insect and bird habitat. I rose to the bait, picked up Zumie, and off we went to the Fairfax Park where a chainsaw was already whining on a yellow-ribboned tree. Zumie inspected the trees and pronounced them healthy. The tree cutter, an unemployed electrician, admitted that peely bark was normal. He said he would go with us and talk to the mayor. Mayor Sousa wasn't in, but Egger was there, and said, "I'll convey the wonderful news to the mayor that all the trees are healthy."

The Ranch has always fed its volunteers well, whether at our annual Mother's Day barbecues, periodic fundraisers, board meetings, or special events like this 1969 dedication of the Ranch as a National Landmark.

Zumie and I then wrote to Mayor Sousa on our impressive Ranch stationary, laced with the names of well-known attorneys and citizens, and sent copies to Ballard and some county agencies. We urged that tree cutting be halted and that the native trees along the creek be preserved. It turned out that Sousa had intended to cut bay trees there also, and to straighten out the stream.

We had the letters hand-delivered to key people and urged the recipients to phone Sousa that evening. The strategy worked. Sousa, angry as hell, stopped the cutting and referred to us in the press as "anarchists."

For more than thirty years Clerin Zumwalt exemplified the spirit of Audubon Canyon Ranch. He was known as the "Sage of Marin County" and helped upgrade its environmental ethic through his scientific knowledge and engaging style. Like Bugs Cain and many other naturalists I've known, he was an unabashed protector of wildlife and wild places. Zumie died on Earth Day, April 22, 1996, at age eighty-five. A memorial service was held in Volunteer Canyon where his friends and family gathered to celebrate his life. His ashes are scattered near Alis' Tree, a century-old Douglas fir named for his wife.

CHAPTER SEVEN

Training the Troops

Recruit and train your troops to carry on when you wear out.

—State Senator Peter Behr of Marin County

Audubon Canyon Ranch was originally concerned with purchasing ranches, establishing wildlife preserves, educating the public, and fighting freeways. But it soon became apparent that our preserves on the Bolinas Lagoon, and later on Tomales Bay, could end up as isolated islands of beauty in a sea of mediocre sprawl so typical of urban California. To prevent this nightmare the Ranch adopted in 1968 a radical shift in policy as yet untried in California: recommending that the entire watersheds of Bolinas Lagoon and Tomales Bay (and later the entire county) be managed to protect their ecological quality. To do this it was necessary to train people who could influence county and state agencies and political bodies on the ecosystem approach to land management practices.

I jumped headlong into the county planning process as chair of the county's Environmental Health Committee for West Marin and a member of the county's new Environmental Quality Committee whose intent was to develop a new Marin Countywide Plan based on ecology.

To help accomplish these ambitious goals, the Ranch created two strategically complementary training programs: first, the Docent Program in Nature Education; and second, the more politically oriented Environmental Forum of Marin. The latter was the first effort in the state to actively train leaders in environmental advocacy and environmental health.

From these two training programs have emerged some nine hundred citizen planners who have become wildlife educators, guides, political leaders, county supervisors, state health officers, agency directors, naturalists, and Ranch board members. Both courses teach the students that ecological quality and sound land-use planning are essential for human health and a healthy environment.

Stan Picher was a genius at securing funding and new talent to greatly

Audubon Canyon Ranch naturalist Ray Peterson trains and entertains Ranch docents in the magnificent outdoor classroom of Volunteer Canyon.

Each spring, students and Ranch visitors can view the mating and nesting behavior of egrets and herons from the Henderson Overlook. In the distance is Kent Island, Bolinas, and the Pacific Ocean beyond. Natural history is taught by trained Docents, Guides, and Ranch Hosts—all volunteers.

expand the Ranch's training programs. On March 18, 1969, at the dedication of the Audubon Canyon Ranch as a National Natural Landmark by the National Park Service, we took the opportunity to launch our new docent program.

We held a chicken barbecue behind the cowbarn in the Ranch yard for three hundred distinguished guests. There, after the Park Service dedication, it was my privilege as chair to announce that the Junior League of San Francisco had granted $44,608 to the Ranch for a training program for Ranch docents. "Stan Picher" I said, "will be supervising the three year program." The crowd went wild with applause.

Behind us, the heronry that had made this wonderful gift possible was in full display with stunning white egrets descending into their nests in the redwood grove.

Stan then explained to the crowd in his crisp and excited manner, "In addition to operating the sanctuary, the Ranch's other mission is education. Last spring there were twenty thousand visitors to the Ranch, with many classes of school children. This great expansion of visitors has created a need for a high quality interpretive program."

Stan never did things in a small way. He continued, "These activities will require trained docents, who will become part of the Audubon Canyon Ranch Volunteer Council, to lead tours at the Ranch and staff the office, a nature store, a display room, and a heronry overlook. School children and teachers will be educated by docents with slide shows in their own class-rooms before they visit the Ranch. In addition, volunteer docents trained in nature education will be placed in cooper-ating conservation organizations, sanctuaries, and parks."

The Ranch hired Mrs. Rembert (Remmy) Kingsley, a well-known environmental educator, to develop the course. Notices of the course were sent to the media, and out of sev-enty applications, forty qualified people were selected. Thus was born the first annual docent training course of the Audubon Canyon Ranch Volunteer Council. Over twenty-five years, some four hundred women and men have been trained. Many of these volunteers have become strong sup-porters of the Ranch programs, have contributed to its fund-ing, and have served on its board and committees. They also provided a powerful constituency intent on saving Marin County.

Docent training programs are now alternated between the Bouverie Audubon Preserve in Glen Ellen and the Bolinas Preserve of Audubon Canyon Ranch. Here is the schedule of the first docent class:

Edris Cole (left) was our only paid office staff in the early years, running the day-to-day opera-tions and later the book-store for thirty years. Skip Schwartz (right) and his late wife Karen were both graduates of the Ranch's docent training program. Skip has been our Ranch Manager since 1974.

> *Lecture 1*—Ecology of Bays and Lagoons, Harold Gilliam
>   Field Trips: Kent Island Salt Marsh, Bolinas Lagoon
> *Lecture 2*—Concept of an Ecosystem
>   Field Trip: San Francisco Bay Tour
> *Lecture 3*—Natural History of Herons and Egrets of Bolinas
>   Lagoon, Clerin Zumwalt
> *Take-home Examination*

By 1997 the course had expanded to twenty training sessions and field trips led by experts in their field and coordinated by graduates Cia Donahue, Betsy Stafford, Jeni Jackson, and Patti Blumin.

Skip Schwartz—CEO

As proof of the quality of the Ranch's docent training course, an early graduate, Maurice "Skip" Schwartz, has become one of California's foremost wildlife sanctuary administrators. For more than two decades he and his family have lived in the historic Bourne house, from which he has overseen the growth of Audubon Canyon Ranch's educational and scientific programs. The annual budget has grown twenty-fold; his staff now numbers fourteen, including three full-time naturalists, and the Ranch endowment fund is growing to ensure long-term fiscal responsibility.

Skip has made sure that the wilderness areas and wildlife habitats in his care are protected, that necessary property is purchased, historic structures are restored, and new ones are constructed in a manner that befits the purpose of Audubon Canyon Ranch and preserves natural habitats.

Debbie Ablin and Nancy Barbour have been active on the Ranch Board since 1962, providing long-term stability and common sense. Their husbands were my medical colleagues.

Skip has overseen the many committee and board meetings that are needed to make a complex organization of this size succeed. He has established effective relations with the community, other environmental groups, and with the four Audubon branches that are the sponsoring backbone of Audubon Canyon Ranch.

In 1996 the Ranch celebrated its 35th anniversary with a formal party where ACR president Len Blumin, Skip, Zumie and I were all dressed in tuxedoes, a far cry from our early years.

Creation of The Environmental Forum of Marin

During the battle for Tomales Bay we decided that every county needs an Environmental Forum, whose purpose is to give people the scientific edge and political training needed to defend their environment. Since its founding in 1972, The Environmental Forum of Marin has selected and trained more than 550 citizens to be effective and influential spokespeople on environmental issues that are usually political in nature.

The need for The Environmental Forum was obvious to Stan Picher and me. At crucial Tomales Bay hearings, we couldn't rally our troops to speak; they didn't know the issues. However, we still urged them to attend as "nodders and frowners." It often boiled down to only a few people who could square off with our opponents, which included some nasty supervisors and developers.

The Environmental Forum of Marin was born at a meeting of Audubon Canyon Ranch board members Stan Picher, Mary Belle Van Voorhees, Howie

Allen, Clerin Zumwalt and me. Miraculously, the Junior League of San Francisco *again* granted the Ranch $44,000 for three years. Entirely separate from their nature education grant, these funds enabled us to employ Remmy Kingsley again. She developed and taught the first course, assisted by Ginny Havel, Nona Dennis, Kathy Cuneo, Phyllis Faber, Maggie and David Cavagnaro, and Ray Peterson. The latter three became full-time Ranch naturalists, Ray for fourteen years. Phyllis later became a founder of the Marin Agricultural Land Trust, chair of the North Central Coastal Commission, and editor of the California Native Plant Society bulletin, *Fremontia.*

Ray Peterson (left) and John Kelly are professional, well-trained naturalists and scientists. Ray manages the education program at the Bolinas Lagoon Preserve, and John heads the ACR scientific program with headquarters at Cypress Grove Preserve.

Later, the Forum became independent of Audubon Canyon Ranch in order to give it freedom to take political action. For its first three years, the Forum concentrated its training on the Tomales Bay watershed, with field trips using the new Countywide Plan and the new environmental studies of Bolinas Lagoon and Tomales Bay by the Conservation Foundation. Ian McHarg's book, *Design With Nature,* was required reading.

I was the first beneficiary of the Forum course when I ran for director of the Marin Municipal Water District in 1973, and Pam Lloyd of the first Forum class was my campaign manager. She succeeded me on the water board and later became a director of the Regional Water Quality Control Board. Many other graduates have had effective environmental careers, and some have been elected to office, including Senator Barbara Boxer. Karin Urquhart became the president and later the executive director of the Marin Conservation League, retiring in 1995. She was succeeded by Jerry Edelbrock, a professional planner and educator. In 1997 the Forum celebrated twenty five years of making environmental history in Marin (*see Appendix*).

Today the Forum course is self-supporting, operated by volunteers who train thirty students a year. The Forum publishes a quarterly bulletin, holds graduation ceremonies, and has an active four-hundred-person phone tree. Every trainee is expected to become an expert in one area of conservation. Zumie and I were made honorary lifetime members in 1992.

The troops are also reaching out to start forums in other counties. Marin Supervisor Harry Moore and his wife, Callita, both graduates, along with officers Julie Grantz and Karol Raymer, helped create a similar model in Sonoma County in 1995 focusing on Russian River water supply issues, which concern both counties.

PART THREE

TOMALES BAY

The Tomales Bay watershed covers about 228 square miles and drains about two-fifths of Marin County into the Pacific Ocean at Bodega Bay through twelve-mile-long Tomales Bay. The Bay is fed partly by Lagunitas, Nicasio, and Walker Creeks, which have been dammed to create six small wilderness lakes that supply drinking water to ten of the eleven cities in Marin. Lagunitas Creek drains the steep northern slope of Mt. Tamalpais and creates the Olema freshwater marsh, a natural filter. Public ownership of the 21,500-acre Marin Municipal Water District's watershed protects both the main sources of drinking water and an extensive wildlife habitat. The battles to prevent subdivisions within the unfinished Point Reyes National Seashore and along the east shore of Tomales Bay triggered California's first major coastal and water supply revolutions. Note the location of Cypress Grove Preserve.

CHAPTER EIGHT

The Tide Turns for Marin

No elected office in California has such a profound effect as Supervisor on the quality of life in Marin, Sonoma, or any county.

—State Senator Peter Behr

Just as The Kent Island Coup was concluding in 1967, securing the southern flank of the National Seashore, we had to begin fighting for Tomales Bay, which protected the Seashore's entry twenty miles to the north. As land acquisition chairman for Audubon Canyon Ranch, I assessed our chances as nearly hopeless. Here's why: Tomales Bay is ten times the size of Bolinas Lagoon and thousands of acres of tidelands had been subdivided into underwater lots and sold by the state years before. Nearly all the shoreline was privately owned except for one of Caroline Livermore's projects, Tomales Bay State Park on the west side. Even Hog and Duck Islands were privately owned. In addition, the area was swarming with developers and the supervisors were pressing hard for a freeway, this time from San Rafael to Tomales Bay and on up the coast into Sonoma County.

Tomales Bay is a long narrow bay about twelve miles long and barely one and one-half miles wide, shallow at its peaceful southern end, and deep near its dangerous oceanic mouth, where huge waves crash over its sandbar, overturning boats and drowning unwary fishermen each year. The bay averages twelve feet in depth and covers nine thousand acres, including tidelands. The dreaded San Andreas Fault goes right down its center, creating the granite cliffs and bishop pine forests of the Point Reyes Peninsula, which the 1906 earthquake jolted northward an astonishing twenty-two feet near the town of Olema. On the east side of the bay, the chewed up continental plate hides landslides. Also, as we emphasized over and over, *there is hardly any available water.* Wells can go down hundreds of feet without hitting a drop.

The hills are kept green all year by "ye stinking fogge," as Sir Francis Drake called it, creating some of the finest dairyland in the state. Butter, cream, milk, and teleme cheese from a dozen large Tomales Bay dairy farms

Subdivisions, malls, high schools, and freeways were projected for the east shore of Tomales Bay (distant) in the 1967 West Marin General Plan, eliminating one of the state's most productive dairy regions. This photo was taken from the Inverness Ridge, which is now part of the Point Reyes National Seashore.

have been prized for a century. So why, we asked the supervisors, kill this golden goose by paving it over? Why not leave it alone?

The bay was historic: it had seen English, Spanish, Russian, and Mexican explorers. The remnants of a railroad track between Sausalito and Cazadero near the Russian River, built by Chinese labor, follows the eastern shore, creating brackish lagoons that are home to mallard, pintail, and widgeon. This railroad once brought vacationers to the woodsy village of Inverness and the dairy center of Point Reyes Station, and brought clammers to Cypress Grove midway up the bay. In 1967 the population of the Tomales basin was only five thousand. Why not keep it that way to protect the dairy industry and attractiveness to tourists?

Only a few Marin residents were aware that the superlative wildlife habitat of Tomales Bay was in grave danger in 1967 from the freeways and urban development proposed by the West Marin General Plan.

Although it had no stunning colony of egrets for the Ranch to defend, Tomales Bay was far richer in wildlife and had its own stark, windswept beauty. Unfortunately, though, it was best known for its annual shark derby in which sportsmen caught, killed, and threw back sharks and California bat rays that used the bay as a nursery. Also, the bay boasted tens of thousands of wintering ducks and geese, which attracted large numbers of hunters from outside the county. At the annual "coot shoot," hundreds of coots (small, harmless, black waterbirds) were needlessly killed and left on the marsh. The economic center for many farmers on Tomales Bay was Petaluma in Sonoma County, and many of its visitors came from the Sacramento Valley. Few people in Marin then knew or cared about foggy Tomales Bay.

By 1967 the struggle for Tomales Bay had begun in earnest. The east shore's gentle pasturelands overlooking the bay were ideal for development. Three of the five county supervisors and a sophisticated cabal of wealthy speculators were alarmed by the success of Audubon Canyon Ranch at defeating growth around the Bolinas Lagoon. Mary Summers prepared a master plan for the east side of Tomales Bay, entitled the West Marin General Plan, which the supervisors adopted by a three-to-two vote. It was far more grandiose than the one she'd done for the Bolinas basin six years before. The more colorful the map, we soon learned, the worse the concept. This plan allowed for a new city along Tomales Bay, with a population of some 150,000 people, more than half the total count for the county. Housing tracts and miles of freeway would urbanize the hills overlooking Tomales Bay.

The water supply for this new city would come by pipeline from the Russian River, which would be swollen with water from the proposed Warm

Proposed Sonoma-Marin Russian River Aqueducts

to SEA RANCH

HEALDSBURG

Russian River

WOHLER PUMPS

Coastal Aqueduct
(never built)

JENNER

SEBASTOPOL

SANTA ROSA

Existing Aqueducts

Connecting Aqueduct
(never built)

BODEGA BAY

COTATI

SONOMA

PETALUMA

Sonoma-Marin Aqueduct
(defeated by Marin voters in 1971; approved in 1992 but never built)

NOVATO

POINT REYES STATION

Existing Pipeline
from Novato to Corte Madera

SAN RAFAEL

MARIN MUNICIPAL WATER DISTRICT

The Sonoma-Marin Aqueduct, proposed in the 1960s, would have provided water for development all along Highway 101. In addition, a connecting aqueduct was to be built to supply a coastal aqueduct, which would provide water for development all along an expanded Highway 1 on the Marin-Sonoma coast. A huge nuclear power plant was planned in 1962 for Bodega Bay. Explosive growth would follow, and some thought fortunes could be made.

Springs Dam. Such large development would be used to further justify plans for the dam.

Love That Benthos

Tomales Bay was relatively unpolluted in 1967 except for leaching from septic tanks, the new West Marin Sanitary Landfill, and from the heavy manure runoff during winter rains. Our biggest ace in the hole was that the Pacific Marine Station monitored the bay mud, "the benthos." Under the direction of Professor Edmund Smith, they identified thirty-six of the three hundred or more species of tiny bottom creatures that formed the start of the food web. Smith was my hero for persuading the Bay Area Regional Water Quality Control Board, of which he was a member, to prohibit sewage wastewater discharge into Tomales Bay or the ocean as being possibly lethal to these organisms. This was bad news for the subdividers: they might have to pump sewage out of the Tomales basin at a prohibitive cost.

Although Tomales Bay was deemed pristine, the biology of the upper

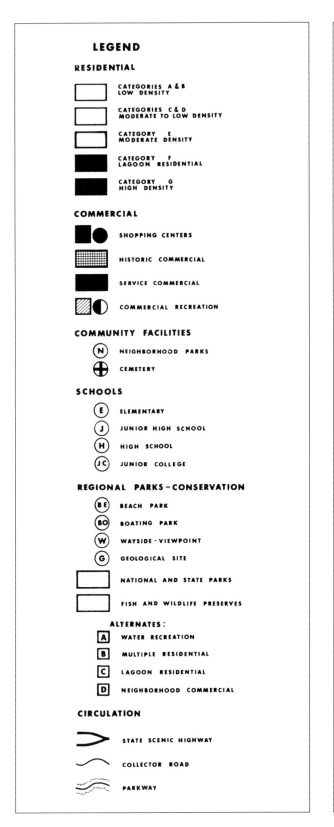

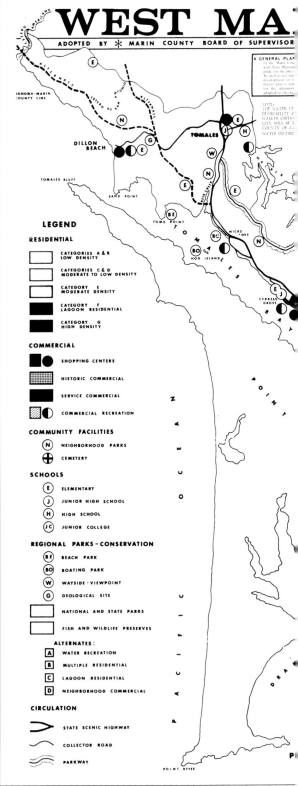

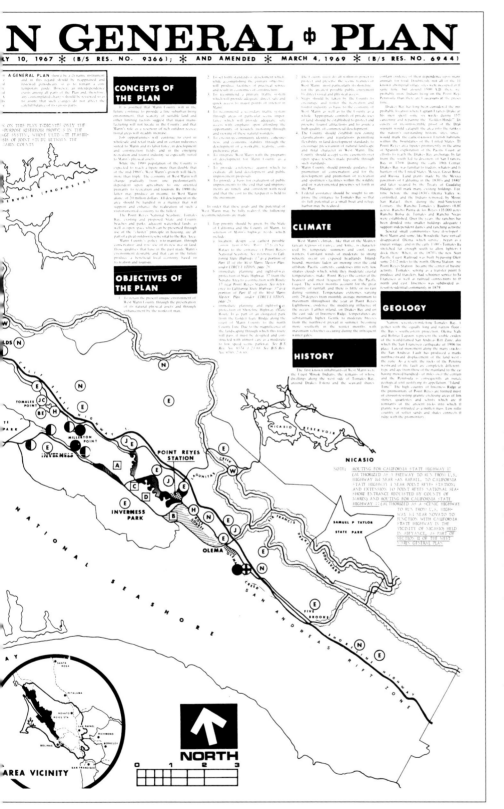

CONCEPTS OF THE PLAN

OBJECTIVES OF THE PLAN

CLIMATE

HISTORY

GEOLOGY

NICASIO

NICASIO RESERVOIR

POINT REYES STATION

INVERNESS PARK

OLEMA

SAMUEL P TAYLOR STATE PARK

NATIONAL SEASHORE

SAN ANDREAS RIFT ZONE

FIVE BROOKS

AREA VICINITY

NORTH

This absurd 1967 West Marin General Plan called for urban development for 150,000 people, threatening 130,000 acres of productive dairy and farmlands, inflating land values, and compromising the purchase of the National Seashore. Schools and shopping centers would punc-tuate the residential countryside, served by parkways and a major "scenic" highway. The Plan required a coastal aqueduct from the Russian River for water and outfalls for treated sewage directly into Tomales Bay.

In the early seventies several "canoe-ins" raised public awareness about saving the wildlife habitats in Tomales Bay's marshes and tidelands. In 1972 The Environmental Forum of Marin was created by Audubon Canyon Ranch. Over the next twenty-five years, The Forum trained more than six hundred citizen advocates in how to protect their county.

bay for native oysters had been ruined by the construction of dams that decreased the freshwater flow of Lagunitas Creek, which filtered through the large Olema freshwater marsh before entering the bay. However, commercial oyster farms for imported Eastern and Pacific oysters did well elsewhere in Tomales Bay, and we let the supervisors know that we would defend these oyster farms from pollution at any cost, as they were among the last in California.

To the east of Tomales Bay, the Walker Creek watershed, the second-largest in the county, had been overgrazed and deforested for more than a century, resulting in heavy erosion. This in turn created a huge delta that protruded alarmingly into the bay. Still, the delta remained rich in salicornia marsh, which attracted egrets, herons, willets, and other shorebirds. Any roads or house pads cut into the hills above the bay would be totally unacceptable, we warned, as they would increase erosion and eventually cut the bay in half.

Privately owned Hog and Duck Islands near the mouth of Tomales Bay were still pristine. The rich tidelands surrounding them bore oysters, cockle clams, and abundant fish, all drawn by great upwellings of ocean nutrients. Seals hauled out on Hog Island but, we discovered, were run off by party fishing boats from Lawson's Landing at the mouth of Tomales Bay. The bay needs management, not more development, we said. The oceanic end of the bay supports great forests of eelgrass, which are the spawning grounds for schools of the herring threatened by overharvesting for the Japanese market. Also, black brant, a smaller relative of the Canada goose, rely on the eelgrass for food.

Several species of shark and rays use the bay as a nursery, and huge sea lions enter the bay to dine on fish. In fact, on a high school outing in 1937, a friend and I made our first and only attempt to swim across Tomales Bay.

Midway across, a sea lion suddenly loomed up, giving us a good scare, then followed us. A Marconi Station guard spotted us and sent out a rescue boat.

Three Blind Supervisors

All in all, Tomales Bay added up to one of the most productive and varied wildlife habitats on the Pacific Flyway. But the county supervisors weren't impressed by the facts, even when we told them that the annual Christmas bird counts on the bay were among the highest in the nation. The West Marin General Plan, prepared by County Planner Mary Summers and her husband Harold, a retired state freeway planner, and supported by three blind supervisors, appeared to spell doom for the seals and sting rays, the steelhead and coho salmon, the benthos and the black brant of Tomales Bay.

All the supervisors seemed to care about, and argue over endlessly at public hearings, was the density of houses per acre. They saw the wildlife habitat of the bay as expendable and gave no thought to how subdivisions and a freeway would defeat the underfunded National Seashore by pushing land values out of sight, how the views from the Seashore would be marred, how dairy farmers would be turned into land speculators overnight, or where the water for 150,000 people would come from, and where their wastewater would go. Master plans once adopted are hard to repeal; however, they're not carved in granite.

The Campaign for Supervisor Heats Up

Diagnosing a desperate situation, Ted Wellman of the Marin Conservation League recognized that the best strategy for saving Tomales Bay and the National Park was a political one: we had to replace one county supervisor. This would provide the three-to-two vote needed to support the completion of the National Seashore, overturn the West Marin General Plan, stop the freeway, delay or kill the dam, and rezone the east shore of Tomales Bay for agriculture. A new Board of Supervisors would hold the power to make these policy changes.

The leading supporter of the West Marin General Plan of 1967 was a powerful, outspoken supervisor with a booming voice, Ernest "Kett" Kettenhofen, who wanted Marin County and the developers to cash in on the proximity of the National Seashore. Kett was up for reelection in 1968, and he seemed likely to win since he had split the conservation vote by helping me obtain Kent Island for a county park. But Kett's support of the General Plan had aroused the ire of the Roger Kent family, including their relatives next door, Jane and Stanleigh Arnold, whose friends numbered in the hundreds.

In 1968 Roger Kent called an emergency meeting of sixty conservation leaders from the entire county at his estate in Kent Woodlands. Its purpose was how to oust Kettenhofen from office. We gathered in Alice and Roger's Victorian parlor with vistas of Mt. Tamalpais beyond. He said, "In the century my family has lived here, the development of West Marin is the greatest threat the county has ever faced."

Roger was chair of the State Democratic Party. He sent each of Kett's financial supporters a personal letter urging them to defect in the interest of saving West Marin from a freeway. Roger, a kingmaker, almost ran for Kett's place on the Board of Supervisors himself but changed his mind and persuaded Peter Arrigoni, former mayor of Fairfax, to run instead. In a second masterful letter, dated March 8, 1968, to the members of the Marin Conservation League, he said of Arrigoni bluntly, "I think Arrigoni can win and if he does we'll be glad he's on the board. If he loses, we lost plenty."

Kettenhofen was incensed. He wrote to his supporters protesting Roger's tactics, but he nevertheless strengthened Arrigoni's hand by supporting several critical proposals that would have opened West Marin to staggering urban growth, including:

- building an expressway (Highway 17) from the Richmond Bridge across Marin to Olema (Highway 1), then up the coastline into Sonoma County and down the coastline to the Golden Gate Bridge,
- allowing for more than one house per acre in the West Marin General Plan, and
- building a parkway on the Bolinas Ridge crossing Mt. Tamalpais from Mill Valley to Olema. (Kettenhofen owned a 1,400-acre ranch on the Bolinas Ridge near Olema.)

The damage these endorsements inflicted on Kett's hopes for a second term was characterized by a cartoon, reprinted widely, showing him giving the victory sign in front of a maze of freeway overpasses. Arrigoni, a stockbroker and outdoors man, ran a spirited campaign and his wife Pat, a talented author, handled publicity that wisely emphasized that the county's beauty was at risk.

The Political Turning Point for Marin County

Peter Arrigoni turned out to be a knight in political armor. With the support of Kent and the Marin Conservation League, he won two successive

The fight for the crucial swing vote on the Board of Supervisors in 1968 featured a caricature of Ernest Kettenhofen (bottom left) as the freeway czar. It helped candidate Pete Arrigoni win this seat for two four-year terms, a turning point in the battle to save Tomales Bay and Marin County.

IT'S YOUR CHOICE
THIS KIND OF MARIN

BULK RATE
U.S. POSTAGE
PAID
San Anselmo,
Calif.
Permit 16

649 SAN ANSELMO AVE.
SAN ANSELMO, CALIF. 94960

... OR THIS

The County's Future
Is in Your Hands

Our County as we know it now is in danger of being destroyed. If we who live here are willing to stand up and protect it, it can still be saved. If not, it will become just another urban sprawl.

Marin's hills and valleys will be covered by overbuilt subdivisions. Concrete freeways will slash through its meadows and forests. Wandering creeks will turn into concrete ditches. Marin's beauty will vanish irrevocably.

That prospect is the underlying issue of the supervisorial election this Tuesday. It is at the core of today's problems . . . sky-rocketing taxes and county government costs . . . jammed commuter and local traffic . . . virtually complete breakdown of county planning because of lack of policy from the Board of Supervisors.

Peter Arrigoni asks for your support at the polls. He invites you to study his record, his public service experience, his concerns. Compare these with his opponent's record, experience and concerns.

Then make your choice.

ELECT PETER ARRIGONI SUPERVISOR, 2nd DISTRICT!

Lobby the Board Today

This verse was written by Douglas Maloney, long-time county counsel for Marin, on the occasion of the Marin Conservation League's sixtieth anniversary in 1994. He was the key appointed official who kept The Plot to Save Marin on track through ever-changing makeups of the Boards of Supervisors. (Sung to the tune of "Marry the Man Today" from the musical *Guys and Dolls*.)

At many meetings held in Marin
A lesson we've been taught:
You can't get any action on something
You haven't sought.
At any regular meeting,
From Bolinas to Ross,
You mustn't count on success
'Til you've insured against loss.
Corner them all,
And lobby the Board today.
So we just convince them of the better things,
Respectable, conservative and clean.
Conservation
Fiscal restraint
Harvest mice
Terns
Salt marshes
Marin green
But lobby the Board today

Handle them meek and gently,
Lobby the Board today,
And bug them subsequently.
Carefully expose them to your best issues,
And if they ever try to stray from you,
Have a talk fest
Have a meeting
Send a letter
Send two
Hundreds, thousands,
Stop.
Lobby the Board today,
Rather than sigh in sorrow,
Lobby the Board today,
And count their votes.
And change their votes.
And change their votes.
Tomorrow!

elections for a total of eight crucial years, 1968-1976. He was joined on the Board in 1968 by Michael Wornum, a conservationist who replaced another leading conservationist, Peter Behr.

Then followed the remarkable but hoped-for political turn-around. On November 3, 1970, the Board withdrew its support of the Marincello Plan, a proposed city of 25,000 people and seven-story buildings on the Marin Headlands. Instead, Huey Johnson obtained its two thousand acres for The Nature Conservancy, and it is now part of the Golden Gate National Recreation Area.

In August 1971, by a three-two vote with Arrigoni the new swing vote, the Supervisors repealed the West Marin General Plan which envisioned 150,000 people along Tomales Bay. Then again in 1971 and 1972, with the support of Arrigoni, Arnold Baptiste, and Michael Wornum, the supervisors requested that the state withdraw its Highway 17 plan for coastal Marin County from Highway 101 to Tomales Bay, which they did. Then in a grand finale in 1971, the supervisors adopted a precedent-setting ecological study called *Can the Last Place Last?*—the basis for the Marin Countywide Plan adopted in 1973 *(see box on page 110)*.

With these profound changes in county policy, the coastal freeways and the new cities were dead, the wildlife of the Bolinas Lagoon and Tomales Bay were safer, and the completion of the National Seashore was more likely.

Next, despite vigorous protests from developers, agricultural zoning that allowed only one house for each sixty acres was enacted by Supervisors Arrigoni, Wornum, and Baptiste in March 1972 for the east shore of Tomales Bay, extending to the border of Sonoma County—one-fifth of the county. Prior to this some ranches could be subdivided into two-acre parcels, destroying viable agriculture. Gary Giacomini came on the Board on January 1, 1973, and served for twenty-four years, spearheading subsequent agricultural and coastal preservation. The supervisors also helped stall Warm Springs Dam, delaying completion until 1983. To date, however, no freeway or water pipeline carrying Russian River water has invaded West Marin or the Sonoma coast, nor should they ever.

To me, the 1968 supervisorial election was the true political turning point in modern Marin County and North Coast history. The defeat of the cross-county and coastal freeways had enormous implications in saving the wild coastline of Marin, Sonoma, and Mendocino counties. For the first time in more than a century, the public, not the real estate developers, was in control of planning in Marin County. We learned from this election that it is

Karin Urquhart, a graduate of the first class of The Environmental Forum, served as the director of the Marin Conservation League from 1980 to 1995. A talented musician, she ushered in an era of musical/political extravaganzas with supervisors and county officials spoofing themselves on stage at sold-out annual dinners.

The Supervisor's Ecological Revolt, 1967–1974

STRONG MEDICINE FOR MARIN'S POLITICAL FUTURE

County supervisors *can* limit growth, prevent sprawl, and insure the quality of life if they are backed by alert citizen planners. Between 1967 and 1974, during the transition from a developer-driven county to a citizen-controlled county, the majority of Marin County Supervisors took several key actions in three crucial areas:

Land Use Planning

Hired ecologically trained Planning Chief Paul Zucker
Appointed new City-County Planning Team
Appointed 20-member Environmental Quality Team
Prepared new ecological Marin Countywide Plan, adopted 1973
Adopted 60-acre minimum agricultural lot size for one-fifth of the county
Created Open Space District to buy 21,000 acres of community separators

Slowing Growth

Accepted gift of Kent Island, sinking the Bolinas Lagoon Marina, 1967
Killed Marincello, a new city for 25,000 on the Headlands, 1970
Repealed West Marin General Plan for 150,000 people, 1971
Withdrew support for freeways from Highway 101 to Tomales Bay and along the coast, 1971
Supported Peter Behr's Save Our Seashore campaign and the completion of two National Parks, 1972

Limiting the Water Supply

Voted against Dos Rios Dam on the Eel River, 1969
Helped stall Warm Springs Dam and Russian River aqueducts
Supported Senator Behr's 1972 Wild and Scenic Rivers Act to protect the Eel, Trinity, Klamath, and Smith Rivers

most cost- and time-effective to put all one's energies into electing the right supervisor. Until voters in every county recognize this fact, they are doomed to "good old boy" politics, pollution, over-development, and mediocre planning. Sonoma County is a sad example of this.

Today in Marin County all elected and appointed officials—supervisors, mayors, city council members, planning commissioners, and water and sewer agency directors—are scrutinized by the informed voters with great attention to their environmental credentials. Job creation, environmental planning, water conservation, wastewater recycling, and bird watching are held in high esteem, and a candidate who can't identify a pickleweed marsh might have trouble getting elected.

In my view, Marin can—and should—serve the rest of the nation as an example of how intelligent voting, careful planning, environmental education, and volunteer stewardship can protect our most vital resources.

Before these major countywide changes took place, however, Audubon Canyon Ranch sent me forth to see if we could purchase and preserve any of the rich wildlife habitats along Tomales Bay.

Canoeists enjoy the wild beauty of the Estero Antonio, a long estuary draining into Bodega Bay near the Marin-Sonoma border. We fought a large subdivision near its mouth, called Oceana Marin, approved by Marin supervisors before the State Coastal Act of 1976. Currently there is a battle to keep Santa Rosa's wastewater out of the Estero Americano to the north.

Can the Last Place Last?

In 1967, Marin County hired Paul Zucker, a young land-use planner who was not only inspired by Marin's natural heritage but also was willing to put himself out on a limb to save it. When the balance of power on the Board of Supervisors shifted in 1968, he was preparing a revolutionary Marin Countywide Plan, which used "designing with nature" as its method for preserving Marin's extraordinary landscapes and preventing its cities from sprawling together.

This Plan was prepared by the Marin County Planning Department under the direction of the City-County Planning Council of Marin for the eleven cities and the county of Marin. The Plan went through fifty-seven public hearings and was adopted in 1973 after a superb user-friendly guide was sent to every home, and published in three Marin County newspapers, the *Independent Journal*, the *Point Reyes Light*, and the *Pacific Sun*.

The Plan was the inspiration of talented county planners Paul Zucker and Al Solnit. Zucker later lost his job after he lost a supervisorial race, and Solnit was the victim of vicious attacks by developers and hostile editorials. But the Plan was embraced by the public and has prevailed through minor revisions for over twenty-five years. The countywide plan addressed Marin's major problems: rapid population growth, economic sameness, and deterioration of environmental quality due to sprawl.

Can the Last Place Last? *was the Environmental Quality Element of the Marin Countywide Plan. Its pioneering use of "ecological planning" is a model for other counties.*

The Plan divided the county into three distinct corridors: coastal/recreational, inland/rural and agricultural, and eastern/urban. As one of the twenty-member Environmental Quality Committee that

We lost the battle to save the lush Corte Madera Creek marsh near Marin General Hospital. Here I'm inspecting the only clump of salt-loving pickleweed that survived millions of cubic yards of dredged mud dumped there by the Army Corps when they moved and channeled the creek for a condo project— without a public hearing.

helped develop this plan, I was astounded that the urban corridor, stretching from Sausalito to the Sonoma County border along Highway 101, was given the highest priority for open space. I had mistakenly assumed it was hopelessly lost for wall-to-wall tracts. Instead, the plan recommended that thirteen magnificent community separators of unblemished ridges, some grassy, some forested, all rich in wildlife habitat and totaling 21,774 acres, be acquired by a new Open Space District. Today, much of the area has been preserved, and Barbara Salzman of the Marin Audubon Chapter and others are working on a Bayland Protection Corridor for tidelands along the eastern edge of the corridor.

Marin's Countywide Plan has been published on a stunning poster and can be obtained from the Marin County Planning Department. Its effect is shown on pages 148 & 149.

CHAPTER NINE

Yellow Ribbons Threaten Tomales Bay

In any conservation battle you must bell the cat: identify your opponents and publicize their works.

—David Brower, Archdruid, The Sierra Club

As Smiley's Saloon in Bolinas had been a crucial place of intelligence-gathering for saving Bolinas Lagoon, so my dentist's chair in Kentfield became my source of intelligence for the battle of Tomales Bay. I almost bit my dentist's hand when he told me in 1965 that he had bought 1,700 acres there for a future subdivision.

It was also in the dentist's chair, in 1966, that I first heard about a group of bright, young, rich executives, mostly from Ross, who called themselves Land Investors Research. They were buying up any ranch they could on the ridge that overlooked the full sweep of the National Seashore directly across Tomales Bay. They even had the audacity to purchase the 2,500-acre Pierce Point Ranch, which lay totally in the proposed Seashore boundaries. They were also buying up ranches encircling the Sonoma State University campus, thirty miles northeast, that would eventually become a warren of subdivisions in Rohnert Park.

This 1966 tax shelter ad by Land Investors Research attracted speculators in ranches along Tomales Bay. The most beautiful spot on the eastshore was Cypress Grove (left) whose Victorian cottages drew duck hunters not so long ago.

Having sold partnerships to raise funds, Land Investors Research tied up some eleven ranches, mainly on the east shore of Tomales Bay, by optioning or buying 7,805 acres. This plan for miles of subdivisions was frightening.

It seemed impossible for Audubon Canyon Ranch to repeat on Tomales Bay what we had done on Bolinas Lagoon—the land was too expensive. Nevertheless, a phone call put me on Land Investors Research's mailing list, unleashing a flood of fancy, embossed brochures. We learned that Gordon

Land Investors Research
*Speculative Land Syndicates 1965-1971**

Land Name & Location	Acres	Acquired
1. Tomales Bay Ranch Syndicates		
Cypress Point Farm	326	1966
Pierce Point Ranch	2,500	1966
Millerton Point	800	1965
Furlong Ranch	600	1969
Tomales Bay Associates	160	1969
Bay Ranch	500	n/a
Marin French Cheese Co.	700	n/a
Cypress Point Associates	700	1967
Deep Cove Beach Assoc.	570	n/a
[Unidentified] Associates	589	n/a
Rancho Estero Americano	360	1965
2. Rohnert Park Ranch Syndicates		
College Land Associates	34	1968
Cotati Rancho	26	1969
Crane Seventy Three	73	1969
Golf Lake Estates	75	1968
North Cotati Rancho	56	1969
Rohnert Park Associates	20	1969
Sonoma Campus Co.	200	1968
Sonoma College Partners	29	1968
Sonoma Property Associates	70	1967
3. Petaluma Ranch Syndicates		
Lake Ranch	2,500	1968
Petaluma 100	100	1969
Petaluma Partners	106	1969
Petaluma 29	29	1971
Petaluma 213	213	1970
4. Santa Rosa Ranch Syndicates		
Santa Rosa Valley Farm	206	1969
Windsor Orchards	124	1969

*Source: Land Investors Research, 1971

Large ranches were syndicated by Land Investors Research in Petaluma, Rohnert Park, and Santa Rosa as well as the 7,805 acres on Tomales Bay.

Pusser, Webster Otis, and Van Norden Logan, all of Marin, were founders and that the list of investors included Marin County physicians, dentists, lawyers, a judge, many ranchers, and even my minister. The smell of money was rampant in West Marin.

In any conservation battle you identify and expose your opponent, called "belling the cat." By clearly drawing the battle lines, you bring in supporters. Land Investors Research, with their grandiose brochures, belled themselves. They didn't need any help from conservationists.

Yellow Ribbons Everywhere

Van Norden Logan was Land Investors Research's architect and planner. As with Norman Gilroy's plans for Bolinas Lagoon, Logan's vision of marinas and carving up the east shore of Tomales Bay into thousands of view lots put him on a collision course with Audubon Canyon Ranch. Logan was a gentle, persuasive young man, the type you'd like to have for a son-in-law. Whenever I saw him and his handsome young associates in their suits and ties walking the hills above Cypress Grove with a surveyor, however, I felt sure that Tomales Bay, like Rohnert Park, was doomed. For three years rows of survey stakes and yellow ribbons could be seen marching up and down hills on thousands of acres bordering Tomales Bay and at Pierce Point. The ribbons and stakes delineated building parcels, roads, water lines, sewage spray fields, and reservoirs. To me, it felt as though each flagged stake cut a notch in my coronary arteries. One ranch family that didn't sell was Bill and Ellen Straus, who became my contacts on Tomales Bay and who have been stalwarts in the battle to save family farms in West Marin.

Water? The North Marin Water District based in Novato nearly twenty

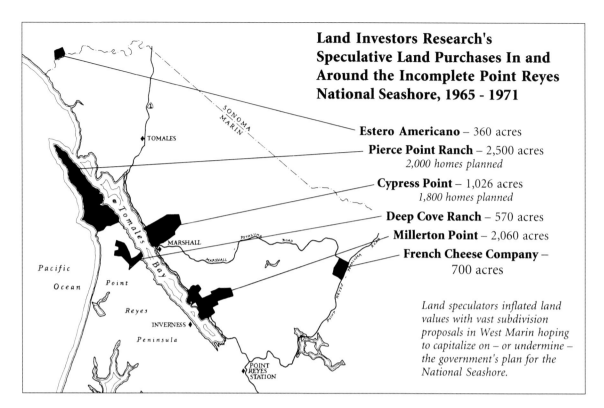

Land Investors Research's Speculative Land Purchases In and Around the Incomplete Point Reyes National Seashore, 1965 - 1971

Estero Americano – 360 acres

Pierce Point Ranch – 2,500 acres
2,000 homes planned

Cypress Point – 1,026 acres
1,800 homes planned

Deep Cove Ranch – 570 acres

Millerton Point – 2,060 acres

French Cheese Company –
700 acres

Land speculators inflated land values with vast subdivision proposals in West Marin hoping to capitalize on – or undermine – the government's plan for the National Seashore.

miles away had annexed the ranchlands of the east shore of Tomales Bay and would furnish water for subdivisions. The first were to be supplied from small reservoirs and later by pipeline from the Russian River. Sonoma County Water Agency planned a pipeline from near Sebastopol to Bodega. From here pipelines could be extended down the coast to meet the needs of West Marin, and up the coast to Jenner and Sea Ranch, if development occurred there. The Sonoma County Water Agency wholesales water; the more water sold, the more money made.

Audubon Canyon Ranch in 1970 had a formidable team: Howard B. Allen was chair, George Peyton was legal advisor, Stan Picher managed finances, and I led the land acquisition efforts. My fellow board members encouraged me to devote my efforts full-time to the desperate plight of Tomales Bay.

The accompanying box lists the ranches that Land Investors Research syndicated between 1965 and 1971 in the hope of cashing in on the disastrous West Marin General Plan, which would have allowed a huge city on the east shore of Tomales Bay overlooking the National Seashore. Did the investors know they were driving up the price of the park by their speculations?

Land Investors Research syndicated clusters of ranches totaling 7,805 acres within the proposed National Seashore boundaries and along the east shore of Tomales Bay. With such sophisticated and well-financed development interests at work in 1967, saving Tomales Bay and the National Seashore looked hopeless.

Several miles of Tomales Bay tidelands on both sides of Cypress Grove (right center) were owned by Norwegian oysterman Oscar Johannson. The hills behind were slated for subdivisions by well-tailored young developers carrying briefcases.

Conflicts of Interest?

There were cries of protest when the *Independent Journal* disclosed in 1971 that Land Investors Research was possibly affecting the government's ability to buy land for the Seashore through their connections in Washington, D.C. That year Webster Otis, president of Land Investors Research, was appointed as assistant to a fellow Ross resident, John W. Larson, in the US Department of the Interior. The newspaper revealed that the Pierce Point Ranch, which the Department of the Interior was trying to buy for the seashore park for $1.7 million, was being ransomed by Land Investors Research for five million dollars. They planned more than 2,000 view-homes on its 2,500 acres, which had fabulous vistas through the fog and wind of both the ocean and Tomales Bay. The purchase price was eventually settled by negotiation.

Our biggest brush with Land Investors Research came in early 1971, the year the West Marin General Plan had been overturned. They just wouldn't give up. I received a map and pitch for the sale of seven parcels of the scenic

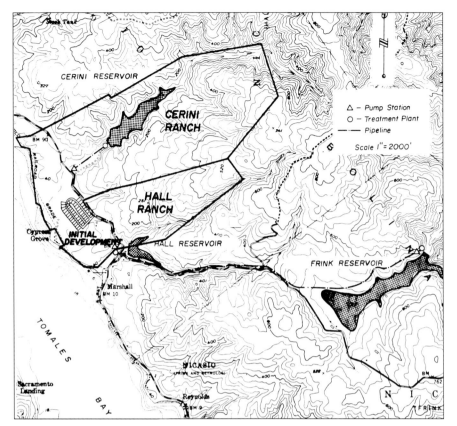

Cypress Grove (far left), a ten-acre forested bluff commanding Tomales Bay and owned by architect Clifford Conly, Jr., was threatened by a freeway and by two large tracts proposing 900 houses, complete with their own dam and reservoir.

Millerton Point Ranch, which overlooked twin salt and freshwater lagoons. If this small subdivision went through, it could set a precedent.

Alarmed, I rushed to the Civic Center and looked over the general plans for the project with Supervisor Pete Arrigoni. The County determined that the project didn't meet subdivision requirements for roads, water, and sewers, which meant that the subdivision was non-conforming. Land Investors Research was notified and agreed to stop sales on March 8, 1971. To this date there are no houses on this subdivision.

These experiences tipped us off to the fact that Land Investors was having problems and that their timing was off. Their hopes for Russian River water and a freeway had all been dashed. We saw that it was now or never. Audubon Canyon Ranch had to buy Tomales Bay land and establish a wildlife sanctuary while Land Investors was unable to sell its lands and before new supervisors were elected.

I had already started buying tidelands in 1970 before the West Marin General Plan was killed. Ruth Corwin at the county planning department had furnished a map and a list of all the property owners on Tomales Bay.

Herring boats on Tomales Bay haul in large catches off Cypress Grove, where the fish spawn in the eel grass on the bottom.

Land Investors owned much of the east shore uplands but not the tidelands, which they would need for recreational access to the bay. Nor did they own the critical jewel called Cypress Grove, a small 10-acre promontory in the middle of the east shore, which reminded me of Rosie's strategic bluff on Richardson Bay. My job was clear: Audubon Canyon Ranch would have to buy as many miles of privately owned tidelands as possible and then try to purchase Cypress Grove. The owner of four miles of tidelands was Oscar Johannson.

Oysters Keep Johannson Young

I called on Oscar Johannson in early 1970. He lived in a little red house near the West Marin Sanitary Landfill. He was a weathered, slightly bent, powerfully built Norwegian who had been oystering on Tomales Bay for decades. He served me a plate of delicious raw oysters with a dash of Tabasco. We talked for a while about the yellow flags along the bay. Then I asked, "Would you sell us your tidelands if you could keep on working them?" He jumped at the chance. "I'm tired," he said, "and I want to get married." I pledged him to secrecy.

Then began several months of trying negotiations with his son, Edward, who lived in Sebastopol. Edward, who would inherit the property, wanted to give us a lease, but I wasn't interested. During this time, Land Investors

Research got wind of our negotiations, but Oscar Johannson wanted Audubon Canyon Ranch to get his property. Edward finally agreed to a sale of his father's six tideland parcels, all former oysterbeds, totaling thirty-two acres and stretching in segments (four miles in all) for ten miles along the bay. We paid $25,000 cash. Some would argue that we didn't need these tidelands since in theory the bay belonged to the public. However, in 1970 a legal conveyance of title in tidelands still had a powerful effect.

The final agreement, drawn up on September 2, 1970, by our attorney, protected the tidelands from development or filling and kept them as open space but allowed oystering and the raising of other mollusks, a policy that is now under study by Audubon Canyon Ranch whose goal is to protect the ecological quality of the Bay. Most important, the purchase cut off access to the bay for two of the ranches held by Land Investors Research.

The cost of those tidelands, mostly submerged, alarmed some of our board members, but we never got a better bargain. Oscar Johannson was delighted. Within a month after getting his check, he retired. He was married on his eightieth birthday.

Oysterman Oscar Johannson displays a string of oysters on his eightieth birthday. His tideland oyster beds on Tomales Bay became the strategic parcels we needed to block the proposed subdivisions from access to the bay.

In the Nick of Time—The Shields Salt Marsh

Out of the blue, in 1970 I received a phone call from William Page Shields of San Mateo offering to donate ten thousand dollars to the Ranch—if we had a use for it. He had read in the *San Francisco Chronicle* about the long history of diking and straightening of Lagunitas Creek that ran through the 1,000-acre salt marsh owned by Waldo Giacomini at the upper end of the bay. It had been sold by the state before the turn of the century.

Twelve years earlier I had been unsuccessful in helping Captain Adolph Oko, a courageous real estate broker of Inverness, in first trying to save the salt marsh, which was nearly as large as Bolinas Lagoon, from diking. Oko's attempt earned him ridicule from the powerful West Marin farm lobby. (Feisty Oko had earned his title running refugee ships through blockades to Israel at the end of the war.)

Now Giacomini was seeking a permit to dike off another 132 acres of salt marsh and convert it to pasture for his dairy, which had provided superb milk to the Bay Area for decades. But by 1970 Marin's attitude toward salt marshes had changed, in part because of the Ranch's educational programs and a canoe-in along the marsh led by Jerry Friedman, founder of Environmental Action Committee of West Marin. Waldo's request was turned down at a tumultuous county Planning Commission hearing, where Al Bianchi, Waldo's attorney, challenged the county to buy the salt marsh if Waldo couldn't develop it.

So when Shields phoned me I said, "Mr. Shields, Audubon Canyon Ranch can use that check today to buy four acres of salt marsh extending out from Sir Frances Drake Boulevard north of Waldo's salt marsh that the Inverness Garden Club has to sell. We'll establish the Shields Salt Marsh Study Area, give it a lot of publicity, and see if we can persuade Audubon Canyon Ranch to purchase the Giacomini marsh adjacent to it."

Stan Picher inspects the William Page Shields Salt Marsh Study Area in 1972. Audubon Canyon Ranch bought it as leverage to help save the state's adjacent 500-acre Tomales Bay Ecological Preserve from filling.

Unknown to me, after the public hearing George Collins, with the financial help of Conservation Associates, had quietly taken an option to buy five hundred acres of the Giacomini marsh in 1970.

In 1972 the state Wildlife and Conservation Board took over the option and bought the property with an appropriation of $248,000 obtained by Marin's Assemblyman Bill Bagley. It is called the Tomales Bay Ecological

Preserve and today the entire south end of the bay is being restored to health. The Shields Salt Marsh is the home of a rare salt marsh plant species, Point Reyes Birds' Beak, the subject of a scientific paper by Audubon Canyon Ranch naturalist John Kelly and Dr. Grant Fletcher, a medical school classmate of mine.

The Shields Salt Marsh, the Johannson tidelands, and the Giacomini Marsh were the first pieces of the gigantic Tomales Bay puzzle locked into place in the race to save Tomales Bay from the yellow ribbons.

Clifford Conly's Crown Jewel: Cypress Grove

Yellow Ribbons (Sung to the tune of "Yellow Rose of Texas")

Those yellow rows of ribbons
They will not go away
They mark the subdivisions
Along Tomales Bay.

The Audubon is coming
They're marching down the Bay
To take those yellow ribbons
And throw them all away.

The most rewarding phone call of my wildlife career was the one I put in late at night in September 1970. Flushed with the success of buying miles of Johannson tidelands for the Ranch, I was particularly excited that two of its parcels protected the vulnerable flanks of Cypress Grove. I thought that Cypress Grove would make a fine headquarters for a new wildlife sanctuary on Tomales Bay, if we could obtain it.

Cypress Grove, a ten-acre cypress knoll on the shores of Tomales Bay, is a mystical place with adjacent salt and freshwater marshes teeming with waterbirds, six Victorian cottages, and a lovely main house standing within its borders. The grove brings to mind "Alice in Wonderland"; one expects the Mad Hatter to pop out between the long rows of trees at any moment. A parade of harbor seals, terns, gulls, and brown pelicans streams noisily past Cypress Grove each winter, following the herring that spawn in the eelgrass beds extending south from Hog and Duck Islands. This often foggy, windy paradise was formerly a stop on the old North Pacific Coast Railroad from Sausalito to Cazadero, and in the 1890s a wood-burning engine brought hunters to the cottages there to hunt brant and mallard ducks.

Clifford Conly's Cypress Grove became Audubon Canyon Ranch's headquarters in 1971 in the battle for Tomales Bay, the northern gateway to the still-incomplete Point Reyes National Seashore.

A Midnight Phone Call

None of us had met Clifford Conly nor set foot on Cypress Grove, but something told me one evening to call him. I had just returned from a medical meeting and didn't realize how late it was. At midnight Conly picked up the phone. "Mr. Conly," I said, "This is Dr. Griffin with the Audubon Canyon Ranch, and we've been purchasing lands along Tomales Bay. We thought you would be pleased to learn that we just bought the Johannson tidelands on both sides of you." There was a long ominous silence. I thought, my God, I've blown it, but I continued on. "We've heard that Cypress Grove might be for sale, and we'd like to make you an offer and purchase it."

"Look, Dr. Griffin," Clifford said, "I've heard of you and I've heard of Audubon Canyon Ranch and I like what you're doing, but do you know what time it is? It's midnight, and I'm standing here starkers on a cold floor. I have no intention of selling my property. Now, if you'll just let me get back to bed, I'll promise to *give* Cypress Grove to Audubon Canyon Ranch!"

That's how it happened, I swear it! The story of my midnight phone call has been told and retold and has become legend. That gift opened up a whole new thrilling era in the saga of Audubon Canyon Ranch and turned the battle to save Tomales Bay our way.

Needless to say, the grumbling among board members about my Johannson purchase stopped. They were overwhelmed by Clifford's generosity and electrified by this strategic gift. Preserving Tomales Bay was within our grasp. Our attorney, George Peyton, worked out the details with Clifford, and percentages of ownership were deeded over to Audubon Canyon Ranch over a period of years.

Late one night in 1970 I phoned Clifford Conly, and he offered to donate his ten-acre Cypress Grove to Audubon Canyon Ranch if I'd let him get back to bed. Later, he became a valuable board member.

With the Clifford Conly gift of Cypress Grove arranged, and the deed of the tideland purchase signed by Oscar and Edward Johannson, Stan Picher and I met with the press. The Marin *Independent Journal* headline on October 18, 1971, was in a special orange ink reserved only for disasters: AUDUBON BUYS 42 ACRES ON TOMALES BAY. The article described Clifford's ten-acre gift and the thirty-two acre purchase of tidelands from Johannson, and gave dire warnings that we "might tie up the future of the bay for the birds."

In 1992 Clifford, then seventy-eight years old, and his ranch foreman, Bill Tykodi, moved to an early California home they had restored near the plaza in the town of Sonoma, and the Ranch took over the management of Cypress Grove. It is now Audubon Canyon Ranch's educational and research flagship on Tomales Bay.

Tying Up the Bay for the Birds

However in 1971, Clifford was worried about his encircling and aggressive neighbors. Yellow ribbons still fluttered everywhere he looked. He was alarmed by the marinas and condominiums proposed to the north and by subdivisions proposed to the east and south. In a personal letter to me, he asked Audubon to purchase acreage surrounding Cypress Grove in order to protect it. "Cypress Grove," he wrote, "is an island surrounded by alligators." The Johannson tidelands we had just purchased were critical because they blocked water access to large ranches owned by Land Investors Research on each side of Cypress Grove which were slated for more than nine hundred homes.

The key parcel Clifford wanted us to buy was a marshland and bluff just north of Cypress Grove already owned by Land Investors Research. I walked over it with him and Bill Tykodi one sparkling morning and agreed it would be a superb addition to Cypress Grove. It included the freshwater marshes and the wetlands along Cerini Creek extending to Highway 1, and the broken berms of the old railroad along the bay that I felt could be restored to enclose the freshwater marsh. I realized that if water and building permits were available, this twenty-six-acre mesa and marshland overlooking the National Seashore would be ideal for condominium development and a marina. Nevertheless, Land Investors Research needed cash.

I knew that if I didn't act quickly the land would be sold to others and lost forever. Fortunately, my relations with Van Norden Logan, the architect for Land Investors Research, were good. With some trepidation I phoned and asked the question, "Will you sell?" When he answered, "Yes," I almost dropped the phone.

Cypress Grove foreman Bill Tykodi slices a ten-foot-long sandwich for an Audubon Canyon Ranch board meeting. Grilled salmon and oysters simmered in the shell were also served, along with Hop Kiln Chardonnay.

The group agreed to sell Audubon the twenty-six acres we wanted for $29,000 cash. But there was one condition: that we give them a fifty-foot easement to the bay across the former Johannson tideland parcels to other lands they owned. This condition caused me anxiety because I feared a Pandora's Box. However there was no choice and, on December 4, 1971, I held the yellow-ribboned stakes that would delineate the twenty-six-acre addition to Cypress Grove while Van Norden Logan drove the stakes home. I held my breath until this delicate transaction was concluded. Clifford Conly and I were ecstatic, and we celebrated with a bottle of champagne. We had

Audubon Canyon Ranch purchased this twenty-six-acre fresh water marsh from Land Investors Research, who had planned to develop 7,805 acres along the bay but ended up with zero. We named the marsh after Caroline Livermore.

preserved the bayside and the northern flank of Clifford's ten-acre crown jewel. This area is now known as Livermore Marsh in honor of Caroline Livermore, whose family donated twelve thousand dollars through the Marin Conservation League toward its purchase.

Strategy: Vanquishing the Alligators

If Cypress Grove was to become a great wildlife sanctuary in 1972, we had to raise more money and enlarge its boundaries quickly while the land speculators needed cash. Marin County resident George Collins, formerly with the San Francisco division of the National Park Service, was one of the masterminds who conceived of the National Seashore. Financed by a group called Conservation Associates led by Doris Leonard and Dorothy Varian, he quietly bought ranches on the east shore threatened with subdivisions and turned them over to the state parks. Often these were ranches where Audubon Canyon Ranch had helped delay earlier plans for subdivisions. I knew that Collins, representing Conservation Associates, was trying to acquire the Giacomini marsh, Millerton and Tomasini Points, and the

Angress ranch (at that time slated for a motel and condominium project) all on the eastern shore for state parks. We worked together and gave him parcels we owned to round out state park boundaries. Our joint goal was to acquire all the available land between Highway 1 and Tomales Bay for a stretch of eleven miles for Audubon Canyon Ranch or the California State Parks system.

Stan Picher and the board went on a crash fund-raising program. In rapid succession, spurred by Clifford and me, the Ranch purchased the fourteen-acre Marshall Creek delta protecting Cypress Grove from the south. Then we purchased fifty-seven acres of the Cerini Ranch and forty-one acres of the Hall Ranch, which separated Cypress Grove from Highway 1. These two parcels were already mapped for subdivision by Land Investors.

We were also fortunate to purchase our lonely sentinels on Tomales Bay, Hog and Duck Islands, for forty thousand dollars from Mike Gahagan, owner of the weekly *Point Reyes Light.* These islands, slated for beach houses, guard the eelgrass beds and seal haulouts of the oceanic end of Tomales Bay.

The Clifford Conly Center for ecological research and education, dedicated in 1993, is in Clifford's restored Victorian home overlooking Tomales Bay. From the right: Zumie, Clifford Conly, Bill Tykodi, and me.

These acquisitions added up to 182 acres of superb tideland, freshwater, and coastal chaparral habitat surrounding our Cypress Grove Headquarters. These were further secured when in 1990 the Point Reyes National Seashore purchased the forty-acre Dunn Ranch to the east next to Marshall Creek. This purchase was facilitated by Senator Barbara Boxer and Audubon Canyon Ranch manager Skip Schwartz. In 1996 the Ranch donated Hog and Duck Islands to the National Park Service.

While we still had the fund-raising urge in 1972, we also purchased the forty-two-acre Olema Marsh at the southern end of the bay for $51,500. This was part of the largest freshwater marsh in the county. Then we purchased the entire delta of Walker/Keys Creek, 96.7 acres, for $15,500 from a friend of Clifford's to prevent any future lagoon housing tracts and to deter a proposed freeway headed east to Sonoma County. We also bought five acres on Keys Creek estuary for thirteen thousand dollars and donated it to the California Department of Fish and Game for a fishing access.

In 1985 Margaret Quigley donated to Audubon Canyon Ranch seventy-acre Toms Point, a spectacular promontory with half a mile of shoreline overlooking the entrance of Tomales Bay. It had been designated in the 1969

Stewards of the Land

Edgar Wayburn, my instructor in medical school, with his wife Peggy, was a leading proponent of a fully funded Point Reyes National Seashore and Golden Gate National Recreation Area.

The two great National parks, the Point Reyes National Seashore and Golden Gate National Recreation Area, plus the Gulf of the Farallones National Marine Sanctuary, have their longtime stewards, including Dr. Edgar Wayburn, who was also behind the Redwood National Park and the Alaskan National Parks; Amy Meyer, the sparkplug behind the Golden Gate National Recreation Area; and Peter Behr, the Savior of the National Seashore, among many others, who helped make them possible.

Many organizations are also working to ensure that the magnificent bays and parklands of West Marin are permanently protected and to provide a powerful citizen's constituency and lobbying force. Each has its own field of expertise, but together they represent thousand of citizens in Marin and throughout the Bay Area.

These groups include the Environmental Action Committee of West Marin, the Tomales Bay Association, the Inverness Association, the Point Reyes Bird Observatory, Audubon Canyon Ranch, Marin Audubon Society, Marin Conservation League, Coastwalk, Trout Unlimited, the Marin Agricultural Land Trust, Friends of the Estuary, the Sierra Club, and others. These groups meet with representatives from several governmental agencies and with political bodies as required. For years their Dean, the late State Senator Peter Behr of Inverness, brought together farmers and environmentalists to help save agriculture and to take responsibility for preserving the natural treasures of West Marin.

General Plan for a sewer pipeline outfall into Tomales Bay from subdivisions on the east shore.

Clifford Conly was more than pleased; all the alligators surrounding his Cypress Grove paradise had been vanquished and we owned 432 acres of superb parcels strategically located around 9,000 acres of contested tidelands that really belonged to the public. Meanwhile, there were far larger alligators at work across Tomales Bay.

The Senator Who Saved the Seashore

Peter Behr, a liberal Republican, started up the political ladder as a Mill Valley City Councilman. In 1962 he barely won a seat on the Marin County Board of Supervisors in a contentious recall election against a county supervisor who had voted to cut the National Seashore to 20,000 acres. The loser had mistakenly thought he could compensate for the loss of these parklands by building a fishing pier on Elephant Rock on San Francisco Bay. He had also voted to turn the famous Frank Lloyd Wright Civic Center into a hospital.

At that time the Point Reyes National Seashore and Cape Cod National Seashore were the first national parks to be purchased from private landowners; the rest had been carved from the public domain. This meant that unless the Marin County Board of Supervisors supported the proposed Seashore, there was little chance of Congress appropriating the money. For six years Behr was a minority on the board, but he managed to persuade his fellow supervisors to support the fragile National Seashore Project.

When Behr retired as supervisor in 1968, the Point Reyes National Seashore had exhausted all funds for acquiring land and was still short $38 million dollars to complete its land purchases. William Tevis' Lake Ranch was being logged and cut up into forty-acre parcels. The National Park Service had plans to sell off certain Seashore lands to developers for controlled subdivisions, and to use the money to buy the remainder of the park or other parks. Behr was furious, and in 1969 he started his Save Our Seashore (SOS) campaign. It electrified the entire region. His broadly based team quickly obtained a half-million signatures on petitions, distributed by County Planning Commissioner Margaret Azevedo, appealing to President Nixon to complete the park purchase. Until then, Nixon had adamantly refused to release funds and bills in Congress had put the park on hold.

Then Behr shaped a brilliant stroke. He sent the immense signature list

Senator Peter Behr of Marin, known as the Happy Warrior, rides his five-speed to work in Sacramento in 1973. There, he changed California's legislative process forever by requiring a published roll call vote on every bill. This was a direct frontal attack on the powerful old boy network of timber, water rights, and mining interests. When Behr died in 1997, at the age of 81, there was an outpouring of praise for one of the most effective and respected statesmen in California's history.

Audubon Canyon Ranch Strategic Acquisitions on Tomales Bay, 1968-1985 — 432 Acres

Cypress Grove Preserve Headquarters

Located between Tomales Bay and Highway 1, with a commanding view of the Point Reyes National Seashore and Tomales Bay, Cypress Grove's restored Victorian hunting lodge houses educational and research facilities for salt and freshwater marsh and chaparral habitats. The Preserve is a major resting area for migratory birds on Pacific Flyway.

1. *Cypress Grove Promontory,* a stop on 1875 Sausalito-Russian River railroad, 10-acre gift from Clifford Conly, Jr. in 1971.

2. *Johannson Oyster Tideland* purchases, 20.3 acres protecting Cypress Grove and access to bay, cost $25,000.

3. *Delta of Marshall Creek,* salt marsh and willow creek habitat, 14.53 acres protecting southern boundary of Cypress Grove, cost $14,756.

4. *Livermore Marsh,* fresh and salt water habitat to the north, 26 acres protecting the delta of Cerini Creek, cost $29,000.

5. *Part of Cerini Ranch* (rolling grasslands) between the bay and Highway 1, 57 acres protecting northern boundary, cost $68,601.

6. *Part of Hall Ranch,* 41 acres of chaparral habitat, between Cypress Grove and Highway 1, cost $52,986.

This map by Ane Rovetta depicts Audubon Canyon Ranch properties purchased or donated along Tomales Bay.

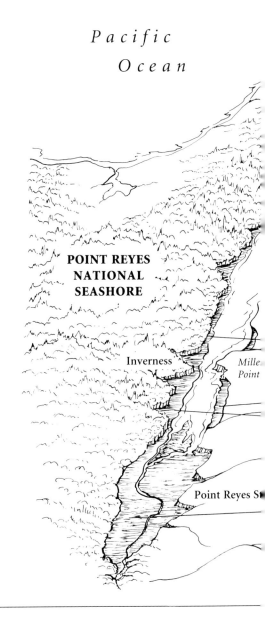

Pacific

Ocean

POINT REYES NATIONAL SEASHORE

Inverness

Mille Point

Point Reyes S

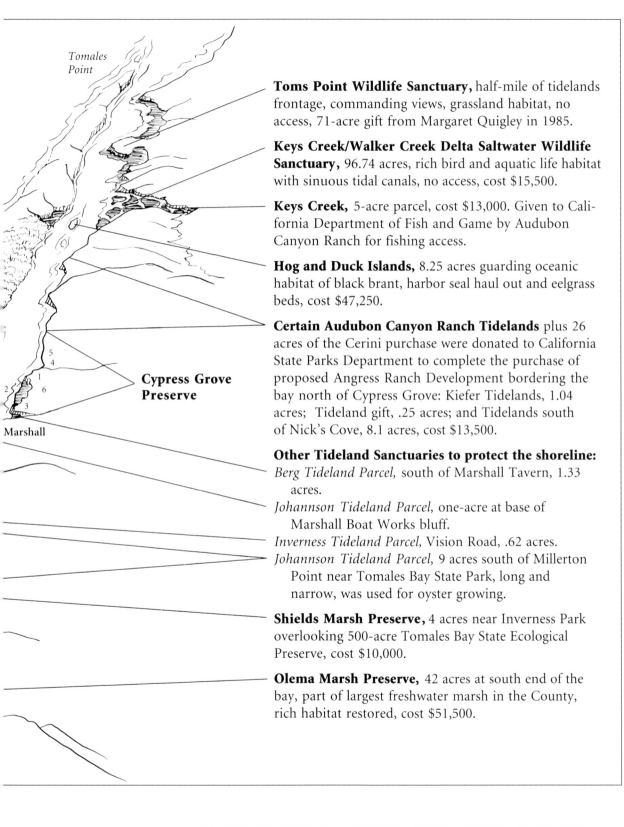

Toms Point Wildlife Sanctuary, half-mile of tidelands frontage, commanding views, grassland habitat, no access, 71-acre gift from Margaret Quigley in 1985.

Keys Creek/Walker Creek Delta Saltwater Wildlife Sanctuary, 96.74 acres, rich bird and aquatic life habitat with sinuous tidal canals, no access, cost $15,500.

Keys Creek, 5-acre parcel, cost $13,000. Given to California Department of Fish and Game by Audubon Canyon Ranch for fishing access.

Hog and Duck Islands, 8.25 acres guarding oceanic habitat of black brant, harbor seal haul out and eelgrass beds, cost $47,250.

Certain Audubon Canyon Ranch Tidelands plus 26 acres of the Cerini purchase were donated to California State Parks Department to complete the purchase of proposed Angress Ranch Development bordering the bay north of Cypress Grove: Kiefer Tidelands, 1.04 acres; Tideland gift, .25 acres; and Tidelands south of Nick's Cove, 8.1 acres, cost $13,500.

Other Tideland Sanctuaries to protect the shoreline:
Berg Tideland Parcel, south of Marshall Tavern, 1.33 acres.
Johannson Tideland Parcel, one-acre at base of Marshall Boat Works bluff.
Inverness Tideland Parcel, Vision Road, .62 acres.
Johannson Tideland Parcel, 9 acres south of Millerton Point near Tomales Bay State Park, long and narrow, was used for oyster growing.

Shields Marsh Preserve, 4 acres near Inverness Park overlooking 500-acre Tomales Bay State Ecological Preserve, cost $10,000.

Olema Marsh Preserve, 42 acres at south end of the bay, part of largest freshwater marsh in the County, rich habitat restored, cost $51,500.

directly to President Nixon and showed the list to California Senator George Murphy who was running for re-election. Murphy is said to have told his good friend President Nixon, "Dick, get me this park; it will help me get re-elected." So, in 1970 Nixon freed $38 million that was there all along in the Land and Water Conservation Fund, and the remainder of Point Reyes National Seashore was purchased by 1972. Ironically, Murphy lost the election to John Tunney.

George Collins of Ross, formerly a director of the National Park Service, conceived the Point Reyes National Seashore Project. After his retirement he helped the state acquire lands on the east shore of Tomales Bay to prevent subdivisions.

When Nixon was running for a second term in 1972, he was successfully lobbied by Dr. Edgar Wayburn, Amy Meyer, Huey Johnson, and now State Senator Peter Behr to create the Golden Gate National Recreation Area as part of his campaign strategy. Nixon won, released more money, and the new parklands, including federal army lands, were rapidly acquired on both sides of the Golden Gate extending in Marin from the Marin Headlands to Tomales Bay. These now total about 74,000 acres along 28 miles of coastline in Marin, San Francisco, and San Mateo counties.

All the SOS publicity helped Peter Behr win his election to the California Senate in 1970 and re-election in 1974, where he became such a legend that when one observer first saw him riding to work in Sacramento on his bicycle, she cried, "My God, it's the Senator who saved the Point Reyes National Seashore."

In West Marin today, there are about 150,000 acres of national, state, county, and city parks, Marin Municipal watershed lands, Audubon Canyon Ranch properties, and protected tidelands reaching from the Golden Gate to the Sonoma County border. These make up the greatest wilderness park in the nation adjacent to a large metropolitan area.

In the heart of this wilderness preserve, I am proud to say that Audubon Canyon Ranch operates two magnificent wildlife sanctuaries, the Bolinas Lagoon Preserve and the Cypress Grove Preserve on Tomales Bay, as well as two smaller groves in Muir Beach and Bolinas, which each winter harbor thousands of migratory monarch butterflies. The Muir Beach Preserve is named in honor of Elizabeth Terwilliger.

With the sales of some of their valuable lands to Audubon Canyon Ranch safely in escrow, our former adversaries in Land Investors Research slowly began to fade away. To my astonishment, I never lost the friendship of my minister, my dentist, or several physicians, all of whom were investors. I

think that they knew I was sincere, didn't attack them personally, and most of Marin County was on our side; and perhaps they came to realize that what they had wanted to do was not right. By the end of 1973 this saga of Tomales Bay was nearly over.

The Yellow Ribbons Disappear

For years, meaningless rows of yellow surveyor ribbons fluttered forlornly as the Land Investors parcels reverted to their original owners or were bought for state parks, the National Seashore, or by Audubon Canyon Ranch. In 1976 the new California Coastal Commission gave added protection to fifty-six miles of Marin's coastline by setting protection and access requirements. By then the county supervisors we had helped elect voted to protect the farmlands along the eastern shore of Tomales Bay with agricultural zoning, establishing a strict, development-deterring sixty-acre minimum lot size.

Currently the Marin Agricultural Land Trust, created in 1980, is buying conservation easements (development rights) to preserve agriculture permanently in West Marin. To date MALT has acquired some twenty-four

The filling of these rich Tomales Bay tidelands —and most other tidelands in California— was stopped permanently by the 1972 Marks vs. Whitney public trust lawsuit won by Peter Whitney of Inverness. This was a major turning point in saving coastal California's bays; it also should have protected the state's rivers.

Marks vs. Whitney Tidelands Decision—A Pinnacle

A far-reaching California Supreme Court decision affecting every California citizen took place during the battle for Tomales Bay: *Marks vs. Whitney* affords the permanent protection of state tidelands, marshlands, and submerged lands. This important legal precedent was accomplished by Peter Whitney of Inverness in a lawsuit against developer Larry Marks to prevent the filling of Tomales Bay tidelands. (Peter Whitney's grandfather was the state's first geologist and Mt. Whitney, the highest pinnacle in the Sierra, was named in his honor. Whitney's team was among the first to survey Tomales Bay.)

Marin Superior Court Judge Sam Gardiner, my relative, ruled against Peter Whitney, but his decision was overruled by a California Supreme Court decision filed in Marin County on December 9, 1971. The decision declared that tidelands sold by the state after 1868 are protected for public use and wildlife under the Doctrine of Public Trust.

Where this wading egret feeds on Tomales Bay scientists have discovered some seventy species of benthic invertebrates ranging up to 120,000 individuals per square meter of bottom.

A key section written by the most conservative justice on the court was a blow to Judge Gardiner. It read:

One of the most important public uses of tidelands—a use encompassed within the tideland trust—is the preservation of those lands in their natural state, so that they may serve as ecological units for scientific study, as open space, and as environments which provide food and habitats for birds and marine life, and which favorably affect the scenery and the climate of the area.

This case and the Mono Lake case, *National Audubon Society vs. Los Angeles Water and Power* decided on February 17, 1983, were two of the defining Public Trust lawsuits of this century. In 1994 the Mono Lake Committee presented its Defender of the Public Trust Award to Audubon Canyon Ranch attorney George Peyton who had rallied the National Audubon Society behind the Mono Lake lawsuit.

thousand acres, comprising more than thirty-five ranches, extending from Tomales Bay east to the Sonoma County border. This is about twenty-five percent of the prime agricultural lands in the county. One of the first to join the Land Trust was the Straus Ranch, now the region's premier organic dairy.

In 1995 Congresswoman Lynn Woolsey and Marin County Supervisor Gary Giacomini proposed the federal acquisition of conservation easements on forty thousand additional acres of ranch lands along the east shore of Tomales Bay, expanding the National Seashore from Point Reyes Station to near Bodega Head in Sonoma County. This park would both preserve agriculture and become Sonoma's first national park. The Marin Agricultural Land Trust would handle the new easement acquisitions. As I write, Congress is still considering the measure.

Persistence Pays

Under Stan Picher's leadership, the Ranch had raised some $1.5 million by 1973 from thousands of donors through a dozen large fund drives. It used these funds to preserve for wildlife some thirty properties totaling more than sixteen hundred acres on both bays. The lessons we learned were that persistence, organization, and a large informed constituency pay off. The ripple effect from our first purchase of Canyon Ranch twelve years before had vast and unanticipated consequences in saving the West Marin paradise.

George Peyton of Oakland was Audubon Canyon Ranch's legal advisor and board member for over thirty years. He was instrumental in completing the purchase of Audubon Canyon Ranch, arranging the gift of Cypress Grove, and negotiating the gift of the Bouverie Audubon Preserve in Sonoma County. He also brought the National Audubon Society into the Mono Lake battle, ensuring victory.

Today, Tomales Bay looks precisely the same as it did when I tried to swim across it as a boy and was chased by a sea lion. The shoreline is undeveloped, the water is clean, and the sea lions still swim up to the mouth of Lagunitas Creek to fish for coho salmon each fall.

So far, our part in the revolt against the greedy real estate engine was a success. Our purchases had helped secure both approaches to the Point Reyes National Seashore, and had initiated the scientific management of the Bolinas Lagoon and the Tomales Bay watersheds with the Tomales Bay Environmental Study (see box). Later, Audubon Canyon Ranch Preserves on Bolinas Lagoon became inholdings of the Golden Gate National Recreation Area, saving the nation millions of dollars in purchase costs.

To make Marin's slow growth permanent, it was necessary to block the Warm Springs Dam on the Russian River and the pipeline planned from the Russian River to Marin. That was my next adventure.

A Landmark Watershed Study for Tomales Bay

The *Tomales Bay Environmental Study* is a simple, inexpensive approach we used to assess Marin's largest watershed and how best to manage its resources for sustainability. This was one of the first ridgetop-to-ridgetop management studies in the country and remains a useful model for other counties.

As usual, Marin County claimed it was broke, but the planning chief still assigned county planner Ruth Corwin full-time to the project. The study was conceived by lead scientists Rowan Rountree and David Walker of The Conservation Foundation

Dr. Robert Cooper (left), Professor of Landscape Architecture Robert Twiss (right), and other UC Berkeley professors used facilities in West Marin to conduct the Tomales Bay Environmental Study. Center is David Walker of The Conservation Foundation, who was chairman of the project.

of Washington DC, which was funded by the Ford Foundation. Much of the basic work was done by landscape architects and their students in the UC School of Environmental Design. Audubon Canyon Ranch, the Marin Conservation League, and others raised fifteen thousand dollars toward expenses. Jerry Friedman of Inverness and I co-chaired the advisory committee that worked with a panel of thirteen scientists who were experts in their respective fields. Some were so enthusiastic about the project that they donated their services.

Fortunately, I was working toward a master's degree in Public Health at the time and was able to convince my professor, Robert Cooper, to write the segment on the Environmental Health of Tomales Bay. This included the crucial issue of sewage disposal.

The scientists and team members used Cliff Conly's Cypress Grove as their base on Tomales Bay. The University of the Pacific Marine Station at Dillon Beach lent us their biological studies of the bay. Much of the field work was done by volunteers. To keep the scientists and their families happy, we had delightful barbecues at the

Jerry Friedman of Point Reyes Station was co-chair with me of the 1973 Tomales Bay Environmental Study. Jerry founded the Environmental Action Committee of West Marin and served for eighteen years on the Marin County Planning Commission, appointed by Supervisor Gary Giacomini to keep the new Countywide Plan on track.

Ranch and at Cypress Grove.

The final two hundred page book with maps and photos was released in 1972 and strengthened the Marin Countywide Plan, adopted in 1973. For the first time most of the essential features of the watershed and Tomales Bay were described in one place, including a legal review of the ordinances and laws affecting the watershed along with its geology, hydrology, human history, land use, soils, climates, aesthetics, wildlife, plants, fisheries, aquatic biology, agriculture, and public health.

It was truly a remarkable study for its time. Unfortunately, the Foundation never completed a second volume detailing management goals, but the County enacted direct positive management in the form of agricultural zoning, waterway ordinances, and the Countywide Plan with environmental corridors and resource conservation zones.

CHAPTER ELEVEN

A Water Moratorium Stops Sprawl

. . . when you add a couple of freeway lanes, cars come out of nowhere to fill them. It was the same with water; the more you develop, the more growth occurred, and the faster demand grew. California was now hitched to a runaway locomotive.

—Mark Reisner, *Cadillac Desert*

During 1973, five humbled men—myself among them—learned that being an elected member of a public water district is not for the faint-hearted. We found ourselves in an inferno at the height of the water wars between Marin and Sonoma counties, accused by angry developers of "controlling growth with water."

Actually, this accusation was at least partly true. In the absence of any effective land-use planning controls in Marin, there were three ways to cap unchecked, developer-driven sprawl: prohibit freeway construction into West Marin, limit sewerage hookups that would pollute the bays or ocean, and deny new water permits during a water shortage. Marin voters chose all three methods, but water was the most controversial.

Shortly before Christmas 1972, attorney Tom Thorner phoned me to suggest that I run for a vacant slot on the board of the Marin Municipal Water District. Thorner, along with Barbara Boxer (later a supervisor, then a Senator) had been a leader in "The Plot to Save Marin." This was a slogan of the campaign against the 1971 ballot measure to pipe Russian River water to Marin, opening the way for explosive growth. The ballot measure was defeated by an astounding nine-to-one margin. The voters had said "No" to further growth by refusing to rely on Russian River water.

But even without Russian River water the developers demanded even more building and water permits. Both Tom Thorner and Ted Wellman, water supply expert for the Marin Conservation League, filled me in on the

Lagunitas Lake, in the shadow of Mt. Tamalpais, is part of the public's watershed that provides drinking water for most of Marin. In 1967 Marin Municipal Water District supported a new dam on the Russian River and an aqueduct to import massive amounts of water—enough for sprawling growth. Marin was about to be hitched to a "runaway locomotive."

issues: the failure of the county and its cities to control growth and the failure to conserve and recycle water. In addition, they said that Marin would continue to be targeted by out-of-county developers and the state water lobby. They said these outsiders needed to spur the rapid growth of Marin and Sonoma counties to force the completion of Warm Springs Dam in Sonoma County.

Warm Springs Dam was to be built on Dry Creek, a tributary of the Russian River near Healdsburg, by the US Army Corps of Engineers for the Sonoma County Water Agency. The Corps had been planning this so-called "flood control project" since 1940. None of the water was to be used for agriculture; all was slated for municipal use, if it was built. The combination of the subsidized dam, cheap water, and a pipeline through Sonoma County into Marin was a developer's dream come true. It could accommodate urbanization of the counties from border to border.

My family encouraged me to run for the water board seat, even though I would have to work full time to overcome the powerful bi-county, pro-dam, pro-growth lobby that backed the Army Corps of Engineers. Pam Lloyd, a bright young Mill Valley resident fresh from the Environmental Forum class we had just started at Audubon Canyon Ranch, agreed to be my campaign manager and John Anton, a financial genius and neighbor, would be my finance chairman. Before the election campaign was over, our opposition had spent some $100,000; our costs had been about $25,000. Jerry Hauke, an engineer from Mill Valley, was my main opponent, and we both ran to win. At stake was Marin's future.

The Marin Municipal Water District is the pioneer municipal water district in California. It is highly democratic and the public can vote on its water projects. Its regularly scheduled meetings are open to the public and covered by the press. State-chartered in 1912, it consists of a general manager and five elected directors from its five divisions, which are all located in the southern half of Marin. It includes ten of the eleven cities in Marin. Novato to the north is served by the North Marin Water District, whose water comes from the Russian River. My district included Kent Woodlands, Corte Madera, Alta Valley, and Mill Valley.

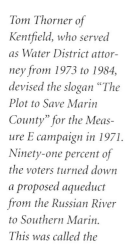

Tom Thorner of Kentfield, who served as Water District attorney from 1973 to 1984, devised the slogan "The Plot to Save Marin County" for the Measure E campaign in 1971. Ninety-one percent of the voters turned down a proposed aqueduct from the Russian River to Southern Marin. This was called the single most important vote in stemming runaway growth in Marin County.

A Wilderness Watershed Preserved

I was no stranger to the 21,500-acre water district lands. They included the timbered watershed of Lagunitas Creek and reached to the top of Bolinas

Ridge, almost to Audubon Canyon Ranch. In fact, our home was on the edge of water district lands.

Owing to the tremendous rainfall on the north slope of Mount Tamalpais, the Marin Municipal Water District had always been self-sufficient in water captured in its reservoir lakes along Lagunitas Creek. The largest recorded rainfall was ten feet at Alpine Lake during the winter of 1889-1890. However, there were dry years back-to-back when the rainfall over the twenty-eight-square-mile watershed was a scant nineteen inches. Because the watershed of the Russian River was fifty times larger—1,450 square miles with a runoff of more than one million acre-feet a year—the district manager, Bill Seeger, looked there for future supplies.

The public-spirited district operated eight major recreational areas and maintained hundreds of miles of trails. They protected the land against invasions of non-native plant species, fire, feral pigs, four-wheelers, and eventually, mountain bikes. Its remote woods supported an astounding diversity of native plants, birds and other wildlife, a paradise for cougar, bobcat, and osprey.

During the strenuous six months of my campaign for office, I ran four-miles cross-country each afternoon from Kentfield to Fairfax, through chaparral and Douglas fir forests alive with iris, all on water district lands. I ended at Pete Arrigoni's bar for a beer and waited for a ride home. I loved these wild lands so close to cities. They made me mourn for the beautiful canyon the Oakland Boy Scouts had sold for development so long before.

DON'T LOS ANGELIZE MARIN

★ ★ ★

VOTE NO ON MEASURE 'E'

E = L.A.²

A vote against the Sonoma-Marin Aqueduct (Measure E) in 1971 was also a vote to discourage high dams on the Russian and Eel rivers which would divert large amounts of water to Sonoma and Marin counties and to Southern California.

Marin County is lucky. Only one percent of all the public water districts in the US are said to own their own watersheds and can readily protect their source of drinking water.

"Good Old Boys" at Work

What convinced me to seek the Marin Municipal Water District seat were the land uses the "good old boys" who then ran the district allowed. For a small fee, the district leased 167 acres of its lush meadows and woods to the privately owned Meadow Club for a golf course. They leased six thousand acres to a hunting club. But the rumor that chilled me to the bone was that if fifty thousand acre-feet of water, enough for about 300,000 people, reached southern Marin by pipeline from the Russian River, the thousands

Water Board Race Poses Key Question

Should Supply Be Limited To Control Development?

L. MARTIN GRIFFIN
Kentfield internist

JEROME C. HAUKE
Planning engineer

ROSS S. SHADE
Public accountant

Residents of the Marin Municipal Water District's Division Four will have the chance to decide if they want the district to restrict population growth by limiting water supply when they go to the polls Tuesday to choose a representative to the MMWD board.

There are 17,019 registered voters in Division Four.

Three candidates, with diverse views on that controversial question, are seeking to replace Director Eugene A. Miller — who resigned last November — as representative for the division which includes Mill Valley, and parts of Tamalpais Valley,

Corte Madera and Kentfield.

Dr. L. Martin Griffin, physician and conservationist, believes that limiting supply may be the only way to curb population, since he thinks the proposed county-wide plan may not be effective in stopping overdevelopment.

Two other contenders for the board post, Jerome C. Hauke, a civil engineer and former Mill Valley city councilman, and Ross S. Shade, a certified public accountant, contend that planning and responsibility for limiting development should be left to the county's planning agencies.

THE QUESTION of a moratorium on new connections — particularly for large developments — has also been one of the major campaign issues.

The district board has considered a connection ban on at least three occasions — always before large audiences —, but the proposal has failed to pass.

There has been considerable controversy on that subject among district residents, with one group believing that the district is facing a water shortage and should curtail new connections and another which contends there is enough water to grant all new services until additional supply is found.

Since Miller's resignation, the four-man MMWD board has often split 2-2 on the granting of

Griffin, former chief of medicine at Marin General and Ross Hospitals and co-founder of the Ross Valley Clinic, left his medical practice in 1971 to return to U.C. where he obtained a Master's Degree in public health, specializing in environmental health sciences.

He now devotes his time to working for a better environment in many different ways, including serving as a member of the environmental quality committee of the city-county planning council and lobbying for passage of Sen. Peter Behr's Wild Rivers Bill while a delegate to the Eel River Water Council.

Griffin is currently chairman of the Tomales Bay land acquisition for the Audubon

only to small projects — like single-family homes — until a new supply is developed.

The district should use the legal means it now has at its disposal to help implement the goals of the county-wide plan, particularly the growth control objectives, according to Griffin.

One of the tools he mentioned is a new amendment to the government code which makes it positive for the MMWD to take a planning role for all water-related resources, such as marshes, estuaries and watersheds. The new regulation could permit the district to have an official voice in dealing with development proposed for these areas, he said.

Griffin said there are currently efforts to undermine the

I won this superheated election on the premise that the Water District could prohibit new water hookups if there was insufficient water. In 1973 our board voted to ban new hookups in Marin, a moratorium that lasted for three years and enabled the county to implement strong city-county planning controls, slowing county growth.

of acres of the Marin Municipal Water District watershed would no longer be needed and might be declared surplus and sold for development.

I learned that the district had been secretively selling off portions of its lands. There were even rumors that a water district director had bought ten choice acres overlooking Fairfax. This was despite a far-sighted county ordinance sponsored by Supervisor Peter Behr in 1964 that classified water district lands as public open space. The measure was violently opposed by Sam Gardiner, then water district attorney, whom Behr called "a fly in the ointment" in his oral history.

During my campaign, I came to know hundreds of my well-educated constituents. They were almost unanimously opposed to the rapid growth that since World War II had been filling the marshes and eroding the steep slopes with poorly planned subdivisions. They were outraged by the difficulty and high costs of providing public services such as schools, fire and police protection, and transportation for leap-frog subdivisions. They insisted that we rely on our water supplies from Mt. Tamalpais and not *steal* water from distant watersheds such as the Russian or Eel rivers. This became one plank in my campaign.

But a more fundamental issue haunted me. The promise of inexpensive water from the Russian or Eel rivers would serve the developers to drive up the population of Marin. Between 1950 and 1970, the population of Marin County had grown from about 85,000 to 209,000, and the Army Corps of Engineers projected a population of 650,000 by 2010. A large part of that devastating growth was still planned for the east shore of Tomales Bay, and the shallow tideland areas on the east side of the county. By 1997 the population of Marin stabilized at 245,000 with no significant change projected by 2010.

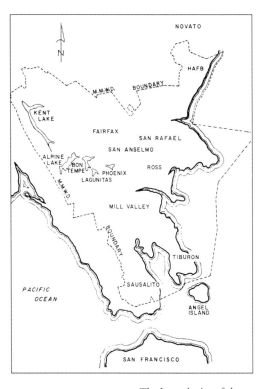

Turning Off the Spigot

When I made my bid in 1973, manager Bill Seeger, who had been president of the Eel River Water Council, was still actively pushing the Russian River Warm Springs Dam Project. He wanted to continue exploiting a Pacific Gas and Electric tunnel diverting 160,000 acre-feet a year from the Eel River into the Russian River, enough water for nearly a million people. To me, this was stealing Mendocino and Humboldt counties' water and using it to pump up the real estate prices of Marin and Sonoma Counties. It also meant sacrificing the salmon and steelhead that had for centuries spawned in the Eel river.

Seeger saw his duty as supplying water to meet the population estimates of the Army Corps. The best sources of water for the future, he felt, were dams to be built on the Eel River in Mendocino County to augment large dams on the Russian River. Neither Marin nor Sonoma residents had a vote on the dams, although part of the water from those dams was earmarked for Marin and Sonoma counties, and the rest for southern California. If this plan were to succeed, Los Angeles would grow even larger, and our two counties would grow ever more like it.

As I saw it, this type of advance, large-scale water planning by pro-growth advocates was ruining our rivers, killing our wildlife and salmon, creating urban sprawl, and destroying large parts of California as decent places to live, all with very little public input. These destructive dams and water transfers were the reason the state's population had been able to soar from four million to thirty-two million people in my lifetime.

My relative, Sam Gardiner, lawyer-developer and later Superior Court

The boundaries of the Marin Municipal Water District (dotted lines) included miles of shallow tidelands in San Francisco Bay which previous boards had approved of filling for development. After my election as a Water District director in 1973, we curtailed this practice.

judge, had been attorney for the water district for years. He was followed by his partner, attorney Bob Elliott, who supported Seeger's views. I figured it was time to step in and throw the family weight in a different direction.

A Revolution in Water Policy

Pam Lloyd helped me draft a strong campaign platform that championed slow growth relying on Marin's water supply alone. The plan emphasized water conservation and wastewater recycling, and a takeover by our water district of local sanitary districts to end the dumping of sewage, sludge, and poorly treated effluent directly into the bays. We promised to prohibit water pipelines that would be used for the development of tidelands in Marin. New hookups would be prohibited if water was insufficient for existing customers. I also promised to charge the Meadow Club, of which Seeger was an honorary member, full rent and to enforce Peter Behr's ordinance to preserve water district lands.

The platform appealed to the conservationists of Marin but outraged most realtors, some of whom were my patients and friends. The county supervisors were concerned that if I won, my swing vote on the water board would cause a construction slump by prohibiting new water hookups. Even so, Supervisor Pete Arrigoni had appointed me in 1972, before the election, to represent Marin on the Eel River Water Council, replacing Bill Seeger. Much to Bill's disgust, the supervisors eventually followed my recommendations in support of Senator Peter Behr, our champion in the state senate, to oppose the Warm Springs Dam, support the state listing of our north coast waterways as Wild and Scenic Rivers, and *dissolve* the Eel River Water Council. This was one major revolution against state water policy.

My campaign didn't have to struggle to catch the public's interest. We didn't have to spend anything on advertising since there was demand from environmental and homeowners groups for me as a speaker and local newspapers featured numerous stories. Wherever I spoke, I was taped by the opposition, obviously hoping or trying to trip me up or catch me saying something I'd regret later. The Sierra Club, Audubon Society, Marin Conservation League, and many other organizations backed me and offered advice.

The week before the election, Jerry Hauke's team organized a costly phone campaign to contact every voter in the district. Pam's team counteracted this effort by arguing endlessly with the callers, tying up their phone lines. I won the election in a landslide in April 1973, and I stepped right into a hornet's nest.

My campaign for the Water District board was on a growth-control platform. Marin voters had overwhelmingly approved the limiting of development to the available water supply in 1971. The California State Water Code now encourages this kind of planning.

The Moratorium

My election broke a two-two tie on the water board. Jordan Martinelli and Jack McPhail were long-established businessmen who still favored a pipeline from the Russian River, even though it had been overwhelmingly defeated by the voters. Jack Felson, a youth camp operator, and Ron Stafford, a Sausalito physician, opposed Russian River water and favored a moratorium on new hookups while new sources of water were found within the county. At my first meeting, we asked Bill Seeger and his staff to give us an accurate rundown on our water supply and the demands on it. The press was there, and we wanted them to hear directly from the manager how desperate was the water shortage we faced.

Bill's graphs showed an overdraft of about four thousand acre-feet per year over safe yield. Alarmingly, even though there was no surplus water available, some two thousand applicants had been promised water hookups, pending the results of the election.

My position as swing vote was not a good one from the standpoint of my health, security, and equanimity. However, at that first meeting, in a room packed with burly construction workers, our board voted unanimously for a moratorium on new water hookups until a new water supply could be obtained. Board members Martinelli and McPhail had been convinced of the water shortage and joined the aye votes. I felt vindicated.

Immediately, we asked Bill Seeger to develop a model water conservation program and to obtain 4,300 acre-feet of surplus Russian River water that the district had bought some years before. This was to be supplied through a pipeline extending from Novato in the North Marin Water District to San Rafael.

It was obvious that the new board makeup did not have the support of water district attorney Bob Elliott. In anticipation of litigation from his former law partner, Sam Gardiner, Jack Felson and I visited Elliot and asked him to resign. He did this graciously, and the board interviewed several attorneys, appointing Tom Thorner who proved to be a superb choice—cool under fire, well-organized, bright, and fair-minded. He served until 1985, when he resigned.

A Dreadful Mistake

With a unanimous vote for a moratorium, our board felt secure in meeting an onslaught of lawsuits (for damages) charging the loss of the right to

develop property. But at that point we made a dreadful mistake. Bill Seeger talked us into holding a public meeting and a re-vote on the moratorium in the county supervisors' chambers. It turned into a mob scene. Construction workers who were given the day off got drunk on beer in the civic center parking lot and hung me in effigy. Even worse, after angry threats against their businesses before a packed chamber, Martinelli and McPhail changed their votes. However, the vote remained three-to-two for a moratorium. Somewhat shaken, my wife and I were escorted home late that night by the sheriff.

During the next few days lawsuits were filed against the three of us (Felson, Griffin, Stafford) as individuals and against the water district itself. Sam Gardiner sued me personally for $25 million, claiming that "old settlers were discriminating against new settlers."

Thank God for Tom Thorner. He reassured us that we had followed the mandate of our electorate and that we had every right—indeed the duty, considering the lack of water—to call a moratorium. There were letters of support from all over the state. To advise us, we hired an attorney from the Goleta Water District in Santa Barbara which had established a water mora-

Angry, sign carrying construction workers picketed this 1973 meeting of the Marin Municipal Water District board where the five elected directors voted for a moratorium on new water hook-ups. I'm on the left, next to Jack McPhail, Jordan Martinelli, Manager Bill Seeger and Jack Felson. Director Ron Stafford is not shown.

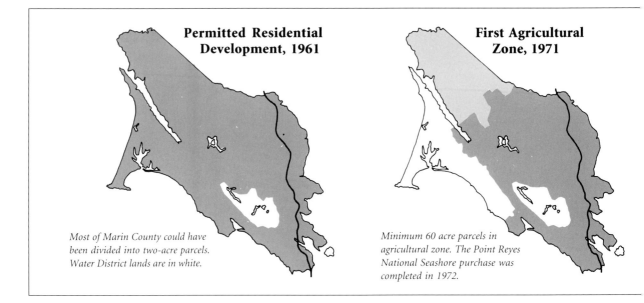

Permitted Residential Development, 1961

Most of Marin County could have been divided into two-acre parcels. Water District lands are in white.

First Agricultural Zone, 1971

Minimum 60 acre parcels in agricultural zone. The Point Reyes National Seashore purchase was completed in 1972.

torium after residents voted against tying into a state aqueduct.

Our board hired the competent firm of Ferguson and Capri to defend us from the lawsuits filed against us. Doug Ferguson's wife, Jane, was on the board of the Audubon Canyon Ranch. We never had to go to court or give depositions. We lost our first hearing in Superior Court, presided over by Warren McGuire, but won on appeal. Gradually the lawsuits were dropped. The accusation that we were "controlling growth with water" have persisted to this day, but are less volatile now since numerous communities throughout the state, having run out of resources such as water, sewage disposal, and even clean air, have enacted their own moratoriums.

In stories and editorials in the Marin *Independent Journal,* Wishard Brown and Jack Craemer attacked the water hookup moratorium. Craemer was on the board of the California State Automobile Association, which pushed freeways for West Marin and up the Sonoma coast.

The moratorium on new water hookups lasted until 1976. Warm Springs Dam, which barely survived attacks on many fronts by the growing bi-county Warm Springs Task Force, was repeatedly delayed until it was finally completed in 1983. This delay, however, gave Sonoma conservationists time to slow down their coastal development, to secure a state coastal commission in 1976, and to spur state purchase of coastal parks.

During this period of water shortage, Marin residents learned to rely on their own water resources. The Marin Municipal Water District enlarged Kent Lake, built a new reservoir on Walker Creek, put in a temporary

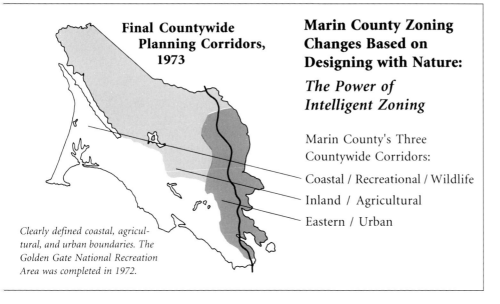

Final Countywide Planning Corridors, 1973

Marin County Zoning Changes Based on Designing with Nature:

The Power of Intelligent Zoning

Marin County's Three Countywide Corridors:

Coastal / Recreational / Wildlife

Inland / Agricultural

Eastern / Urban

Clearly defined coastal, agricultural, and urban boundaries. The Golden Gate National Recreation Area was completed in 1972.

The map on the left shows how much of the county after World War II was ripe for development; even its tidelands could be cut into two-acre parcels. 136,000 acres of agricultural lands (center map) extending east from Tomales Bay to the Sonoma County border were initially protected by 60-acre minimum zoning in 1971. The map on the right shows how the Marin County-wide Plan divided the county into three zones: 1) coastal, recreational, and wildlife; 2) rural and agricultural; and 3) the urban corridor.

pipeline from the state water project in the East Bay, and undertook extensive water conservation and wastewater recycling programs. In 1974 the board hired Dietrich Stroeh, a young engineer, as manager. He replaced Bill Seeger and successfully implemented Marin's water revolution, one of the first in the state to link population growth to the available water supply.

Growth and Sprawl Hit Sonoma

As the construction of the Highway 101 freeway proceeded north, developer-driven Sonoma County, with unlimited Russian River water supplies and no effective city or county growth controls, erupted with freeway sprawl just like Los Angeles, Walnut Creek, and San Jose. It encouraged city, industrial, and shopping-mall growth along its water transmission lines that paralleled the freeway, checker-boarding and leap-frogging thousands of acres of prime agricultural land and spawning freeway gridlock. A notable exception was the town of Petaluma, which pioneered growth controls that were challenged in court.

Today, the hard line that southern Marin voters took in 1971 to prevent its water agency from building a pipeline to the Russian River has been vindicated. While Marin has its problems, including too many cars and economic sameness, the slow growth mandated by the voters allows the people of Marin to strengthen land-use control, improve education, enhance their economy, and protect their farmland, open space, and wildlife resources. If

Marin had not helped prevent Eel River dams and delayed Warm Springs Dam for eleven years, both counties might be criss-crossed today by freeways and subdivisions, eliminating much of the Russian River wine grape valleys and the beauty of the unspoiled coast.

By 1992, with planning controls in place, southern Marin voters bonded themselves for $33 million dollars to build a pipeline and bring ten thousand acre-feet of off-peak water a year from the Russian River (with no guarantee of water quality), enough for sixty thousand new residents. However Sonoma County taxpayers, who own the Russian River Water System, were not allowed to vote on whether to sell their water. To date, the State Water Resources Control Board has not issued a permit for this water transfer, declaring that the Russian River may be fully appropriated if adequate flows for salmon, and eighty other applications, are met.

The Plot to Save Marin from the big dam builders and developers had worked. Marin's huge block of wild watershed lands protecting the source of its drinking water remained intact. In 1992 the *San Francisco Examiner* commended Marin County's growth control strategy as a model for California.

Now, with Sonoma County next door being overrun by the very forces Marin had controlled, it seemed of critical importance to protect the Russian River watershed, a major wildlife habitat and the source of drinking water for both counties.

PART FOUR

SONOMA &
THE RUSSIAN RIVER

The resource-rich Russian River watershed drains 1,450 square miles into a long estuary and the Pacific Ocean at Jenner. With over thirty steep gravel bed tributaries, it is the third largest river basin on the North Coast, and was renowned for its supreme steelhead fishery. Since 1908 water from the Eel River (top) has been diverted by tunnel into the Russian River, whose water flows are regulated by Coyote Dam. This was one of the first large interbasin "water thefts" in California. Warm Springs Dam regulates Dry Creek, and Big Sulfur Creek drains the immense Geyser Geothermal Power fields along the Mayacamas rift. The wild canyons of Digger Bend spill onto the vineyard-covered, nine-mile Middle Reach gravel aquifer, properly the Sonoma-Marin Aquifer, which naturally filters drinking water for both counties. On the lower right is the urbanizing 240-square-mile watershed of the Laguna de Santa Rosa, previously a biotic wonderland of meandering creeks, vernal pools, and a large lake. Note the location of the Bouverie Audubon Preserve in the Valley of the Moon, and the Griffin Riparian Preserve on the Russian River.

CHAPTER TWELVE

David Bouverie's Gift:
A Sonoma Creek Watershed

*The fields of Bouverie wildflowers are waves of meadow foam and
buttercups, clover, larkspur, lupine and poppies, deep yellow
fiddlenecks, magenta vetch blossoms, pink and white wild radish.*

—Gaye LeBaron, *The Press Democrat*, Santa Rosa, Spring 1995

In the late sixties, in search of some relief from the stress of the exhausting battles to save West Marin, I became involved in wildlife projects in Hawaii and Nepal with various international conservation groups, including The Nature Conservancy and the Sierra Club.

Actually, I was more in demand for my medical skills than as a naturalist and leader. On the Nepal treks in the early seventies, I conducted clinics each day on the trail for sick or injured natives brought from remote villages and for our porters, sherpas, sherpanis, and trekkers. On Maui, I worked as a physician deep in the rainforest for The Nature Conservancy in establishing the Kipahulu Wildlife Preserve, one of the last unspoiled rainforests on the deforested islands. Those experiences opened my eyes to the rapid destruction of natural resources worldwide. When I returned to the US, I decided to take a degree in Public Health at UC Berkeley.

This was a turning point in my medical career. I took courses that gave me a worldwide perspective. I was captivated by the Geography of Disease, Epidemiology, Designing with Nature, and Environmental Science. On entering the school, I looked and thought like an old man, but at graduation, my vigor had returned and I was prepared for a new career in Public Health. But where? The Russian River seemed to be calling to me.

When I moved north to Sonoma County in 1974, as my term on the Water Board was expiring and in the midst of a marital breakup, I was fortunate to find a job as Public Health Officer at the state hospital for brain-damaged patients in Glen Ellen, the largest of its kind in the country. My

This one-hundred-foot high Stuart Creek waterfall, sacred to Native Americans, is part of the 570-acre Bouverie Audubon Preserve, which David Bouverie began donating to Audubon Canyon Ranch in 1976 for wildlife education. Pristine Stuart Creek is a tributary of Sonoma Creek, a steelhead spawning stream that flows into San Francisco Bay.

plan was to work for a year or two to equip my new winery, but the job was so intellectually rewarding that I stayed for fourteen years.

At that time Hepatitis B, a contagious blood-borne disease, was endemic throughout the state's eleven psychiatric and developmental hospitals. At Glen Ellen, with nurses Arlene Poteracke and Gloria Colgrave, we developed a system for testing and, eventually, immunization that controlled the spread of this costly and debilitating disease. In 1981, I was appointed chair of the Hepatitis B Task Force, and later the AIDS Task Force, for all state hospitals in California. Dr. Lois Lowden, an astute state psychiatrist, was assigned to help me. By 1989 when I retired, we had cut the incidence of Hepatitis B in the state hospital system to nearly zero. This experience of finding my way through the maze of regulatory agencies in Sacramento proved invaluable to me in later watershed and river battles.

The rolling, wildflower-covered hills of the Bouverie Audubon Preserve are backed by chaparral-covered Mayacamas Ridge. The property adjoins the 1,700-acre Sonoma Developmental Center, where I worked, and the 1,000-acre Preserve donated to the Sonoma Land Trust by Otto Teller.

A New Medical Career in Public Health

My job took me to many parts of California where I got an eye-opening education in the monumental health, social, and environmental problems the state faced from its rapid, unplanned growth. The entire state, I felt, was on a downward spiral from the inhumane automobile-dominated sprawl that had severely damaged the natural environment and ruined the landscape in county after county. The same fate, I feared, awaited semi-rural Sonoma County, which reminded me of Orange County, where developers controlled the county government.

On our hospital rounds in southern California, Dr. Lowden and I visited the once-pastoral Patton State Psychiatric Hospital in San Bernadino County. Here disturbed patients who couldn't stand trial for their crimes were impounded behind steel fences topped with blood-stained, coiled razor-wire that couldn't keep them within. The fences were designed to protect their frightened neighbors whose dreary, lonely housing tracts reached into the foothills of the smog-bound mountains. Near the huge Metropolitan State Hospital in Orange County, where the bulk of its psychiatric patients came from the concrete wasteland of Los Angeles, the orange groves that I had admired as a boy had been replaced by subdivisions built with no regard for preserving the area's once-robust agricultural heritage.

Near the large psychiatric and developmental Camarillo State Hospital in Ventura County for both children and adults, the truck farms of the fertile valleys were a mish-mash of leap-frogging tracts, cut off from creeks, ocean frontage, and each other. At Atascadero, where the state's most dangerous psychiatric criminals are flown in by armed helicopter, I was appalled at the disorganized development that was chopping up San Luis Obispo farmlands and extending north into the fertile Salinas River Valley of Monterey County, where huge prisons were being constructed far from population centers. Here I saw that the river where I had camped with the Boy Scouts had been cleared of its streamside forests by farmers, and the thrilling dawn chorus of songbirds was lost forever.

California not only held the nation's largest mental institutions, but also was busily building the largest and costliest prison system of any industrialized nation, sometimes in the wildest corners of the state. These new prisons attracted thousands of employees, visitors, housing tracts, and freeways to formerly undeveloped areas, putting more stress on endangered ecosystems.

The medical consequences of the rapid, mismanaged growth were also overwhelming the once-superb state medical care system; millions of citizens could no longer afford health care and were losing their access to the healing power of nature. I knew from my studies that human health and sanity depend on ecological factors like those identified in Marin's Countywide Plan, and that long auto commutes made participation in local county land-use decisions impossible.

Architect David Bouverie stands in front of the stunning Docent Center he designed. The Bouverie Audubon Preserve trains thirty docents a year who introduce wildlife and ecological concepts to Sonoma and Napa County schoolchildren in their classrooms before they visit the spectacular Preserve.

I found it tragic that, through chaotic, developer-driven pseudo-planning, the citizens were allowing their state, their watersheds, and their homes to be turned into a giant prison with a degraded natural landscape, unsustainable agriculture, spoiled rivers, polluted air and water, and diminished quality of life outside the institutional walls and razor-steel coils.

The Squire of the Valley of the Moon

Back in Sonoma, my office was located on the grounds of the seventeen-hundred-acre Sonoma Developmental Center, one of the most scenic, historic, and wildlife-rich public properties in California. Said to be selected by Governor Leland Stanford's wife, it has creeks, lakes, a freshwater marsh, redwood groves, and fossil redwoods. It includes both Indian and inmate

David Bouverie made his gift to the children of Sonoma County. Born in England, he bought his ranch in the Valley of the Moon before World War II. He permanently protected it before he died in 1994 at age 83, and he set aside a sum of money for the docents to hold a levitation party for him after his death.

burial grounds, and adjoins the twelve-hundred-acre Jack London State Park, both on the heavily wooded eastern slopes of Sonoma Mountain in the Valley of the Moon. Through the valley runs steelhead-spawning Sonoma Creek on its way to San Francisco Bay, where diked off tidal marshes are being restored. These two wilderness properties are owned by different state agencies, but the Center's rolling hills are coveted by developers and vintners, and I had to fight repeated state efforts to sell or lease parts of the Center property while I worked there.

On my rounds as guardian of the state hospital's water supply, I saw how the Sonoma Creek watershed was being devastated by erosion and siltation from vineyard terracing operations on steep adjacent ranches.

Directly across the valley floor and next to the Center's property was the equally wild and unspoiled five-hundred-seventy-acre ranch of David Pleydell-Bouverie, which extended up into the mountain range, an uplift of the underlying fault. The ranch included a hundred-foot waterfall on Stuart Creek, an unspoiled tributary of Sonoma Creek.

One day in 1978 Stan Picher called and said, "David Bouverie is thinking about giving his ranch to Audubon Canyon Ranch and is willing to endow it. Please give him a call." I made an appointment to see him, and he expressed admiration for Clifford Conly's 1971 gift of Cypress Grove that I had obtained for the Ranch on Tomales Bay. David had become thoroughly informed about the Ranch's training and education programs by his neighbors, Ranch board members Flora Maclise and Phyllis and George Ellman.

In 1979 David, then seventy years old, donated his ranch as the Bouverie Audubon Preserve. Although it lies forty miles northeast of Bolinas Lagoon, it has become an integral part of the Audubon Canyon Ranch wildlife preserves and educational programs. John Peterson, a talented artist, became its first naturalist.

A Splendid Gift, Well Endowed

David Bouverie was born in England of a noble family, trained as an architect, emigrated to the US and bought his ranch in 1938. His family history is depicted in the docent assembly room, Gilman Hall, a stunning barn that he designed and restored. David once threw fabulous parties for his café society friends who visited from the east. He had been married into the Astor family, and he maintained an apartment in New York for the winter social season as well. David also built a Spanish cottage on his ranch for his friend, noted food and wine writer M. F. K. Fisher. She died there in 1991. *House Beautiful* magazine featured his home, bell tower, and the hollow redwood tree on the trail to the waterfall, where a hidden bottle of chilled champagne and crystal flutes awaited his guests.

Over the ensuing years David Bouverie gave much of his personal wealth and persuaded his friends to help endow his wildlife preserve and education center. Board members Paul Ruby and Jack Harper began a drive to raise three million dollars.

During my years at the hospital I often walked with David through his fields of wildflowers. He was the picture of a gentleman farmer, dressed in a neatly pressed shirt and blue jeans with a gingham bandanna around his neck. He was slender and witty, with an iron will and the self-discipline to carry out his plan to protect his rolling oak woodlands and lovely creek for all time. He confided to me his fears of mortality and of dying alone. "Marty," he said, "the reason I gave my ranch to Audubon was so I'd have a family, and know that this property will be preserved forever." The Preserve's loyal and devoted docents became his family and brought him great pleasure.

He agreed that the Bouverie Preserve should become the catalyst for the scientific management and restoration of the Sonoma Creek watershed, as Audubon Canyon Ranch had been for the Bolinas Lagoon and Tomales Bay watersheds. In 1995 Angela Morgan, a Bouverie docent and Sonoma Ecology Center biologist, obtained a $10,000 grant to develop such a management program.

John Peterson, a talented artist, has been the full-time naturalist for the Bouverie Audubon Preserve since its inception. The property is an example of the stewardship ethic that Audubon Canyon Ranch seeks to inspire in other landowners.

The Bouverie Audubon Preserve has become one of Sonoma County's most successful wildlife education programs. It has a fine docent training program, and its spring wildflower display is one of the county's spectacles. There is a wealth of plant and animal species, and its creek teems with newts, other aquatic life, and the occasional spawning steelhead. The entire ranch exudes the elegant character and personality of its generous benefactor, David Bouverie. As noted in *The Press Democrat* editorial on December 5, 1994, upon his death at the age of eighty-three, "He gave back the most enduring gift on Earth, a piece of Earth itself."

CHAPTER THIRTEEN

Wild Rivers–Who Needs 'Em?

In the world made for the car, the landscape, the past, the air simply vanish. California is the edenic holocaust, the disappearing place.

> —Professor Daniel Solomon, Landscape Architect, *Rebuilding*, 1993

There were more than eighty wild, undammed rivers in California in 1920 when I was born. Today some of the last relatively wild rivers lie to the north of Marin—the Smith, Klamath, Trinity, and Eel. There is still some hope for the Russian River in Sonoma County, which borders Marin to the north. Within these rivers' 22,000 square miles of steep watersheds are the largest of the state's deer herds, one-third of the state's steelhead and salmon habitat, half the state's timber, and about forty percent of the state's water. The deep, bountiful river valleys are sacred to numerous Indian tribes.

These rivers were worth fighting for. Nothing is so beautiful as drifting silently in a canoe or rubber raft through their deep canyons or hearing the roar of distant rapids. Each stretch of the river reveals scenes of swift shining water, golden streamers of wild grape vines, and distant vistas of forest ridges looming above misty waters alive with rolling salmon and clouds of insects hatching along the gleaming gravel bars.

Talk about controlling growth with water! These great rivers had dams planned that would force sprawling growth along the entire 1,100-mile coast of California. In the 1950s the Bureau of Reclamation planned an enormous dam twelve miles from the mouth of the Klamath, the second-largest river in California, that would back up the river for more than one hundred miles, drowning Ishi Pishi Falls and backing up into the Trinity Gorge, flooding the Hoopa Indian's sacred valley. Another high dam was planned near Lewiston that would block the upper Trinity River for 127 miles.

Of these two dams only the Trinity Dam was completed, creating Lake Claire Engle in 1964. This dam severely altered the river ecology and ruined the steelhead and salmon fishery. It did little or nothing for Trinity County,

Native American women washed clothes on this natural gravel bar on the Russian River near Healdsburg around 1910. The gravelbed rivers of the North Coast nourished a cornucopia of salmon, clams, deer, elk, waterfowl, fruits, acorns, and roots that once fed countless generations.

the county of origin, and diverted ninety percent of the upper Trinity River water to southern California. President John F. Kennedy dedicated this unworthy project shortly before he was assassinated.

The Plot to Save Marin largely depended on preventing the Eel and the Russian rivers from becoming dammed and used as water tanks for Los Angeles, Marin, and Sonoma counties. To accomplish this feat, Marin County miraculously produced two men who by 1967 had the political mastery to challenge the might of the state water lobby: Norman B. "Ike" Livermore, son of Caroline, and Peter H. Behr, soon to become State Senator.

What Is a Gravelbed River?

The exquisite salmon rivers of the north coast are called gravelbed rivers by ecologists. They are endless conveyor belts, bringing rocks of varying size and vibrant color from the mountain headwaters to the ocean estuaries, smoothing and polishing them, depositing them on the riverbed or on gravel bars on the inside of the river bends along the way.

During high water the river sorts the gravel by size and rearranges gravel bars, often moving them downriver sometimes as much as three-hundred feet in winter.

The gravel settles into beds, gravel bars, and older, deeper deposits called aquifers; all are priceless parts of nature's fabric and essential to the health and habitat of steelhead and salmon. Actually, hundreds of microscopic

This cross-section of a gravelbed river shows the underground gravel aquifer containing 20%-40% water which flows slowly (sometimes only twenty feet a day) under the riverbed and its flood plain. This is where the river water is cleansed and made colder, and it is the start of the food web. To destroy the aquifer by gravel mining is to destroy the river's ecosystem and its cold water fisheries.

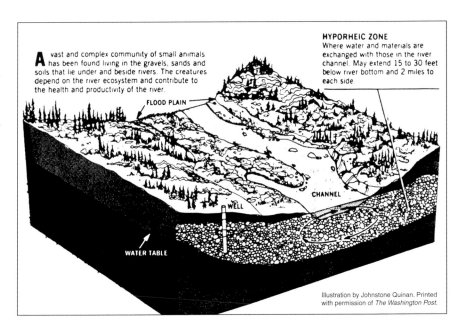

HYPORHEIC ZONE
Where water and materials are exchanged with those in the river channel. May extend 15 to 30 feet below river bottom and 2 miles to each side

A vast and complex community of small animals has been found living in the gravels, sands and soils that lie under and beside rivers. The creatures depend on the river ecosystem and contribute to the health and productivity of the river.

FLOOD PLAIN

CHANNEL

WELL

WATER TABLE

Illustration by Johnstone Quinan. Printed with permission of *The Washington Post.*

species of aquatic life live within the gravel aquifer, filtering and purifying the river water and making it safe to drink. The aquifer also adjusts the river's chemical content and cools the water. Gravel bars form the edges of deep, cold pools. The teeming insects and algae nurtured among the gravel and sand are the start of the food web for fish, birds, and other wildlife along the river. This complex ecosystem is a new frontier for river biologists.

Gravel beds are an essential, life-filled part of the river ecosystem that also includes its flood plain, the area where the river migrates back and forth as part of a dynamic system. To alter or destroy this natural system with dams that halt both water and gravel flow, and with channelized levees that cut off the life-filled meanders, devastates the diversity of life within the ecosystem.

To save our gravelbed rivers from becoming straight, open ditches, river expert Aldaron Laird warned, "The flood plains of the main stem and the tributaries should be preserved from encroachment within *river protection zones,* allowing the river simply to *be a river.*"

During the summer of 1957, Dr. Val Jaros and I set out on the wild Klamath River in our war surplus rubber raft to explore, camp, and fish for steelhead. The huge Ah Pah Dam was planned for twelve miles from the river's mouth and would have destroyed the second largest gravelbed river in California.

There are numerous tree-lined coastal rivers, large and small, between Marin County and the Oregon border which belong to the Pacific Ocean. These are crucial migratory pathways for anadromous fish—steelhead and salmon—and other wildlife. The waterways have great diversity of plant and animal species. These sparkling gravelbed rivers, tumbling through deep timbered canyons and across broad floodplains, are complex ecosystems related to the whole, the essence of life on our water planet.

The Water Thefts Begin

The story began in 1905 when Los Angeles was deep in a water crisis. Its population of 250,000 people couldn't grow unless its Los Angeles Department of Water and Power found a new source of water. This led to the biggest water theft of that time, and caused the drying up of the beautiful high Sierra Owens Valley and the national treasure, Mono Lake. By 1913 more than one-half million acre-feet of water, enough for three million people, was being exported every year to Los Angeles via the 250-mile Los Angeles Aqueduct. The Owens Valley water made the deserts around Los Angeles bloom with housing tracts, raising land values tremendously.

By 1955 the Metropolitan Water District of Southern California, by now the largest wholesaler of water to booming south coast cities, set its sights on the Klamath, Trinity, and Eel Rivers. The District hired Bechtel Engineering of San Francisco to analyze Round Valley on the Middle Fork of the Eel River for a dam to be called the Dos Rios that could feed southern California's enormous growth.

Bechtel recommended a seven-hundred-foot-high dam be built which would flood Round Valley and create a 150-square-mile reservoir. Critics said it would drown eighteen percent of Mendocino County's best farmland, with no significant flood protection benefits downriver. About 900,000 acre-feet of that water would be diverted each year via a twenty-six-mile tunnel through the Coast Range into the Sacramento River, then through the Delta and by aqueduct to Los Angeles. This was enough water for five million or more people. Excess water would be available for the growth of adjoining north coast counties—Marin, Sonoma, Lake, Mendocino, and Humboldt.

During World War II the 3,500-square-mile Eel watershed became one of the most abused in the nation. Vast forests were clear-cut using thousands of haul roads dreadfully bulldozed into the steep, friable ridges of not only the Eel but also the Klamath and Trinity. On frequent canoe trips down the Eel with family and friends over a twenty-year period, I saw bulldozers dragging logs down tributaries, stripping them of rocks and shade in the process. The steelhead and salmon spawning grounds were destroyed as the water warmed from lack of protective shade. To this day, these wild rivers still disgorge great plumes of mud each winter far out into the blue Pacific.

What our north coast rivers needed, I concluded, was not dams for flood control but careful management, tributary restoration, and reforestation. These three measures were considered heresy by the Eel River Water Council, whose offices were located in Santa Rosa in Sonoma County, and who kept their funds with the Sonoma County Treasurer, and whose president was a Sonoma County supervisor. Overseeing this formidable force was engineer Gordon Miller, who headed the Sonoma County Water Agency and was trained by the Los Angeles water lobby.

Saving the Eel River

I got in on the tail end of the fight to save the Eel River as a "Wild and Scenic River" from damming in 1972 when Supervisor Pete Arrigoni appointed me to represent Marin on the eight-county Eel River Water Council. It was a front set up by the state water lobby in 1965 to help them build three huge dams on the Eel River—Dos Rios, English Ridge, and Yellow

Jacket—as part of the California State Water Project. These monstrous dams would turn this superlative gravelbed river into a series of warmwater lakes, destroying its runs of steelhead and salmon which were one of the greatest in the state.

The weapons that the council members used were directed at the public's fear of flood and drought. They espoused dams as the greatest good for the most people—salmon and Indian tribes be damned—and full speed ahead while they had the governor's support.

For more than a year I had an insider's seat and a vote on the river battle that was to shape the future of California.

The water lobby, as I knew it, was led by the octopus-like Metropolitan Water District of Southern California. Its members included the State Department of Water Resources, the US Bureau of Reclamation, the Army Corps of Engineers, PG&E, and the Sonoma County Water Agency. There were also international engineering firms such as Bechtel and Kaiser, large construction firms, banks, and agribusinesses that controlled millions of desert acres. Their political clout was personified by their man, the "Silver Fox," a water titan and state senator named Randolph Collier of Yreka. He was also known as the "Dean of the State Freeway System."

This was one of the nation's most powerful water lobbies, yet they acted like the Los Angeles Chamber of Commerce. They had no concept of the

This wild area of the Eel River in Humboldt County would have been buried under 700 feet of water by the Yellow Jacket Dam. The 300-mile-long Eel carries 6.3 million acre-feet of water a year, exceeded by the Klamath with 12 million acre-feet. The Russian carries 1.5 million acre-feet. (An acre-foot is 327,000 gallons, enough water for five or six people a year.)

wildlife habitat they were destroying in their greed for more water. Their job was to help build the largest assortment of dams, tunnels, and pumps ever conceived by civil engineers—the State Water Project. Their goal in 1968 was to build Dos Rios Dam on the wild Middle Fork of the Eel River, just one hundred and fifty miles from Marin County and six hundred miles from Los Angeles.

Martye Kent, left, Larry Halprin, famed landscape architect, and other protestors stand in front of a huge bulldozer scoop poised to dig up Tamalpais Creek in Kentfield and channelize it for flood control. Martye, granddaughter of Congressman William Kent, lost this 1969 battle but helped transform the Army Corps' channelization policies.

Lt. Col. Frank Boerger of the San Francisco Division of the US Army Corps of Engineers was selected to build the Dos Rios Dam and also to carry out several large creek channelization projects in Marin County for flood control. Boerger proceeded to enrage people in Marin when he began to put tiny Tamalpais Creek, that had never flooded, into a thirteen-foot-deep concrete channel bordered by steel fences. Public demonstrations organized by Martye Kent and her uncle, attorney Roger Kent, failed to stop the channelization, but their highly visible opposition had made its point. Strict creek protection was written into the new Countywide Plan and Marin's 1972 Tidal Waterway Protection Ordinance. More important, however, the negative publicity produced by their grassroots revolt changed the Corp's channelizing policy nationwide and haunted Col. Boerger's Dos Rios Dam Project on the Eel.

Boerger also vexed a wealthy young cattleman, Richard Wilson, whose ranch in Round Valley near Covelo would be flooded by the dam. Wilson formed the Save the Eel River Association, became the head of the Planning and Conservation League in Sacramento, and got the ear of one of the state's most influential leaders, Norman "Ike" Livermore of Marin.

Ike was one of that rare breed, a moderate Republican, an admirer of John Muir, and a leader in the Sierra Club. He was also an executive with the Pacific Lumber Company, a large redwood lumber firm with holdings on the Eel River. (Pacific Lumber was later captured by Charles Hurwitz of Maxxam in a leveraged buyout.) Ike believed in roadless areas, wild rivers, and sustained-yield logging. His brother Putnam was chairman of the State Republican Committee.

In 1967 California Governor Ronald Reagan, who had eyes on the presidency, shrewdly appointed Ike Livermore his State Secretary of Resources (1967-1974), whose responsibilities included the State Department of Water Resources. This agency was headed by aggressive, square-faced William

Tamalpais Creek (above) was wild and unspoiled before it was channelized. The Army Corps of Engineers also gave its "Environmental Treatment" to Corte Madera Creek (left) on the College of Marin campus, complete with ineffectual depressions in the concrete for steelhead and salmon to rest. Marin County residents were outraged and helped to defeat the Corps' Dos Rios Dam on the Eel River in 1969.

Gianelli whose job was to implement the State Water Project, which called for numerous dams on the Sacramento, San Joaquin, Klamath, Trinity, and Eel Rivers.

Livermore recalled that Giannelli was the only agency chief in California who was chauffeured about in a Cadillac limousine. This calls to mind the definitive book on the western water wars, *Cadillac Desert* by Marc Reisner of Mill Valley.

The Water Clash of the Century

The clash between these two men—Gianelli, the belligerent, cocksure water exporter, and Livermore, the kindly, careful, and resolute resource manager—led to a great cliff hanger: would the Dos Rios Dam be built? The battle exposed the opposing water philosophies that were tearing the state apart politically, ruining its rivers, making its cities unlivable, creating incredible profits for land speculators, and causing the collapse of the salmon fishery—a holocaust in Eden.

This mind-boggling story is told in Ted Simon's book, *The River Stops Here*, and in *The California Water Atlas*, produced in 1978 under Governor Jerry Brown and his Resources Secretary Huey Johnson.

In 1969 Livermore put his job on the line by informing Governor Reagan that he would resign if the Dos Rios Dam was built. Fortunately, he succeeded in persuading Reagan to look for alternatives to meet the state's water contracts. Reagan had a perfect out: he said that he refused to break old treaties with the Indian tribes of Round Valley, thereby killing the Dos Rios Dam and securing both the racial minority and the environmentalist vote. And he kept Ike on his team.

Gianelli was furious. The Los Angeles Chamber of Commerce de-

"Dag's Bag" appeared in the liberal Pacific Sun, *which began during the hippie and Vietnam War eras. Many conservationists invested in this alternative newspaper to give us a voice in the rapidly growing county.*

nounced Livermore. However in a speech before them a few days after Reagan announced his decision, Livermore told his hostile audience that the days of the big dams were over, that environmental concerns ranked equally with damming rivers to promote development, and that the south had too many people.

Ike would have made his mother proud.

Senator Behr's Wild and Scenic Rivers

Another Marin County man, Senator Peter Behr of Inverness, besides saving the Point Reyes National Seashore, is credited as "the father of wild rivers." Behr, a boyish Yale Law School graduate, commanded naval ships in the Pacific during World War II. He served as Marin County Supervisor from 1962 to 1968 when the board was mainly pro-growth, often gaining a consensus by the force of his intellect, quick mind, and sense of humor. In 1970 he was elected to the State Senate, where he astounded Sacramento by introducing his brainchild, the Wild and Scenic Rivers Bill (SB107), on his third day in office. None of these rivers were in his district—all were in the district of Yreka's Silver Fox who, according to Behr, turned red, white, and purple with rage when he read the bill.

While State Secretary of Resources, Norman B. "Ike" Livermore of Marin persuaded Governor Reagan to kill the 700-foot-high Dos Rios Dam proposed for the wild Eel River. The diverted water would have stimulated growth on both the north and south coasts.

Behr's bill was beaten the first year, but with superb lobbying from the California Committee of Two Million (fishing-license holders), headed by public relations genius Joseph Paul, it passed in 1972. The bill protected the Smith, Klamath, and Trinity rivers, and put a twelve-year moratorium on dams on the Eel, until 1984. In 1981 the Eel, Smith, Klamath, and Trinity were given federal Wild Rivers protection through the work of state Resources Secretary Huey Johnson.

Gianelli and Collier went all out to kill Behr's bill, Gianelli denouncing environmentalists at an Eel River Water Council meeting I attended in 1972 in an infamous last speech called "Wild Rivers, Who Needs 'Em?" Later, Gianelli predicted the Dos Rios Dam would be back in the year 2000, a chilling reminder to the North Coast counties to be on guard. After that, the council dissolved, and I lost my insider's seat on the water lobby.

Another Marin County citizen, Kentfield businessman Alf Heller, also helped save the wild rivers with his exquisite monthly magazine, *Cry California*. Heller's publication brought together the state's brightest minds to work for a Master Plan to Save California. If only this plan, which called for

California Committee of Two Million

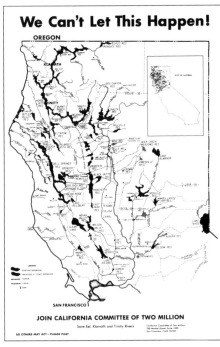

Joe Paul of the California Committee of Two Million printed this startling map showing the large number of dams, reservoirs, and tunnels proposed by the State Water Project in the 1960s for nearly every river on the North Coast.

The California Committee of Two Million was the inspiration of Joseph Paul, a fly fisherman born in Eureka, and California Trout, a fish protection group. As a public relations expert, Joe mobilized two million owners of fishing and hunting licenses to join in the crusade to establish Wild and Scenic River status for the Eel, Trinity, Klamath, and Smith rivers. Damming these wild rivers would have ruined the state's greatest salmonid fishery and urbanized the North Coast counties. He went right for the jugular, exposing the California Water Resources Association, a Los Angeles water lobby, and naming names of those who would profit from the dams and their exported water. He also exposed the Army Corps of Engineers as a false prophet advocating dams for flood control.

Joe never gave up, and after Senate Bill 107 (SB107) was defeated the first time in 1971, he helped Senator Peter Behr reintroduce it in 1972 and obtained support statewide for its passage.

His educational press releases were classics of brevity and vital information, as was his newsletter, *The Wild River*. His graphics and maps were impeccable.

If only we'd had Joe on the Warm Springs Dam battle, which followed the Wild Rivers battle, we might have won. But he died suddenly of a heart attack at age fifty-seven, just before SB107 passed. His organization never recovered without his relentless drive, but his greatest achievement, the Wild and Scenic Rivers legislation, lives on.

Governor Ronald Reagan signs the 1972 Wild and Scenic Rivers Act. From the left are Bill Quinn and Ed Henke of California Trout, Peter Behr, Ike Livermore, Reagan, Richard May of California Trout, Mrs. Joseph Paul, and David Hirsch of The Planning and Conservation League.

slow growth, ecological planning, and rebuilding the mean streets of Los Angeles, had been adopted, California would be a far better place to live today. However, it started at the state level rather than the county level and was more easily doomed.

Marin and Mendocino counties can be proud of their roles as the Cradle of River Conservation in California. Richard Wilson, Ike Livermore, Peter Behr, and Joe Paul turned back the State Water Lobby, revolutionized state water policy, and helped end the careers of Gianelli and Collier.

Damming the Eel River

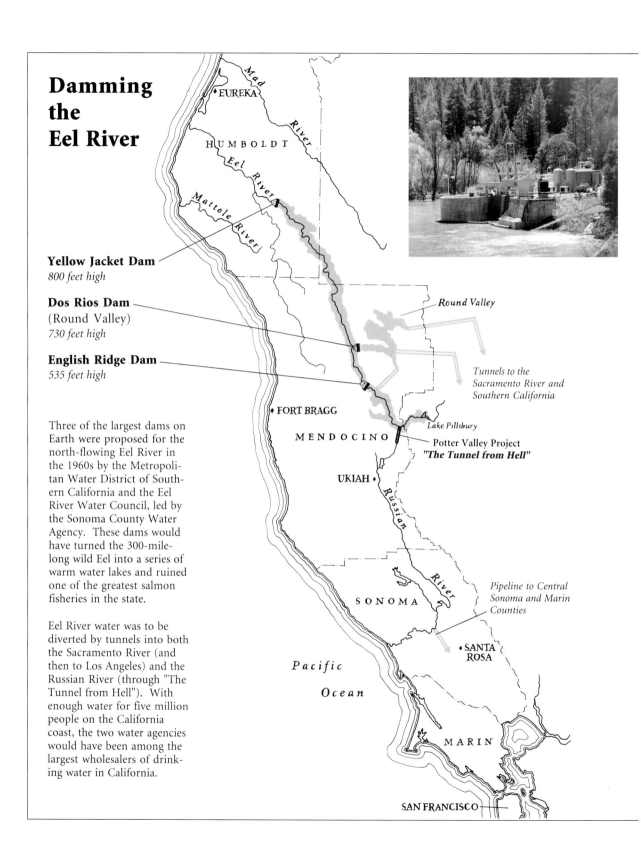

Yellow Jacket Dam
800 feet high

Dos Rios Dam
(Round Valley)
730 feet high

English Ridge Dam
535 feet high

Mad River

EUREKA

HUMBOLDT

Eel River

Mattole River

Round Valley

*Tunnels to the
Sacramento River and
Southern California*

FORT BRAGG

MENDOCINO

Lake Pillsbury

Potter Valley Project
"The Tunnel from Hell"

UKIAH

Russian River

SONOMA

*Pipeline to Central
Sonoma and Marin
Counties*

SANTA
ROSA

*Pacific
Ocean*

MARIN

SAN FRANCISCO

Three of the largest dams on Earth were proposed for the north-flowing Eel River in the 1960s by the Metropolitan Water District of Southern California and the Eel River Water Council, led by the Sonoma County Water Agency. These dams would have turned the 300-mile-long wild Eel into a series of warm water lakes and ruined one of the greatest salmon fisheries in the state.

Eel River water was to be diverted by tunnels into both the Sacramento River (and then to Los Angeles) and the Russian River (through "The Tunnel from Hell"). With enough water for five million people on the California coast, the two water agencies would have been among the largest wholesalers of drinking water in California.

"The Tunnel from Hell"

THE POTTER VALLEY POWER PROJECT

A large, steep, mile-long tunnel was drilled through a Mendocino County ridge by Chinese laborers in 1908 to divert water from the upper Eel River into the Russian River. This diversion, called the Potter Valley Project, dried up the forested canyons of the Eel and wrecked the ecology of the Russian. The original purpose of the tunnel was to generate electricity for Ukiah, but the incredible bonanza of so-called "abandoned water" insured a speculative land boom in Sonoma and Marin counties.

In 1929, PG&E bought the diversion which included Lake Pillsbury, created to provide year round flow through the tunnel. But the warm water lake released predatory squawfish, which ate migrating salmon and contributed to the devastation of the billion dollar North Coast salmon fishery.

In Marin County, we called the diversion "The Tunnel from Hell" because its electric turbines, lacking an effective fish screen until 1995, chewed up juvenile salmon and steelhead trying to find their way down the Eel two hundred miles to the ocean.

The Eel River Tunnel was one of the first big water heists in California—160,000 acre-feet or more each year, enough water for nearly a million people.

The water and hydroelectric rights to the Eel River water diversion are in turmoil. The Sonoma County Water Agency is desperately trying to buy the Potter Valley Project from PG&E while both Mendocino and Humboldt Counties are demanding that their salmon fisheries be restored. Water rights may end up in court.

If Sonoma County's use of Eel River water is decreased or eliminated, the difference could be made up by conserving water, protecting the river's aquifers from gravel dredging, using wastewater for irrigation, cracking down on illegal pumps—and controlling growth.

The photo shows the entrance to the tunnel that diverts water from the Eel River into the East Fork of the Russian River where it's regulated by Coyote Dam, constructed in 1959. Until PG&E built an expensive and complicated fish screen in 1995, migratory salmonids were needlessly ground up in the Project's electric turbines, leading to the name "The Tunnel from Hell."

CHAPTER FOURTEEN

The Sonoma Coast and the Russian River in Peril

*It is hard for me to talk about the Russian River. I've been all over
the world, but never have I seen a river of such resonance, fullness,
and absolute beauty be so utterly violated and dishonored. . . .
Compared with the river it was thirty years ago, today the Russian
is essentially a biological desert.*

—Russell Chatham, *The Angler's Coast*, 1988

In 1930, when I was ten, Dad announced to the family, "Let's go fishing."
So we loaded up the running boards of the family auto and headed for
the Russian River which, he said, had "the finest steelhead fishing in the
state." We arrived at noon on a blister-hot day at the Healdsburg Plaza, just
thirty-one river miles from the coast.

We headed east up the winding gravel road between the Russian River
and Fitch Mountain toward Digger Bend, a hairpin loop in the river where
Dad had rented a vacation cabin for a month.

The Russian River was paradise. I thought it was the most inviting and
sumptuous river I'd ever seen. Its lazy curves were framed by cobbled gravel
bars and tawny hills, with Mt. St. Helena beyond. Overhanging willows,
alders, and giant cottonwoods gave the river an inviting quality that encouraged us to swim, fish, and frolic as Pomo families must have done before us.
We wondered how such beauty had survived the Spanish, Russian, Mexican,
and American invaders of these lands.

We called it Turtle River because dozens of western pond turtles plopped
into the river from the drooping willow branches that swayed with the current. Overhead Golden Eagles soared and osprey dove for fish. The river was
crystal clear and safe to drink, filtered through miles of gravel between us
and the next upriver village, Geyserville.

At night we sat in the soft, warm twilight listening to Dad's mandolin as

*Summer vacationers
sunbathed and frolicked
in the then-unpolluted
waters of the Russian
River near Guerneville
during the 1920s. The
woman leaning against
the car looks just like
my mother, but we
camped upriver near
Digger Bend.*

The Russian River looked like this when I bought my ranch south of Healdsburg in 1961. A forest canopy shaded the river, protecting the profusion of turtles and wild steelhead and salmon that spawned nearby in Griffin Creek. Then the mining started.

fireflies illumined the hillsides of yellow grass. Then we walked down to an outdoor dance floor where couples swayed and spun under Japanese lanterns to a small band under a full moon. Those evenings made me think of the song "I Love You, California," that I learned in grammar school.

Each day we splashed up the river with our fly rods in hand and found deep, cold pools between the gravel hummocks where trout and river otter lurked. Occasionally we'd see a large steelhead that was summering over. Frogs and polliwogs were everywhere. The evening hatch of insects that arose from the gravel bars was consumed by darting swallows, swifts, and bats that swept the skies and shadows. At night we slept outdoors, lulled to sleep by the murmuring river and strumming cicadas, and were awakened at dawn by a chorus of songbirds.

And the fragrance! The bays, willows, pennyroyal, trout, frying bacon, coffee, hot apple pie, and wild blackberries—what more could a boy want?

That idyllic period was over by the time I next inspected the river in 1961. By then the turtles, frogs, fish, and fireflies were fast disappearing. Farmers were clearing land right up to the river's edge to plant orchards and vineyards. Bulldozers were strip-mining the gravel bars and leaving them flat as a pancake. Huge cranes were in the riverbed dredging pits fifty-five feet deep in the Middle Reach aquifer near Healdsburg. They were after its gravel and sand which were shipped by rail out of Healdsburg to build bridges, freeways, and houses in the growing counties of the North Bay Area, particularly Marin.

Billy Walters Sells Me His Ranch

In 1961 I bought a gorgeous ranch six miles south of Healdsburg on Westside Road from an old timer, Billy Walters, who had been raised there. The ranch lay on both sides of the Russian River, and through it ran a small shaded creek teeming with newts, turtles, steelhead trout, and silver salmon that spawned in gravel beds in the deep canyon pools. It was just what I had dreamed about. The ranch was historic, marking the southern boundary of the huge Sotoyome Mexican land grant which General Vallejo gave to his sister-in-law's American husband, Captain Henry Fitch, and which was later fought over by land squatters when California became a state. Billy Walter's father, Seth, had bought it in 1880. I was only the third owner since 1850.

The ranch's vineyards of Petite Sirah and Zinfandel vines produced fruit from which we made a dark, rich wine not for the faint of palate. We eventually opened the Hop Kiln Winery in the ancient hop-drying barn overlooking the Russian River Valley. Water? I knew I had bought a treasure when Billy's wells gushed more than 1,000 gallons of water a minute from the gravel aquifer below the winery.

I didn't think too much about the gravel mining until 1962, as I visited the ranch only on weekends. However, Billy Walters had leased the floodplain on both sides of the river to a mining firm for twenty-five years to skim—a watered-down word for strip-mining—the gravel bars. One week while I was away they skimmed—cleared—the entire fifty acres of virgin riparian forest, destroying valley oak, cottonwood, elder, four kinds of willow, and rare vines such as Dutchman's Pipe. Wild grapevines fifty feet long and as thick as my arms—were all ripped up. A small colony of great blue herons and a nest of young osprey were destroyed. The trees were bulldozed into great piles and burned with old tires, whose acrid smoke filled the valley for weeks. This devastation was happening up and down the river, perpetrated by both miners and farmers.

We founded Hop Kiln Winery in 1975, restored this historic hop drying barn as a National Historic Trust building, and had Westside Road designated a County Scenic Corridor, protecting its rural character. Five years later we won the Sonoma County Sweepstakes award for our Zinfandel.

Huge trucks bring raw gravel, often dripping wet, from riverbed mines or from deep pits in the Middle Reach aquifer to Syar Industries' giant gravel stockpile at Healdsburg. Public recreational use of the Russian River has been severely affected as the riverbed has dropped substantially.

River Channel, 1940

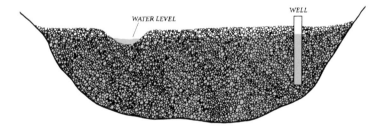

This stylized cross-section of the river channel (right) shows how the riverbed and the water table have dropped many feet in places from repeated, excessive gravel skimming (strip-mining) since the Coyote Dam started trapping gravel flows in 1957. This loss of filtering gravel has depleted and contaminated several public and private wells along the river, leaving some high and dry (right).

River Channel, 1990

After this the miners rerouted the river on my ranch, built a dike to keep it there, and then dredged a gravel pit in the aquifer fifty-five feet deep by a half-mile long and four hundred feet wide. Even though this dredging on state instream lands was illegal, no agency would lift a hand to help. Later, floodwaters filled the pit with silt, and my wells and those of my neighbors were cut off from being recharged by the river. We no longer had gushes of water. Eventually we fought back, long and hard, against the mining.

The Middle Reach Aquifer— Over 11,000 Years Old

The Middle Reach aquifer, where my new ranch was located, is a nine-mile bathtub of gravel about eighty feet deep, one mile wide, and over eleven thousand years old. It extends from Healdsburg southwest along Westside Road to the Wohler Bridge, where there is a narrowing in the Coast Range called the Wohler Narrows. Formed after the last ice age, the aquifer has an underground river running very slowly through the gravel which, along with the organisms living within it, acts as a natural water purification filter, one of the finest on Earth. The gravel aquifer, which is about thirty percent water, fed about one hundred farm wells, the municipal wells of Healdsburg and, later, Windsor and those of the Sonoma County Water Agency.

After 1993 flooding, this vineyard and its irrigation pipes collapsed into the sinking riverbed just above the Geyserville Bridge, near an instream mining site, leaving the grower's well standing alone in the middle of the river (right). In 1996 the County admitted that the miners had excavated five times more gravel than the river could replenish.

I was dumbfounded as, over the years, I saw new gravel pits dug in the aquifer adjacent to the Sonoma County Water Agency's wells and alongside the drinking water wells for Windsor and Healdsburg upriver. I asked myself why in the world would this public water agency allow its only source of naturally pure drinking water to be destroyed along with the well sites it would need in the future?

After researching campaign contributions in the courthouse, I realized that a majority of supervisors' campaigns for office received generous donations year after year from the politically astute gravel miners and developers. Since the supervisors controlled gravel mining and doubled as directors of the Sonoma County Water Agency, the developers had gained control of a bonanza—the Russian River and its resources of water and gravel.

The developers did not consider the river a treasure, or even an amenity, but merely a cheap commodity to be exploited for rapid growth. The

Middle Reach Aquifer contained at least a hundred million tons of cheap-to-mine gravel whose end product was expensive and highly profitable asphalt and concrete. With this subsidized bonanza dredged from river channels that belonged to the public, gravel mining interests could easily afford to hire attorneys and lobbyists and to make generous political contributions.

I had stumbled onto an unprecedented river mining scandal. The supervisors in Sonoma County, still with a frontier, old-boy mentality, were giving away the aquifer that the public owned and depended on for its drinking water without collecting royalties or damage fees of any kind. I figured at one point that, at one dollar per ton in potential royalties, the county had lost more than fifty million dollars.

Even floods didn't stop the mining. On a stormy night in 1964 after days of rain, the bed and banks of Griffin Creek (as the mining firms named it) on my property slid slowly into the deep gravel pit recently dredged in the bed of the Russian River. Overnight the Russian River, Griffin Creek, and nearby Dry Creek changed their courses and their beds slid some seventeen feet as the river broke into other deep pits. This catastrophe is called "pit capture." As a result, bridges over the river were undermined and some twenty farm wells were left hanging in midair as the banks collapsed into the flood waters. The steelhead spawning grounds of Griffin Creek were wiped out. The mouth of Dry Creek widened from thirty to three hundred feet. With each flood over the next few years, the drop in the riverbed increased. The mining firms and the supervisors did not take these events as a warning; they merely called them "acts of God" and looked for more places to dig. Nature's great gift continued to be sacrificed to greed and ignorance.

Gaye LeBaron, long-time journalist and historian for The Press Democrat, *is called "the conscience of Sonoma County." As a young reporter she helped expose the folly of the Bodega Bay nuclear reactor in 1962. In 1997 she was honored by Santa Rosa Junior College with the President's Medallion.*

The Battle of Bodega Bay

Sonoma County's environmental movement began with the Battle of Bodega Bay the same year that the Point Reyes National Seashore and Warm Springs Dam were authorized. The Sonoma County Supervisors were hoping to develop Sonoma's fifty-five mile coastline without public hearings or public access to its beaches, coves, or tidelands.

First, PG&E began digging a hole on the Bodega Bay Headlands in 1962 for the largest nuclear energy plant on Earth—without a permit from the Atomic Energy Commission. They couldn't have picked a worse spot. The "Hole in the Head," as it became known, adjoined an active earthquake fault as well as the Bodega Marine Laboratory, which the University of California had just selected "as the finest site on the California coast." This story of greed and collusion by the Sonoma Supervisors, PG&E, and regulatory agencies is told in *Power and Land in California, The Ralph Nader Task Force Report.*

When PG&E tried to covertly condemn the Bodega Bay ranch owned by Rose Gaffney for their nuclear power plant, Rose raised such a ruckus that the secret leaked out: the Supervisors had issued twenty-seven permits to PG&E—without any public hearings.

"The atomic park," said Supervisor "Nin" Guidotti, "will speed the development of the coast." It would also require enormous tonnages of Russian River gravel for aqueducts, freeways, and new cities, as well as for the plant itself. Incredibly, the only public hearings on this stupendous project were requested by Marin Supervisor Peter Behr, held in Marin, and attended by a busload of Sonoma protesters. The AEC finally killed the project after scientists proved the earthquake fault ran through the reactor site. Today, the five miles of coastline making up the dramatic Bodega Headlands are preserved as state and county parks and the site of the reknown Bodega Marine Laboratory.

Then, in the early 1970s, the Utah Construction Company unveiled plans to dredge the estuary of the Russian River claiming that it needed the gravel for concrete to build the Bay Area Rapid Transit (BART) tunnel under San Francisco Bay. This was the same company whose plans to fill Richardson Bay in Marin County had been thwarted by Caroline Livermore. The opposition this time was led by Virginia Hechtman, a shrewd housewife from Jenner, who worked night and day with her Jenner Coalition to kill this project, which would have dug deep pits near the mouth of the Russian River and excavated Penny Island, now a wildlife preserve. She also helped defeat a 1,500-home subdivision at nearby Willow Creek, which was later turned into a state park.

COAAST Is Born

Another great threat to the Sonoma coastline was the Sonoma County supervisors' approval in 1968 of Sea Ranch, a 5,200-home subdivision on the Sonoma-Mendocino border by Oceanic Properties of Hawaii, which planned to deny public access to eleven miles of coastline except for one county park. If built on the scale proposed, Sea Ranch could have brought a

Bill Kortum, a Cotati veterinarian and political strategist for a half century, was a founder of COAAST (Californians Organized to Acquire Access to State Tidelands) and co-author of the 1972 Coastal Initiative that established the California Coastal Commission. He also created Coastwalk and, later, Conservation Action, a political canvassing group led by activist Mark Green.

four-lane freeway and an aqueduct from the Russian River up the coast. The beautiful Gualala River nearby was to be strip-mined for construction gravel for the project.

This assault on the public's access to beaches inspired the creation of COAAST—Californians Organized to Acquire Access to State Tidelands. This acronym was the brainchild of educator Charles Rhinehart. This citizens' group was led by veterinarian Bill Kortum, Peter Leveque, John Crevelli, and Ernie Smith—all leaders at Santa Rosa Junior College, Santa Rosa attorney Dick Day, Virginia Hechtman, and many others. COAAST developed a powerful constituency in the county and the state legislature, and they won a lawsuit requiring a bluff trail and five access trails through Sea Ranch from Highway 1 to the ocean. They were also successful in cutting the size of the development by half. They then took on Brown and Kaufman, one of the state's largest developers, and were able to cut in half a 1,626-home development at Bodega Bay *after* it was approved by the county supervisors.

COAAST's greatest achievement under Kortum's leadership, and that of Janet Adams of Save the Bay, was a statewide initiative drive by the 105 members of the Coastal Alliance who campaigned to save the California coastline. This led to the passage of Proposition 20 in 1972. This landmark legislation established the California State Coastal Commission to manage the eleven-hundred-mile coastline and to protect its scenic and biotic treasures for all Californians to enjoy. In 1976 the State Coastal Act was passed making the Coastal Commission permanent.

The fertile brain of Kortum also thought up Coastwalk, which gives people the opportunity to walk sections of the coast with trained leaders to acquaint themselves with its riches and to help obtain access to all parts of the coast. Coastwalk, an annual event that now includes every county along the coast, is one of the state's finest environmental education tools. Coordinated by Richard Nichols of Sebastopol, thousands of people have enjoyed the lessons of superb naturalists, the coziness of shared campfires, and the splendid vistas of the remaining wild coast, and even the developed coast, from Oregon to the Mexican border. As historian Gaye LeBaron rightly says, "Sonoma County is the cradle of coastal conservation in California."

A Trumped-up Recall

Bill Kortum's growing credentials alarmed the real estate developers and ranch land speculators who feared that his team would kill the Warm

Springs Dam project. Their anxieties were heightened when Kortum and conservationist Chuck Hinkle were elected county supervisors in the early seventies. The developers engineered a recall election in 1976 that unseated both of them after a costly media blitz. Kortum and Hinkle were accused of being anti-business and anti-jobs because they opposed lot splits into ranchettes that would destroy agriculture. After the recall, a disillusioned Hinkle left the county, but Kortum worked even harder to save agriculture and the coast, to stop the dam, and to decrease dependence on the automobile.

Tragically, the ruthless political upheaval that followed turned Sonoma County away from any possibility of reasonable, planned growth for nearly two decades. The county planning department was decimated, advance planning was eliminated, and much of the county and the Russian River were opened to raw, ruthless exploitation by corporate developers, part-time farmers, and mining firms. The way was being paved to open up the vast agricultural lands and vernal pools along Highway 101 through Rohnert Park, Santa Rosa, and Windsor to the staggering growth and sprawl that would double the County's population between 1980 and 1990—triggered by the promise in 1962 of water from the Warm Springs Dam.

Hikers can enjoy the unspoiled coast on trails for most of the length of California, thanks to Coastwalk. This trail is on the wild 273-acre Black Ranch in Sonoma County which has been preserved by the state Coastal Conservancy. The sparsely-developed, fifty-five mile Sonoma coast is partially protected by parks and preserves, but the rolling hills from Tomales Bay to Bodega Bay are still coveted by developers.

CONSERVATION POOL
ELEVATION 451 FT.

OUTLET WORKS

DAM

SPILLWAY

FISH HATCHERY

BORD BRIDGE

WARM SPRINGS DAM SITE

CHAPTER FIFTEEN

How to Build a Water Empire

*With improved water supply Sonoma County's development
can expect to be similar to that of Santa Clara County.*

> —Stone and Youngberg, Consultants to the
> Sonoma County Water Agency, 1954

The Warm Springs Dam is a chilling example of how a publicly owned water agency was able to disenfranchise Sonoma County voters (and tried to do the same with Marin voters) in order to construct a dam costing $365 million—the last large dam built in California.

The Warm Springs Dam had a forty-three-year gestation: it was conceived about 1940 by the US Army Corps of Engineers for flood control and water supply. Construction was authorized in 1962 by Congress, and the dam was completed in 1983.

Today the dam is a fact of life, a gigantic earthen barrier extending for half a mile across the confluence of Warm Springs Creek and Dry Creek and creating Lake Sonoma to a depth of 315 feet. The entire project includes 16,770 acres of over-cut watershed (some of it severely eroding), a modern state-run fish hatchery, splendid recreational benefits, and a well-run federal park with interpretive Pomo displays.

Despite the benefits, I fought that dam tooth and nail. In my opinion, water-rich Sonoma didn't need the dam, and its flood control benefits couldn't make up for the land speculation that followed in the wake of its proposal, or for the sprawling growth that followed the giant water pipelines south from the Russian River along Highway 101, through Sonoma and deep into Marin.

This pre-construction diagram of Warm Springs Dam shows the vast area filled to create Lake Sonoma. The Dam blocks Dry Creek, its salmon spawning grounds, and natural gravel flow, and releases sediment-starved water, which erodes the river channel and silts drinking water wells.

Who Is Behind It?

As the Golden Gate Bridge was nearing completion in 1937, local development interests began to meet with the US Army Corps of Engineers in

Gravel from the Russian River has been used since the 1930s for the bridges, freeways, and post-war growth of both Marin and Sonoma. Quarried rock could have been used instead of the enormous tonnages of river gravel railed and trucked from Healdsburg each year.

Washington D.C. to take advantage of money available for flood control. Sonoma and Marin, being closest to the bridge, were the highest priority. Once the Corps drew Warm Springs Dam on their maps, the dam became a favored, but unfunded, "flood control" pork barrel for generations of politicians.

The Corps required a local sponsor for its dams, so in 1949 the Sonoma County Water Agency was chartered by the state to manage the Russian River water supply and flood control. A few years later, Gordon W. Miller, a young engineer from the Los Angeles Flood Control District, was hand-picked as the Water Agency's manager. One of his jobs was to get Warm Springs Dam built, along with three dams on the Eel River.

Miller was also a mover and shaker in an aggressive statewide lobby for big dam projects named the California Water Resources Association, formed in 1955 and based in Glendale, near Los Angeles. Miller became a director of the association representing Marin, Sonoma, Mendocino, Humboldt, Trinity, Del Norte, Napa, and Lake counties. These counties were joined as the Eel River Water Council between 1965 and 1973, when it was disbanded. With an annual runoff of 6,300,000 acre feet of water each year, second only to the Klamath River, the Eel was the key to developing these North Coast counties as well as counties on the South Coast.

The Council meant business. They had stunning brochures in red, white, and blue and detailed maps in full color showing dams on nearly every river. They also had a full-time executive director in addition to Gordon Miller, who seemed to run the organization.

I met with Miller in 1972 in the Council's plush Santa Rosa offices when I was a delegate representing Marin County. There I learned that traditionally water agency professionals don't take their dam projects to the voters. They don't need to.

Miller had the full political power of the state water lobby behind him. His mentors were the engineering firms that had built the largest dams and aqueducts on Earth. As befitting an autocratic water developer from Los Angeles, Miller was noted for his white shoes and license plates reading "H2O CZAR."

Kicking Off the Dam Project

One of my great regrets at the time was not attending the kick-off event for the Warm Springs Dam project held by the Army Corps on March 17, 1960. Appropriately, it was held in the nearby Villa Chanticleer in Healdsburg. Three hundred organized supporters unanimously agreed to urge Congress to authorize the dam for "desperately needed flood control." The Corps was anxious to get federal approval before opposition to this dinosaur mounted; there was growing public awareness that damming is the most absolute way to destroy a river.

My immediate reaction to news of the dam in 1960 was dismay. The Army Corps had already damaged the steelhead fishery of the Russian River with the cheap construction of Coyote Dam in 1959 near Ukiah, built with neither a fish ladder nor multiple outlets for coldwater fish. There were miles of severe streambank erosion downriver from the Corps' bulldozing and straightening the riverbed. To top it off, they had cabled huge steel jacks to hold the banks in place where they planted invasive grasses and bamboo, and the whole mess washed out in the first flood.

When President Kennedy signed the Warm Springs Dam bill in 1962, it triggered the first battle to slow growth in Sonoma County, and for good reason. The "firm water supply" promised by the Corps of 115,000 acre-feet was enough to supply a population of about half a million people. Including the 160,000 acre-feet of water diverted for free each year from the Eel River, there would be plenty of water available to export 50,000 acre-feet a year to Marin by aqueduct if Marin bought into the dam. This was more water

Gordon Miller, Chief Engineer of the Sonoma County Water Agency from 1957 to 1979, was the most influential water developer on the North Coast. Miller's primary concern was providing sufficient water for the expected enormous growth.

supply than that available in all of Marin's lakes. I've already told of Marin's political and water revolution in response to this proposal.

The Corp's Warm Springs Dam project was delayed for years by a lack of federal funding. Then in the 1970s opponents began to fight the dam with initiatives and legal challenges while its price steadily rose from an estimated $115 million in 1962 to the final bill of $365 million in 1983.

Colonel James Lammie, District Engineer for the Corps, was in charge of the project. At an environmental review hearing at which I spoke against the dam, he lambasted me as "an outsider." But there was expert testimony that the dam was not needed for water supply and that there was plenty of groundwater available for reasonable growth.

The Corps, however, bamboozled the public with exaggerated flood control promises for the riverside town of Guerneville. In fact, the flood level in Guerneville in 1986, three years after the dam was built, was the highest in history due to dam-induced growth and other factors.

In 1997 an official from the state Office of Emergency Services declared that the Russian River now has the distinction of having the highest and costliest rate of repetitive flooding west of the Mississippi—$130 million in damages in 1995 and 1997 alone.

The voters never had a dam choice. They couldn't vote for or against Warm Springs Dam except by a costly referendum process that required thousands of signatures just to get on the ballot.

So much for the flood control benefits of Warm Springs Dam.

The Warm Springs Dam Opponents

Opposition to the dam was well organized and persistent beyond all expectations. The number and the talent of the people who opposed the Warm Springs Dam was astounding. I can only tell of a few here. Gail Jonas, a feisty and idealistic young woman from Healdsburg just entering law school in 1973, led the Warm Springs Dam Task Force and pitted her talents against Colonel Lammie, Gordon Miller, and the County Supervisors.

Paul Kayfetz, a Bolinas attorney, flew at his own expense to Washington D.C. to obtain a writ requiring an Environmental Impact Report from Supreme Court Justice William O. Douglas, and that was then signed by the entire court. Thousands of hours were volunteered by "no growthers" obtaining signatures for initiatives and getting voter turnout. Nearly all the Dry Creek Valley Association farmers I knew opposed the dam, including leaders Warren Rossiter, Rex Holmes, Charles Richard, and Pomo Native Americans Bill and Sally Smith.

Fishery experts warned that the dam would drown a quarter of all the stream miles utilized by steelhead and coho (silver) salmon for spawning in the entire Russian River watershed. It was predicted that six thousand of the silvery dynamos, weighing up to ten pounds each, would migrate up the main stem into Dry Creek, twenty-eight miles from the ocean, only to butt their heads against the proposed Warm Springs Dam and die. Their only other option was to enter the concrete fish hatchery to be tranquilized, milted, and egged. Hatchery fish were already known to be genetically inferior and to possess fewer survival skills than wild fish. Their fins were eroded from being reared in troughs and they were prone to disease.

In 1973 Warm Springs Dam opponents came close to killing the dam. First, a coalition of nineteen outraged organizations, including the League of Women Voters, confronted the Sonoma County supervisors and demanded that they rescind the sale of Warm Springs Dam bonds because they had been approved without public vote. The supervisors refused. The League's only recourse was to obtain thousands of signatures for an initiative to repeal the bonds and to conduct a difficult, costly campaign. The measure lost at the election by a small margin after a media blitz by the well-funded pro-dam forces. Then Senator Peter Behr, Marin's respected representative

My dad was one of many fishing enthusiasts who opposed Warm Springs Dam. Our claims that it would kill the spawning grounds and destroy the fishery proved all too true. He used to hand-tie his own flies when we fished for steelhead on the Russian, Eel, and Klamath rivers which still had gorgeous, unmined cobbled gravel bars like this one.

The Fallacy of Warm Springs Dam for Flood Control

A DIRE PREDICTION COME TRUE

O f all the things that may be said against Warm Springs Dam, perhaps the most sadly ironic is that the dam conceived as a flood control project may cause greater and more frequent flooding in the lower Russian River channel. With the building of Warm Springs Dam, water will be made available for the rapid development of Sonoma County. Much of that growth will occur on the Santa Rosa Plain, a large flat area drained northward into the Russian River by the Laguna de Santa Rosa. Ten years ago, the plain was found to be about eighty percent permeable to rainwater, there being very little development there. However, with the water made available by the dam, this large vulnerable flat plain will be intensively developed into high-density residential and commercial uses.

Completed Warm Springs Dam and Lake Sonoma.

Now the permeability ratio of the plain reverses itself, becoming eighty percent impervious to rainwater due to streets, driveways, roads, and parking lots. The natural sponge-like effect of the plain is thus lost, having been converted into a hard-surfaced rainwater "catchall basin." During a major downpour, this catch basin will collect millions of gallons of water through runoff and storm drains and discharge it into the Laguna. The Laguna will rise and flow northward, discharging this torrent of rainwater exactly above the stretch of river where the flooding was to have been prevented by the dam! Rio Nido, Guerneville, Monte Rio, and other towns can expect to get more flood water in the river, coming higher and faster than before the construction of the dam and as a direct result of building the dam!

—Bruce MacPherson, Environmental Economist, Santa Rosa, 1974

whose Wild and Scenic Rivers Bill had passed the California legislature in 1972, wrote a letter to Governor Reagan asking him to stop the dam because it had never been approved directly by the voters.

Behr's letter to the governor was squelched by Art Volkerts, editor of Santa Rosa's *Press Democrat*, who wrote editorials for what he called "The Last Great Crusade." By wrongly including the Coyote Dam vote, Volkerts claimed that the public had twice voted for the dam, but Iva Warner, a retired Naval officer in Santa Rosa, rebutted his deceptions in a 1973 issue of *Sonoma Tomorrow*, a publication created to oppose the dam. Her legal strategist was attorney Dick Day, also of Santa Rosa. Warner's research documented how the Sonomans were disenfranchised by their own Water Agency.

In 1949 the state chartered the Sonoma County Water Agency but allowed only indirect public participation by making the county supervisors its directors. In 1961 Gordon Miller quietly achieved state legislative changes that allowed the Water Agency to issue revenue bonds in any amount and to contract with the Army Corps to build the Warm Springs Dam. This maneuver deprived voters of their right to a public vote on the dam or any other

The historic Wohler Bridge south of Healdsburg crosses the Russian River at the Wohler Narrows, which created the Middle Reach gravel aquifer. Above the bridge (right) are two of the five Sonoma County Water Agency water collectors. The river here is dammed to increase percolation, but this creates the long lake shown, which we believe blocks migrating salmonids.

water projects. (In 1971, Miller even attempted to deprive *Marin* voters of their vote on Marin County water projects by changing the State Water Code for Marin, but Marin's angry legislators balked and killed the attempt. The voters of both Marin water districts have fought for and retained their vote on water projects.)

In 1964 the Agency signed a contract with the Army Corps of Engineers obligating county taxpayers to pay for Warm Springs Dam (without a public vote). In 1970, with no public debate, the Sonoma County Supervisors authorized the Sonoma County Water Agency to sell $115 million in revenue bonds but gave no indication where the money would be spent. Warm Springs Dam opponents finally conceded defeat after a second confusing initiative vote lost in 1979.

In 1994 the Sonoma County Supervisors, who are also the directors of the Sonoma County Water Agency, approved a Mining Plan allowing for dredging of two hundred more acres of gravel aquifer directly upriver from the Wohler Bridge wells, potentially destroying its natural water filter and future well sites. From the left are Ernie Carpenter, Nick Esposti, Mike Cale, Jim Harberson, and Tim Smith. The Supervisors are under tremendous political pressure to supply Russian River gravel for development in five counties.

After the dam was completed in 1983, Sonoma was named among the fastest-growing counties in the state while Marin was among the slowest. Iva Warner warned in her final bulletin, "When public agencies don't want public scrutiny, their best strategy is to deny the public the right to vote."

The Sonoma County Water Agency Today

As this is written, this legacy lives on—the Sonoma County taxpayers who own the Russian River Water System are unable to vote on multi-million dollar water contracts, wells, dams, or aqueducts unless the water agency directors decide to put them on the ballot.

The Sonoma County Water Agency is the largest public water agency on the North Coast, operating with its own multi-million dollar budget. Its charter gives it two major duties: to wholesale water and to develop flood control projects. It can also develop sewage projects. In 1994 manager Bob Beach told the Friends of the Russian River its mission was primarily water delivery for economic development, and that it had little responsibility for the health of the watershed.

Supervisor Ernie Carpenter told us in 1995, "As long as the Agency is a cash cow, the supervisors leave it alone." It has about thirty-two million dollars in the bank that is uncommitted money that could be used for watershed management and to acquire and restore the seventy-mile river corridor between Coyote Dam and the Wohler pumps.

It is no secret that for decades the Agency has run its river enterprise not

Russian River Facts & Issues

Length	110 miles in Mendocino and Sonoma Counties
Navigable Length	Approximately 100 miles; Public Trust Easement extends to ordinary high water mark; channels used for Public Drinking Water Supply are unprotected
Watershed	1450 square miles, about one million acres; 95% of watershed privately owned; Drains one-half Sonoma County—1.5 million acre-feet of runoff per wet winter; 160,000 acre feet diverted from Eel River year round
Dams	Two high dams—Warm Springs and Coyote—plus the small Willow (in Mendocino), Healdsburg, and Wohler Dams block gravel flows and fish migration
Water Supply	1,400 private wells; Municipal wells serve 500,000 people; river is overallocated with eighty new applications on hold
Filtration	Drinking water quality depends on depth of gravelbed filtration in the aquifer; in some places little aquifer remains after mining
Mining	Dozens of gravel mines in and along the river are destroying gravel beds and channels used for Public Water Supply and filtration; eleven deep pits in the Middle Reach are rupturing and threaten to reroute the river; estimated 50,000 acre-feet of groundwater storage destroyed
Erosion	Over 1,000 tons per square mile per wet winter; channel downcutting of 9-20 vertical feet below dams; six bridges undermined, two freeway bridges replaced; several municipal wells in Ukiah, Cloverdale, Healdsburg, and Sonoma County Water Agency Well #5 at Wohler are contaminated during high water
Floods	Flooding has worsened since dams were built for flood control; highest rate of repetitive flood damages in California (1995-1997); rated one of the most threatened rivers in America
Waste Water	Discharge from nine cities and industrial sites from October to March; polluted runoff from urban development on the Santa Rosa Plain increases flooding downriver
Channelized Creeks	120 projects to channelize creeks and tributaries (400 miles); approximately 70% of riparian forests lost
Salmonid Fishery	60,000 native spawners in 1940 down to an estimated 300 per year
Overall Management Plan	None (1997)
Who's in Charge?	Mendocino and Sonoma Supervisors regulate land use and gravel mining in their counties. The Sonoma County Water Agency and the US Army Corps regulate the two dams for drinking water and flood control. Jointly the two counties have the power to implement a Comprehensive Watershed and Flood Management Plan.
Litigation	Numerous major lawsuits and Grand Jury investigations (see Appendix)

This 1996 official map shows the unique, billion dollar public water system that is owned by the taxpayers of Sonoma County. Water diverted from the Eel River (top) is regulated by Coyote Dam. From there it flows down the river channel designated for Public Water Supply, joining water released from Warm Springs Dam. At the Wohler Bridge (circle), five Ranney Water Collectors, sunk deep in the gravel aquifer, pump naturally filtered water through aqueducts to Marin and Sonoma. This free gravel filtration saves the taxpayers more than $300 million in artificial water treatment costs. Note that there are no aqueducts along the Marin-Sonoma Coast.

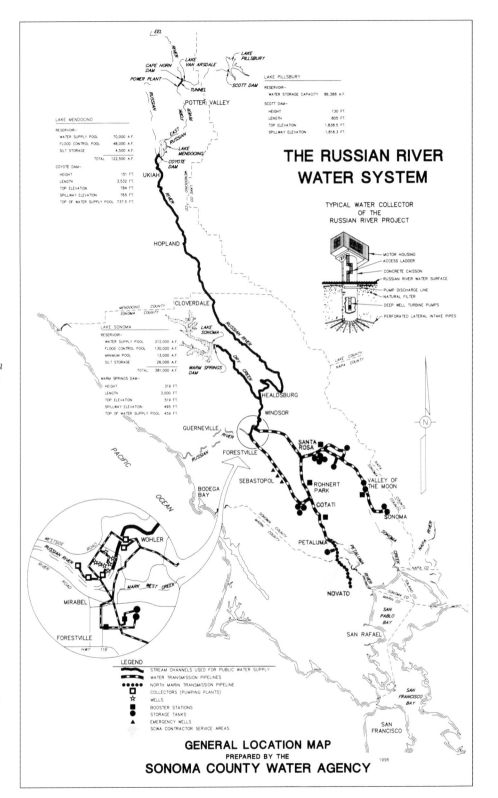

Two huge wells called Ranney Collectors (right), just north of the Wohler Bridge, are sunk sixty feet into the Russian River gravel aquifer. The source of high quality, naturally gravel-filtered drinking water for much of Marin and Sonoma, these municipal wells are seriously threatened by siltation from upriver mining and vineyard erosion.

as a public trust or for the health of the Russian River, but to benefit the developers, cities, and commercial miners. These groups exploit the river in four ways: taking excessive water, strip-mining the gravel aquifer, channelizing tributaries for flood control and development, and dumping wastewater and polluted urban stormwater runoff.

The Sonoma County Water Agency wholesales drinking water to nine regular contractors in Sonoma and Marin, and they then retail the water to their half-million consumers. These contractors are the water districts of Forestville, Santa Rosa, Valley of the Moon, Sonoma, Rohnert Park, Cotati, Petaluma, and North Marin, plus the Marin Municipal Water District which has a separate contract. These water districts each have their own elected boards of directors. In 1994, an attempt was made by three of these water districts to participate in the gravel mining plan for the Russian River. They wanted to do so in order to protect the quality of water they buy, but they were angrily rejected by the Sonoma County supervisors who—wrongly— have control over both mining and the water supply.

For years the Agency has had no overall river management plan and no plan to preserve the aquifer for existing or future well sites. Agency engineer Bob Morrison defended excavation of the Middle Reach aquifer as harmless even though Sonoma County Water Agency's multi-million dollar wells lie in a flood disaster zone which includes a string of mined-out, ruptured, mud-spewing gravel pits and a large illegal demolition dump.

Fife
Creek

Russian River

The Russian River, at the bottom of the picture, floods the town of Guerneville in 1986. Fife Creek, swollen with flood water, is on the upper left. The river reached a record flooding of forty-eight feet three years after Warm Springs Dam was completed for "flood control." Flooding is increasing due to massive building on the Santa Rosa Plain upriver and channelization of the main river and its many tributaries.

What Has Happened to Our Creeks?

In 1957 the Water Agency began receiving federal funding, under the Flood Prevention Act, for Miller's flood control plan to channelize the creeks within fifty-seven thousand acres on the Santa Rosa plain.

That huge block of land was laid out in advance for the subdivisions, offices, and malls sprawling there today. Ironically, studies by Dr. David DeWalle of the Environmental Protection Agency indicate that rapid stormwater runoff from paving each new subdivision adds to flood levels downriver. Also, the channelized creeks have carried enormous amounts of silt from development directly into the Laguna de Santa Rosa—once a sixty-foot deep lake—filling it and destroying its flood deterrent capacity.

Over the years the Water Agency has kept a list that we finally obtained of about 120 flood control creek projects some using what Gaye LeBaron of *The Press Democrat* called "the murderous engineering mode" that may actually worsen flooding downriver. To me, this tragic list reveals the greatest overall loss of freshwater wetlands, vernal pools, wildlife, and fish habitat in the county's history.

Instead of simply requiring building setbacks to allow Sonoma's creeks to meander naturally, the Agency's traditional response has been to capture sections in concrete channels thereby destroying their natural beauty, decimating their salmon and songbird populations, and turning them into debris collectors which are costly to taxpayers to construct and maintain. Fifty-three of these creeks have received what the Agency calls "ultimate channelization"—straightening, removing the trees, planting Bermuda grass, and constructing concrete or rip-rap channels and steel fences. There are another sixty-nine with "less than ultimate" treatment. To our dismay, blanket permits for these projects have been routinely approved by the California Department of Fish and Game.

Recently thirteen miles of Santa Rosa Creek channelized during the concrete craze of the 1960s have been recognized as Santa Rosa's natural treasures and are now being restored for $55 million. Yet some of Windsor's beautiful oak-lined creeks are even now undergoing channelization. These creeks are wonderful community connectors, providing open space, oak forests, wildlife habitat, and a place for children to play while growing up.

Channelizing the Russian River "Conduit"

In preserving its Public Water Supply System, the Water Agency could have prevented enormous channel and watershed erosion by having a qualified fluvial geomorphologist (river expert) on its staff. Instead, their misguided flood control strategy has been to allow the mining firms to *channelize* the river, as with the creeks, deepening and straightening the main river channel from Coyote Dam to the Agency's water pumps at the Wohler Bridge. This is a costly mistake as the dam traps gravel and silt and releases sediment-free "hungry water" with enormous erosive power, adding to channel erosion and speeding floodwaters toward Guerneville. This strategy offers no protection for the 1,400 gravel-dependent wells within this crucial seventy miles below the dam. For many years the Agency labeled the river a "conduit," but on recent maps it has been redesignated a Public Water Supply Channel.

Equally astonishing, the Agency has made no plans to control its massive watershed erosion or to maintain the permeability of the watershed. US Geological Service records show that more than one million tons of topsoil are eroded from the watershed each average winter, about one thousand tons per square mile. During floods, this mud silts public water intakes along the

The Russian River: An Unmanaged and Unprotected Watershed

1,450 square miles in need of a comprehensive watershed and flood management program.

Gravel Mining

Dozens of deep gravel pits dug in the riverbed and flood plain from Ukiah to the Wohler Bridge have severely eroded and sunk the channel in places up to twenty vertical feet, undermining bridges, killing riparian forests, and contaminating wells.

Wastewater Discharge

1,400 drinking water wells that depend on gravel beds along the river are exposed to municipal wastewater discharges from Ukiah to Guerneville, plus polluted urban and farm runoff.

Severe Erosion

More than one million tons of topsoil and silt in an average winter discharge from the eroding watershed into the Pacific Ocean at Jenner. The silt creates a huge plume that spreads into Bodega Bay and Tomales Bay.

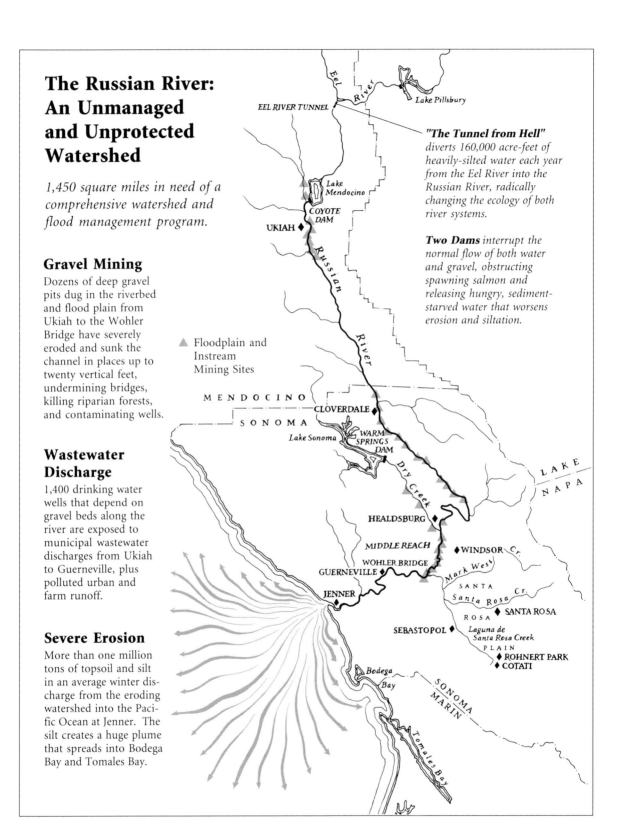

"The Tunnel from Hell" diverts 160,000 acre-feet of heavily-silted water each year from the Eel River into the Russian River, radically changing the ecology of both river systems.

Two Dams interrupt the normal flow of both water and gravel, obstructing spawning salmon and releasing hungry, sediment-starved water that worsens erosion and siltation.

▲ Floodplain and Instream Mining Sites

river and seals the infiltration ponds behind the Agency's wells at the Wohler Bridge, forcing them to excavate enormous layers of silt each spring.

An Agency engineer, Bob Morrison, sat on the Technical Advisory Committee for the county's 1981 and 1994 mining plans that allowed for the digging of a grotesque arc of huge gravel pits across the entire river basin. These are now plugged, eroding, and have the potential for blocking the aquifer half a mile above the Agency's own wells. Incredibly, even the Agency's existing and future well sites were designated for potential mining sites in the 1981 mining plan.

In 1995, 1996, and again in 1997, the Russian River was designated as one of the most threatened major rivers on the continent by the nonprofit river advocacy group American Rivers in Washington D.C. Their 1995 report stated:

The mouth of the Russian River at Jenner is clouded by plumes of toxic muddy silt (right) discharged into the blue Pacific during floods from the unmanaged and severely eroding watershed.

> *The Russian River, as it winds through the wine country and redwood groves of Sonoma County, has been designated as the eighth most threatened river on the continent. It provides a classic example of how incremental, unregulated impacts of human development—dams, water diversions, dredging, pollution and agriculture—have decimated the legendary wild steelhead trout and Coho salmon runs, increasing runoff which contributed to the 1995 and 1986 catastrophic floods, threatening the gravel aquifer which supplies clean drinking water to 500,000 people.*

But the most telling blow is that the California State Water Resources Control Board indicated that the Agency has mismanaged the Public Trust resources of the river and may disallow new allocations until a watershed management program, a salmon recovery program, and a cumulative impact study of water diversions for the Russian River are completed.

After forty-seven years there are signs of change. Randy Poole, formerly an engineer with the Marin Municipal Water District, was hired in 1994 as Sonoma County Water Agency manager. He replaced Bob Beach, who retired and was retained to work on the Potter Valley Project. His first public statement at a landmark public workshop in March 1995, attended by representatives from five North Coast counties, was to announce his "commitment to help save the Russian River." It made headlines. His first act was to hire a fisheries biologist and to undertake the restoration of creeks. Poole hired a water conservation team and adopted an estuary management plan and, in 1997, a *Russian River Action Plan*, forestalling an Endangered listing on steelhead. The Agency now publishes a quarterly *Russian River Bulletin* but there is still no Master Plan, and Poole's advisors include the same engineers whose past policies almost made Sonoma County a replica of San Jose. As *The Press Democrat* editorialized in 1996, the Agency must get used to environmental activism, involve the public in its decisions, and improve its public relations.

Why a Plan to Manage the Russian River Watershed Is Urgently Needed

A few years ago, acerbic Bruce Anderson, editor of the Mendocino County *Anderson Valley Observer* and an outspoken opponent of suburban sprawl, advised his readers to "cover your children's eyes" when driving along the Highway 101 corridor through greater Santa Rosa.

In addition to mega-auto signs and mega-auto rows, there are sixteen (at last count) fake-Italian bell towers trumpeting national mall, motel, and fast food outlets at a Rohnert Park offramp in an area the county once zoned for open space. Before that it was prime agricultural land used for growing seeds and a natural flood retention area.

For all its great natural wealth and beauty, Sonoma County has no Master Plan for its greatest resource, the Russian River. For its size of one million acres (the largest Bay Area county), the county has the lowest percentage of permanently protected farmlands, wildlands, and open space in the Bay Area, according to the Bay Area Greenbelt Alliance. Thousands of acres of prime farmland, nearly one hundred square miles, have been surrendered to intense urban sprawl along both sides of Highway 101, where much of the polluted urban runoff and wastewater discharges into the Russian River.

The tasteless urban growth along Highway 101 from Windsor south to Petaluma is a classic example of hop-scotch, uncoordinated land-use planning between cities and counties competing for tax dollars. Freeway-dominated development is exceedingly unfriendly toward pedestrians or cyclists. Commuter trains are years away, although the old railroad right-of-way has been publicly acquired and a balanced transportation bond issue proposed for 1998.

Santa Rosa's new expansionist general plan, "Vision 2020," was pushed through the city planning office by what the environmental newspaper *EIR Reporter,* published by Juliana Doms, called the "banks', builders', and brokers' lobby." This plan increases Santa Rosa's population from the present 130,000 people to 205,000 by 2020 with no gridlock, stormwater, or wastewater solutions in sight. In 1994 a headline in *The Press Democrat* proclaimed "In Fear of Sprawl," citing a survey of citizens in every city of the county who fear for their quality of life.

A Prescription for Change: Slow Growth and Take Back the Water Agency

For more than forty years the county supervisors and the Water Agency have made unsustainable Russian River policy based on short term economic gain, strongly supported by powerful mining, agricultural, and development interests. There is nothing in the state's charter making the Water Agency the ecological steward of their watershed or protector of the gravel sources of safe public drinking water supplies below their dams.

Krista Rector, water committee chair for the local Sierra Club, has listed various options to reform the Water Agency: removing supervisors as Water Agency directors and electing directors by direct vote, establishing a river authority that would take over the management of the entire watershed, and launching an initiative that controls land clearing, prohibits gravel mining, and outlaws discharges of wastewater and stormwater in a River Protection and Meander Corridor between the Agency's dams and their pumps.

Fake Italian bell towers off Highway 101 at Rohnert Park clutter what was supposed to be Greenbelt and wetlands. In winter the polluted urban runoff from all the paved areas drains into the Russian River adding to downriver flooding.

Instead of degrading the public's rivers and creeks to promote overdevelopment, a reinvented Water Agency would become the steward of our watersheds and ecosystems to ensure a better quality of life and true long-term economic stability for all the people of Sonoma and neighboring counties. My own opinion is that nothing good will happen for the river until mining is banned and the mining firms can no longer exert their influence on the supervisors, the Water Agency, or the Russian River.

Beyond Sprawl

A STATEWIDE AND SONOMA COUNTY PERSPECTIVE

The walled city of Windsor, elevated on pads above the flood-plain and divided into isolated cells, illustrates the sad results of devel-oper-driven sprawl, similar to the freeway-dependent suburbs of Los Angeles. Windsor was invented by specu-lators and the county supervisors who sacri-ficed prime vineyards and rare vernal pools for tract developments. Windsor's sprawl is challenged by escapees from other sprawling cities who are demand-ing slow growth and firm Urban Growth Boundaries.

In an appeal to all Californians to help change the state's patterns of growth, four diverse organizations reached consensus and published the monograph, "Beyond Sprawl," in 1995. Its conclusions may be obtained from its sponsors: Bank of America, California Resources Agency, Greenbelt Alliance, and Low Income Housing Fund.

"Beyond Sprawl" is a guideline that, if followed, will protect public health and the economic, agricultural, and environmental vitality of California. The report says that the state must move beyond sprawl to more strategically managed "smart" growth.

The report concludes that there is no long-term financial benefit from automobile-dominated, leap-frog growth that harms our air, water, farmlands, wetlands, and landscapes. The report predicts economic prosperity and stability from greater investment and better jobs by attracting firms that value carefully planned growth and its resulting quality of life.

Sonoma County is moving in the right direction in protecting its agricultural land and open space from sprawl. At the same time that Marin enacted its revolutionary agricultural zoning in 1973 with sixty-acre minimum lot sizes, Sonoma did the same. However, this zoning can and has been changed by a vote of the supervisors.

In 1990, led by Supervisors Janet Nicholas and Jim Harberson, environmental leaders Joan Vilms, George Ellman, and George Snyder, and members of the business community, the voters passed a quarter-cent sales tax for land conservation that raises some eleven million dollars per year. The county hired David Hanson, who had run Marin's Open Space District, to manage the Sonoma County Agricultural Preservation and Open Space District. To date, more than 21,000 acres have been acquired by purchasing development rights or the

land outright. The goal is to enroll 100,000 acres. However, the County is severely lacking in large blocks of wildlands which protect habitats and can also be used for hiking.

In 1996, Sonoma County voters adopted a network of Urban Growth Boundaries for several cities, firmly fixing their boundaries for twenty years. However, Windsor did not vote and Santa Rosa expanded its boundaries prior to the vote. A companion measure to prevent development in unincorporated areas also passed by a wide margin. The effort was led by Krista Shaw, a young environmentalist born in Healdsburg, who represented the Bay Area Greenbelt Alliance. Both decisions show that voters are more than willing to move Sonoma County land use "beyond sprawl." The Supervisors and City Councils had better pay attention.

CHAPTER SIXTEEN

The Russian River Gravel Wars

The land interests in California, to a significant extent, have bought, intimidated, compromised, and supplied key officials in state and local government to the point where these interests govern the governors.

— Power and Land in California,
The Ralph Nader Task Force Report, 1971 Draft

T he darkly treacherous battles to save the Russian River are far different from the gentlemanly struggles that saved the National Seashore
in Marin County. In Sonoma we are pitted against the state's most
powerful mining interests that supply Russian River gravel to five counties—
Sonoma, Marin, Mendocino, Napa, and Solano. Shortly after establishing
the Hop Kiln Winery in 1975, I joined in a lawsuit with twenty other angry
ranchers on Dry Creek and the Middle Reach who had lost land and wells as
the river banks collapsed into gravel pits during repeated floods. Our water
tables had dropped many feet, drying up our vineyards. Some twenty-five
attorneys led by Ed Wilson of Healdsburg were involved in the lawsuit
against both the supervisors and the mining firms. We finally won in 1979
on the courthouse steps with a cash settlement.

That was a big mistake. We had failed to bell the cat—the Sonoma
County Supervisors who approved mining permits and the compliant
Sonoma County Water Agency engineers.

However, there was a positive result: the ominous clanging of the gravel
dredgers was silenced by our lawsuit while the supervisors prepared an
Aggregate Resources Management (ARM) Plan. In 1980 I worked on that
plan that set aside nearly the entire west side of the river for five miles along
Westside Road, including Griffin Vineyards and those of several other wineries, as a permanent Agricultural and Aquifer Preservation Zone.

Until 1995, the processing plant for Kaiser Sand and Gravel Co. was in the center of the Middle Reach aquifer of the Russian River, away from the main road. This firm is owned by Hanson of London, England, one of the largest multi-national mining firms; it predicts that California will be the largest market for aggregate in the nation.

Betrayal by the Supervisors

The plan promised to phase gravel mining out of the river and into hard rock quarries. The supervisors adopted it in 1981, but by 1989 the plan was a joke. We learned that the Board, led by Supervisor Nick Esposti, was proposing to amend the ARM Plan and to give Syar Industries a permit to dredge a fifty-acre gravel pit in the Preservation Zone sold to Syar by Rodney Strong Winery.

We felt that we and the public had been betrayed by our county supervisors. We had only one vote among the county supervisors; and it seemed that the Planning Department, the Water Agency, and the Water Quality Control Board were stacked with "good old boys" who were unquestioning supporters of the mining firms. In response I spent several days organizing the wineries on Westside Road in case we had to file a lawsuit. We called our group Westside Road Wineries, Russian River Task Force.

After assessing the situation, my prognosis yet again was "nearly hopeless." However we had one strong ally on the Board of Supervisors, Ernie Carpenter, who kept us up-to-date on the mining companies' maneuvers.

This campaign ad was published in Sonoma County newspapers in 1990 by Westside Road Wineries after the supervisors opened five miles of prime vineyards in an aquifer Preservation Zone on our side of the river to deep-pit gravel mining. This betrayal triggered the gravel wars, seven years of litigation against the County and the mining firms.

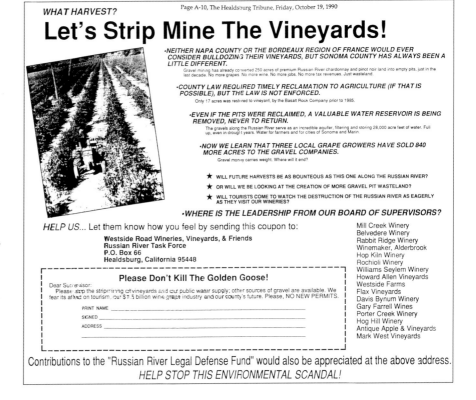

WHAT HARVEST?

Page A-10, The Healdsburg Tribune, Friday, October 19, 1990

Let's Strip Mine The Vineyards!

- NEITHER NAPA COUNTY OR THE BORDEAUX REGION OF FRANCE WOULD EVER CONSIDER BULLDOZING THEIR VINEYARDS, BUT SONOMA COUNTY HAS ALWAYS BEEN A LITTLE DIFFERENT.

  Gravel mining has already converted 250 acres of premium Russian River chardonnay and pinot noir land into empty pits, just in the last decade. No more grapes. No more wine. No more jobs. No more tax revenues. Just wasteland.

- COUNTY LAW REQUIRED TIMELY RECLAMATION TO AGRICULTURE (IF THAT IS POSSIBLE), BUT THE LAW IS NOT ENFORCED.

  Only 17 acres was restored to vineyard, by the Basalt Rock Company prior to 1985.

- EVEN IF THE PITS WERE RECLAIMED, A VALUABLE WATER RESERVOIR IS BEING REMOVED, NEVER TO RETURN.

  The gravels along the Russian River serve as an incredible aquifer, filtering and storing 28,000 acre feet of water. Full up, even in drought years. Water for farmers and for cities of Sonoma and Marin.

- NOW WE LEARN THAT THREE LOCAL GRAPE GROWERS HAVE SOLD 840 MORE ACRES TO THE GRAVEL COMPANIES.

  Gravel money carries weight. Where will it end?

  ★ WILL FUTURE HARVESTS BE AS BOUNTEOUS AS THIS ONE ALONG THE RUSSIAN RIVER?

  ★ OR WILL WE BE LOOKING AT THE CREATION OF MORE GRAVEL PIT WASTELAND?

  ★ WILL TOURISTS COME TO WATCH THE DESTRUCTION OF THE RUSSIAN RIVER AS EAGERLY AS THEY VISIT OUR WINERIES?

- WHERE IS THE LEADERSHIP FROM OUR BOARD OF SUPERVISORS?

HELP US... Let them know how you feel by sending this coupon to:

Westside Road Wineries, Vineyards, & Friends
Russian River Task Force
P.O. Box 66
Healdsburg, California 95448

Mill Creek Winery
Belvedere Winery
Rabbit Ridge Winery
Winemaker, Alderbrook
Hop Kiln Winery
Rochioli Winery
Williams Seylem Winery
Howard Allen Vineyards
Westside Farms
Flax Vineyards
Davis Bynum Winery
Gary Farrell Wines
Porter Creek Winery
Hog Hill Winery
Antique Apple & Vineyards
Mark West Vineyards

Please Don't Kill The Golden Goose!

Dear Supervisor:
Please stop the strip mining of vineyards and our public water supply; other sources of gravel are available. We fear its affect on tourism, our $1.5 billion wine grape industry and our county's future. Please, NO NEW PERMITS.

PRINT NAME _____

SIGNED _____

ADDRESS _____

Contributions to the "Russian River Legal Defense Fund" would also be appreciated at the above address.
HELP STOP THIS ENVIRONMENTAL SCANDAL!

Belling the Cat

Having been through one prolonged mining lawsuit, I was reluctant to start another. So my neighbor, Tom Rochioli, and I met with Supervisor Nick Esposti—the "Gravel Czar"—and asked him to oppose the mining permit for Syar. He told us in so many words that the supervisors were going to give Syar Industries a permit to dredge a deep gravel pit in the vineyard they now owned adjacent to the river, and that there was nothing we could do to stop it.

Those were fighting words.

After leaving Esposti, I met with Barry Dugan, staunch editor of *The Healdsburg Tribune.* I explained, "Barry, thirteen wineries plus several neighbors are filing a lawsuit against the supervisors and Syar Industries. The aquifer they want to dredge without an environmental review filters and stores the drinking water supply for Marin and Sonoma counties and our farm and domestic wells. It's a county preserve, designated and protected as such. If they get away with this, eventually two thousand acres of premium Sonoma County chardonnay and pinot noir vineyards, valued at $40 million, overlaying the aquifer could be dredged, leaving gaping pits taxed as a wasteland."

Barry gave this news a full-page spread with big headlines and a map. For weeks there were stories and maps in *The Tribune* and *The Press*

Democrat. For the first time the entire county was learning about their aquifer and where their drinking water came from. Our Russian River Task Force hired attorney Susan Brandt-Hawley, an expert on the California Environmental Quality Act, who was unafraid to take on large corporations or their allies. The Sonoma Sierra Club chapter, led by Len Swensen, joined our lawsuits which sought to require Syar to complete an Environmental Impact Review (EIR) before receiving permits to dredge. In July 1990 Susan filed our lawsuit in Superior Court.

Susan Brandt-Hawley, an expert in environmental law and an attorney for many mining and logging opponents, speaks to the Russian River Environmental Forum. On her right is Aldaron Laird, river restoration consultant and ecologist from Arcata.

To pay legal bills and our hydrology expert, Dr. Robert Curry, the thirteen wineries put on a two-day fundraiser at the Hop Kiln Winery. Chef Todd Muir of Madronna Manor grilled salmon for four hundred people. We etched "Save the Russian River" on wine glasses and held an auction of premium wines contributed by wineries throughout the county. Pam and Ron Kaiser put on a breakfast at Westside Farms the next day, and we raised enough money to pay our bills. (Later, with each successful lawsuit, our expenses were required to be refunded by the mining firms.) During the year, our members endured harassment, intimidation, threats, and boycotts. These were reported to the police, the press, and the District Attorney.

Much to our dismay, groups of farmers who were selling or leasing their river frontage for gravel mining became our most vocal opponents.

Before the battle started, we had tried to take the precaution of copying every gravel mining packet in the planning department in case they were ever purged of vital agreements. But we had been too late. One of Syar's approved mining plans was already missing from both county and state files. Indignant, I sat down in county mining planner Bob Gaiser's office and vowed not to move until finally they were produced. We complained to the Grand Jury and to the press. The Grand Jury documented how the county was allowing excessive gravel extraction without monitoring or collecting the required fees. Susan discovered that the County Counsel even let Syar's attorney write the conditions of their mining Use Permit.

Gravel vs. Grapes

Susan invited the *San Francisco Daily Journal,* with distribution to law and judicial offices in the Bay Area, to send their best investigative reporters

Gravel Pit

Gravel Pit

Gravel Pit

Gravel Pit

Gravel Pit

Gravel Pit

Russian River

Gravel Pit

to see first-hand the destruction of the river. Their report, "Gravel vs. Grapes," published on October 15, 1990, was the educational and legal tool we needed. We sent copies to all the major newspapers throughout the state.

Thanks to Susan's strategies, we won this long legal battle in Superior Court, and Syar was ordered to do an environmental review as required by law. The firm lost its appeal to the State Supreme Court. The case made history and is widely quoted in other legal cases. The ninety-six page Grand Jury Report of 1990, which referred to our lawsuit, brought in outside auditors who finally exposed the county's practices in this mining scandal. The embarrassed supervisors curtailed deep-pit mining for four years while they prepared a new ARM Plan which they adopted in December 1994, costing the miners a half million dollars.

We had belled the cat. We had successfully challenged a mighty mining firm and exposed their danger to the wine-grape industry, the regional water supply, and the river. And we had belled Esposti. He decided not to run for a fifth term.

The slim and graceful Russian River (far right) meanders past the huge, water-filled pits left over from gravel dredging. Eight hundred acres of eroding mud-lined gravel pits plug the Middle Reach aquifer, destroying future well sites and severely weakening its natural filtering capabilities. Ripping up this 11,000-year-old aquifer is as shortsighted as clear cutting the ancient forests of the North Coast.

The Healdsburg Tribune

Enterprise & Scimitar, Healdsburg, CA

Our 127th Year   Number 17 ©

Wednesday, November 27, 1991   50¢

Kaiser permits ruled invalid

Eastside Rd. gravel pits not reclaimed to ag.

by DAN MURPHY
Tribune Staff Writer

Just two days after the county District Attorney slapped the company with a $1 million lawsuit for mining without permits, Sonoma County planners ruled last Thursday that Kaiser Sand & Gravel lacks a valid permit to mine terrace pits along the Russian River.

But Kaiser officials appealed the decision to the Board of Supervisors Monday. Kaiser plant manager Dennis Ripple said mining will continue at its Pombo gravel pits until county supervisors make a decision.

"Sonoma County has been working on these issues for years," said Ripple.

"Never in all that time has there been any finding that we did not have valid permits."

The 4-1 vote marked the first time, after nearly 30 hours of public hearings, that the commission has said the company lacks a permit for Kaiser's mining.

Kaiser officials, apparently caught off guard by the ruling and waited until Monday to announce their decision to appeal.

"I think that it was a step forward to bring more sanity to control," said Dr. Martin Griffin, chairman of a West County citizen's task force that opposed local gravel companies applying for new permits until reclamation of gravel pits occurred.

"I was surprised, too, that the commission realized that this precious resource has been abused," the county has been very slow in responding to the problem up to this point. Today was a great first step."

River bridge may need rebuilding

Footings under Highway 101 bridge eroding

by BARRY W. DUGAN
Tribune Editor

Years of gravel mining on the Russian River have eroded the footings under the Highway 101 bridge at Healdsburg, and will require costly repairs and possibly a total replacement of the span, according to state transportation officials.

The four-lane bridge over the river is on the state Department of Transportation's "top 20" list to be studied this year, according to Caltrans engineer Bill Lindsey.

In addition, the state agency is also concerned about the seismic safety of the bridge, along with hundreds of others in the state, after the Loma Prieta earthquake.

According to Caltrans, and consultants working for Sonoma County, the river channel under the bridge has dropped 17 feet since it was built in 1959.

Officials say that gravel mining has contributed to the degradation, or lowering, of the river bed in the Healdsburg area.

A Caltrans document states that "Current and historic mining practices have probably aided this degradation...the channel degradation at this structure has exposed the piles below the bridge footings. If this degradation continues, the bridge will require costly mitigation."

Lindsey told the Tribune that the Healdsburg bridge appears on the state's "critical scour list" and needs to be replaced or repaired.

THE PRESS DEMOCRAT, WEDNESDAY, NOVEMBER 20, 1991

Report: Mining changing nature of Russian River

By CHRIS COURSEY
Staff Writer

Gravel is being mined from the Russian River faster than it can naturally be replaced, causing the riverbed to drop as much as 20 feet in some areas and possibly sucking water from the aquifer that supplies nearby wells.

The changing river also threatens the support structure of the Highway 101 bridge over the river at Healdsburg.

Those and other possible impacts of gravel mining are included in the preliminary findings of a report given to Sonoma County supervisors Monday. The report is part of a $440,000 effort to rewrite guidelines on how gravel is mined in Sonoma County.

A Caltrans spokesman said Tuesday the change in the river's flow has exposed footings at the base of concrete supports of the 101 bridge, but a September inspection found "no hazard."

adjacent aquifer and into the river. During periods of high water, the opposite occurs, with the swollen river recharging the aquifer.

While the drop in the river's bed raises questions that haven't been entirely answered by studies thus far, Jordan did indicate Warm Springs Dam has played a major role in the changing conditions of the middle reach.

By stabilizing Dry Creek, the dam virtually has cut off Dry Creek as a source of new gravel washing into the river, he said. While previous studies estimated 770,000 tons of gravel entered the middle reach each year, the latest estimate is just 250,000 tons.

The Russian River's bed at the mouth of Dry Creek now is 20 feet lower than it was in 1940, Jordan said. Beneath the Highway 101 bridge, upstream from Dry Creek, the riverbed is 10 feet lower than 50 years ago

Healdsburg, CA   25¢

Wednesday, January 16, 1991

Grand jury blasts gravel monitoring

County failing to collect fees for regulation

by BARRY W. DUGAN
Tribune Editor

Sonoma County officials have failed to adequately monitor and regulate gravel mining along the middle reach of the Russian River, according to a grand jury report.

Critics claim the report has been suppressed by county officials. But a planning official said he just hasn't gotten around to editing the report.

Gravel critics had called for just such a report earlier this year, but county officials denied the request.

"I think the grand jury report documents in great detail repeated abuses of public funds by the Planning Department," said Dr. Martin Griffin, one of the leaders of the Westside Road Wineries Russian River group. "They've confused..."

on the middle reach aquifer, the nine-mile long, gravel-rich basin that recharges many private and public drinking water wells along the river.

"They've given unfair advantages to them by not requiring them to pay monitoring or inspection fees," he said. "They've unfairly aided gravel..."

The Healdsburg Tribune

Enterprise & Scimitar, Healdsburg, CA

127th Year   Number 13 ©

Wednesday, November 13, 1991   50¢

Gravel firms accused of price-fixing

Boss claims he was fired for not going along

by BARRY W. DUGAN
Tribune Editor

The two biggest players in the county's nearly $30-million per year gravel industry are being accused of a price-rigging scheme that has allegedly caused some aggregate prices to double in Sonoma County over the past three years.

In a lawsuit filed last week in Sonoma County Superior Court, former Kaiser Sand & Gravel executive Rudy Gonsalves claims Kaiser and Svar Industries plotted...

West, Inc., did not return Tribune phone calls to his Dallas office.

Svar officials did not return several Tribune phone calls Monday.

The suit claims fraudulent concealment; restraint of trade; wrongful termination in violation of public policy; and breach of contract.

The lawsuit seeks up to $600,000 in damages for Gonsalves, 64, who was fired from his job that paid up to $200,000...

equipment operator.

Gonsalves' attorney, Daniel Bartley, said Monday that some of the evidence needed to prove his clients claims remains in Kaiser's possession. "I gave them every opportunity to disprove that there was a concerted effort at price fixing, but they elected not to do that," he said.

The alleged price-fixing scheme has cost county builders and developers millions of dollars, Bartley said.

"There's a lot of money, in...

A Second Lawsuit

In 1993 the county supervisors again made a decision against the public interest that led to a second successful Russian River Task Force lawsuit. The supervisors used a standard tactic of amending the old Aggregate Resources Management Plan of 1981 before the new scientific one was completed and gave Syar a permit to dredge a new thirty-five-acre pit (Phase II Pit) far too close to the riverbank without any study of whether the soft levee bank would collapse in a flood. During a tumultuous permit hearing, my wife Joyce read a river poem, accompanied by a recorded clanking of the gravel dredging machines, to the groaning throng of gravel miners, earning her a supportive editorial in *The Healdsburg Tribune*.

With new information from the State Lands Commission and Aldaron Laird, a river expert, Susan filed a new court injunction to stop Syar, but they managed to dredge most of the pit before the judge ordered a study of the safety of their levees. Even worse, before the study could ever get started, all of Syar levees did rupture, as predicted, in the floods of 1995 and again in 1997. Millions of gallons of Healdsburg's sewage wastewater stored in an adjacent gravel pit owned by Syar spilled into the river above the county's drinking-water intakes. Only the depth of the wells into the gravel aquifers averted catastrophe for the Sonoma County Water Agency and the water consumers in Marin and Sonoma counties.

Newspaper headlines (opposite page) provided valuable public education. To further protect the public's interest we created the Russian River Task Force for mining litigation, Friends of the Russian River for education and litigation against polluters and laggard regulatory agencies, and the Russian River Environmental Forum for training agency personnel and citizen leaders.

Gravel Pit / Wastewater Storage Pond

Breached Levee

Russian River

Sewage Treatmaent Ponds

During the flood of 1995, this large gravel pit (center), used by Healdsburg's sewage treatment plant (right, with treatment ponds) for wastewater storage, ruptured its levees, spilling some 800 million gallons of wastewater into the river (bottom of photo) above the county's drinking water wells. Litigation by Friends of the Russian River forced an end to such use.

Threats to Public Health on the Middle Reach of the Russian River

Not only is the ancient gravel aquifer, the region's source of naturally pure drinking water, being plundered by miners, but the river is also being used as a conduit for dumping wastewater, stormwater, and farm chemicals into the ocean.

There is no overall flood management program for the Russian River, which now has the highest rate of repetitive flooding west of the Mississippi. The river is being further exploited to promote rapid growth on the Santa Rosa Plain, which is already built far beyond its human carrying capacity.

▲ Mining Pits in the Aquifer

● Municipal Drinking Water Wells in the Aquifer

Drinking Water

Half a million people in Sonoma and Marin, served by nine water districts, depend on the intact gravel aquifer of the Russian River for safe drinking water. Many municipal wells (circles) are located on the Middle Reach. If these wells fail, then the cost of artificial drinking water treatment plants is estimated at $300 million.

Mining Pits

Floodplain mining destroys the gravel aquifer that supports abundant small organisms. These help cleanse drinking water and are an essential link in the food web that supports all life in the river.

Steelhead Fishery

Steelhead, salmon, and harbor seals (at Jenner) are indicators of the biological health of the river. But 90% of these fish are gone and some seals are diseased. Minute combinations of estrogenic chemicals may affect human and animal health and reproduction.

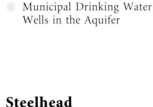

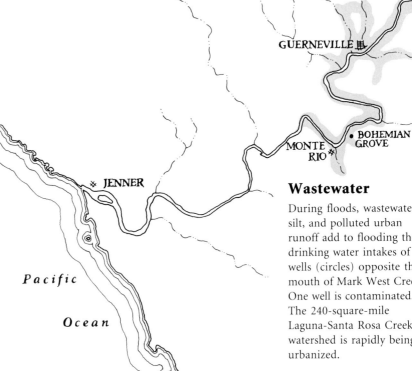

Pacific

Ocean

JENNER

GUERNEVILLE

MONTE RIO

BOHEMIAN GROVE

Wastewater

During floods, wastewater, silt, and polluted urban runoff add to flooding the drinking water intakes of wells (circles) opposite the mouth of Mark West Creek. One well is contaminated. The 240-square-mile Laguna-Santa Rosa Creek watershed is rapidly being urbanized.

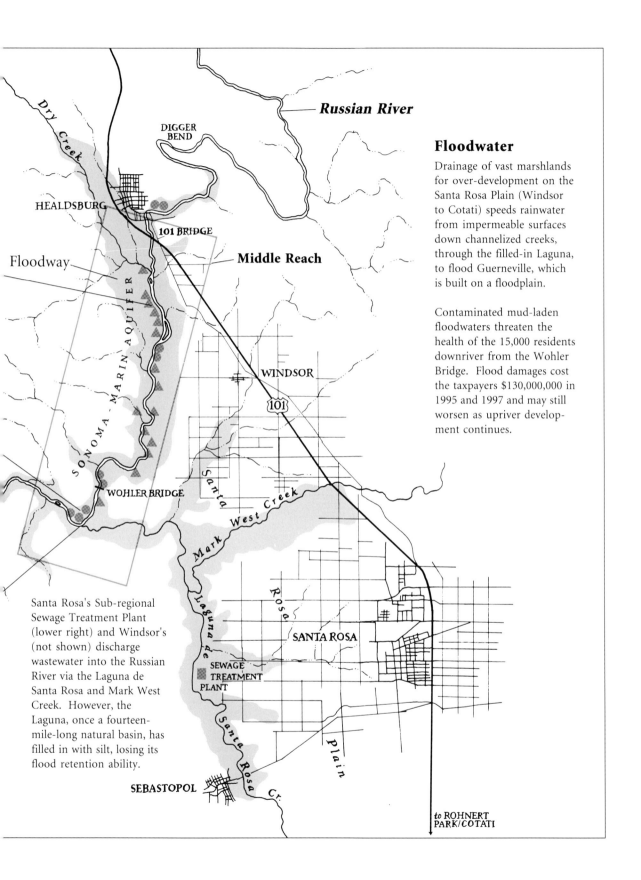

Russian River

DIGGER
BEND

HEALDSBURG

101 BRIDGE

Floodway

Middle Reach

WINDSOR

101

Dry Creek

SONOMA - MARIN AQUIFER

WOHLER BRIDGE

Santa

Mark West Creek

Laguna de

Rosa

SANTA ROSA

SEWAGE
TREATMENT
PLANT

Plain

Santa Rosa Cr.

SEBASTOPOL

to ROHNERT
PARK/COTATI

Floodwater

Drainage of vast marshlands
for over-development on the
Santa Rosa Plain (Windsor
to Cotati) speeds rainwater
from impermeable surfaces
down channelized creeks,
through the filled-in Laguna,
to flood Guerneville, which
is built on a floodplain.

Contaminated mud-laden
floodwaters threaten the
health of the 15,000 residents
downriver from the Wohler
Bridge. Flood damages cost
the taxpayers $130,000,000 in
1995 and 1997 and may still
worsen as upriver development continues.

Santa Rosa's Sub-regional
Sewage Treatment Plant
(lower right) and Windsor's
(not shown) discharge
wastewater into the Russian
River via the Laguna de
Santa Rosa and Mark West
Creek. However, the
Laguna, once a fourteen-
mile-long natural basin, has
filled in with silt, losing its
flood retention ability.

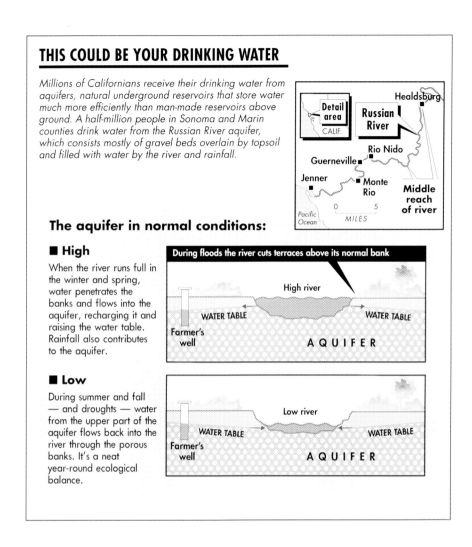

THIS COULD BE YOUR DRINKING WATER

Millions of Californians receive their drinking water from aquifers, natural underground reservoirs that store water much more efficiently than man-made reservoirs above ground. A half-million people in Sonoma and Marin counties drink water from the Russian River aquifer, which consists mostly of gravel beds overlain by topsoil and filled with water by the river and rainfall.

The aquifer in normal conditions:

■ High

When the river runs full in the winter and spring, water penetrates the banks and flows into the aquifer, recharging it and raising the water table. Rainfall also contributes to the aquifer.

During floods the river cuts terraces above its normal bank

High river

WATER TABLE   WATER TABLE

Farmer's well

A Q U I F E R

■ Low

During summer and fall — and droughts — water from the upper part of the aquifer flows back into the river through the porous banks. It's a neat year-round ecological balance.

Low river

WATER TABLE   WATER TABLE

Farmer's well

A Q U I F E R

Detail area
CALIF.

Russian River

Healdsburg

Rio Nido

Guerneville

Jenner

Monte Rio

Middle reach of river

Pacific Ocean

0   5
MILES

A New Campaign Strategy: Drinking Water

In addition to lawsuits, we could see that to win the war we needed a new strategy, one that would further educate the public on the need for safe, clean, gravel-filtered, natural drinking water. We had to bring the Sonoma County Water Agency's incompetence in river management under intense scrutiny by the public and by the Agency's water contractors. I knew from my own contaminated wells that they were risking the quality of drinking water for their half-million consumers. They had even ignored the 1973 warning by their own consultant, H. A. Einstein, famous hydrologist and brother of Albert, to "get mining out of the Russian River" or risk contaminating their wells.

We studied everything about the river we could get our hands on. We

The impact of mining:

The gravel of the Russian River aquifer, both under the river and the terraces on either side, is a mother lode that has been tapped by miners for more than a century. But critics say that mining is among the chief causes of ongoing damage to the aquifer.

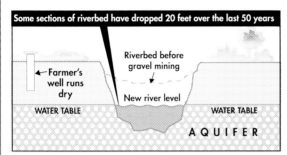

■ Instream mining

Until recent decades, most mining was in the riverbed where giant dredges scooped up tons of gravel, in some places lowering the riverbed 20 feet and more. This dropped the water table beyond the reach of many farmers' wells and contributed to the undermining of bridges.

■ Terrace

Since the 1960s, mining companies have shifted their operations to the terraces on either side of the river. There they have dug into the aquifer, creating pits as deep as 90 feet. Farmers complain that the pit walls silt up and act as dams, diminishing the natural recharge of the aquifer, dropping the water table and drying up wells. But the gravel companies claim their pit walls are porous, and blame damage on vineyard owners who they say farm too close to the river and cause erosion of the banks.

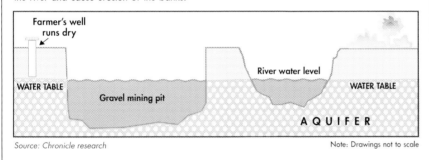

Source: Chronicle research   Note: Drawings not to scale

Harold Gilliam in-cluded this chart by Steve Kearsley of how an aquifer functions in his article "Wrestling Over the Russian River," published in the San Francisco Chronicle *on July 4, 1993. The article gained statewide attention and helped turn the battle our way.*

copied the records of the State Office of Clean Drinking Water in Santa Rosa and learned that the municipal wells serving Ukiah, Cloverdale, and Healds-burg were already depleted of gravel by excessive mining and were contami-nated during high water. A county survey found that thirty farm wells were drying up in the summer on the Middle Reach, but the Water Agency seemed unconcerned that mining and siltation were harming wells along the river from Coyote Dam south, including their own.

We visited wine-grape growers on the river who we thought were allies, but found otherwise. As on Tomales Bay, some farmers supported devel-opment. A number of wine-grape growers had sold their superb vineyard lands which overlay the gravel aquifer for deep-pit dredging: Tom Klein/ Rodney Strong, six hundred acres; Jordan Winery, eighty-seven acres; Geyser Peak, fifty-five acres; and Jay Benoist, seventy-two acres.

Gravel Pit

Gravel
Pit

Russian River

Gravel
Pit

These huge, mined-out gravel pits, which stretch for nine miles along the Middle Reach, are open wounds in the ancient, dying aquifer. In the top photo, the Russian River is the thin band on the left, and Kaiser's processing plant is in the center. The seventy-two acre Benoist pit, deeper than sea level, is at the bottom of the photo, located on the site of a former vineyard where I used to buy cabernet grapes.

Water covers the entire floodplain in the photo at right, merging the Russian River (left, center) with the gravel pits (right) during the floods of 1995. Mud-laden floodwaters backed up from the Wohler Narrows all the way to Healdsburg, rupturing every pit and spilling sewage effluent into the river. Despite severe flood damage downriver, the upriver causes were minimized by the supervisors and the Regional Water Quality Control Board.

Gravel
Pits

Gravel
Pit

Breach

*Russian
River*

Breach

Gravel
Pit

Breach

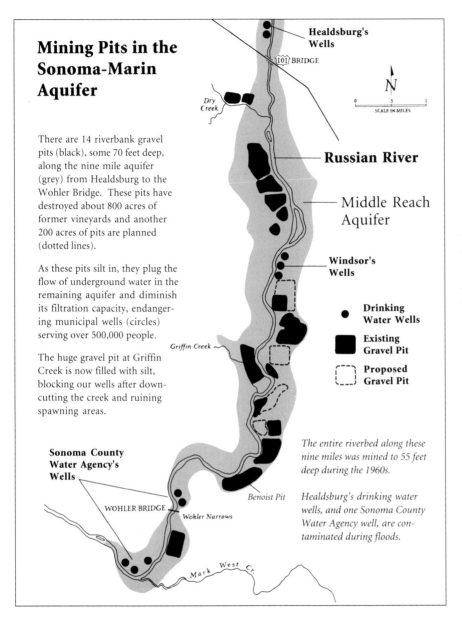

Mining Pits in the Sonoma-Marin Aquifer

There are 14 riverbank gravel pits (black), some 70 feet deep, along the nine mile aquifer (grey) from Healdsburg to the Wohler Bridge. These pits have destroyed about 800 acres of former vineyards and another 200 acres of pits are planned (dotted lines).

As these pits silt in, they plug the flow of underground water in the remaining aquifer and diminish its filtration capacity, endangering municipal wells (circles) serving over 500,000 people.

The huge gravel pit at Griffin Creek is now filled with silt, blocking our wells after downcutting the creek and ruining spawning areas.

Healdsburg's Wells

101 BRIDGE

Dry Creek

N

0   5   1
SCALE IN MILES

Russian River

Middle Reach Aquifer

Windsor's Wells

● **Drinking Water Wells**

■ **Existing Gravel Pit**

⌐ ⌐ **Proposed Gravel Pit**
└ ┘

Griffin Creek

The entire riverbed along these nine miles was mined to 55 feet deep during the 1960s.

Healdsburg's drinking water wells, and one Sonoma County Water Agency well, are contaminated during floods.

Sonoma County Water Agency's Wells

WOHLER BRIDGE

Wohler Narrows

Benoist Pit

Mark West Cr.

These deep, eroding pits are time bombs set to capture and reroute the river as soon as strong floodwaters overflow and break through sufficiently weak levees. Then the entire river bed will be drastically lowered, worsening downcutting and erosion, and threatening wells all along the river. It is estimated that about 50,000 acre feet of irreplaceable aquifer water storage and filtration capacity have been destroyed by excessive mining and siltation. Griffin Creek is used as a means of identifying the large gravel pit at its mouth.

On conferring with the State Lands Commission in Sacramento in 1991, we were told that there were thirty illegal mining operations on North Coast rivers, with no state permits. They gave us costly brochures showing that the state owned the beds of navigable rivers, such as the Russian, under the same Doctrine of Public Trust that protected the tidelands of California's coast from filling and dredging. In 1992 the State Attorney General on behalf of the State Lands Commission made history by suing Syar Industries for obstructing the Russian River and mining on state property *(see Appendix)*.

The piers of this railroad bridge crossing the Russian River at Healdsburg have been exposed by years of excessive gravel mining. Behind the bridge is Syar Industries' stockpile of raw river gravel. The nearby Highway 101 bridge, also undermined, was replaced at taxpayer expense in 1997. Despite these damages, Syar has applied to mine gravel instream at five sites above and below these bridges.

An Undermined Freeway Bridge:
The Turning Point

As the battle grew, we picked up allies right and left. In 1991 I received a call out of the blue from Al Regina, a Healdsburg plumber who lived near the river. "Do you know that the huge piers that support the Highway 101 bridge over the Russian River are undermined and the steel rods that go down to bedrock are exposed?" he asked me. Regina and I notified state inspectors who came out to look at the bridge underpinnings the next day. Syar officials were furious, claiming trespassing, but the news was out: the massive freeway bridge was in danger of collapsing in a flood or earthquake. Years of excessive gravel mining had lowered the riverbed about seventeen feet, undermining the piers. Caltrans estimated the cost to the taxpayers of replacing this bridge at $11 million. We recalled that the Grand Jury report had stated that the twice-annual aerial surveys of the riverbed, which could have prevented this disaster, had not been reported to the State Department of Mines and Geology for ten years by Bob Gaiser or Bob Morrison, despite repeated requests by that Department.

Photographs of the undermined bridges were published in *The Healdsburg Tribune.* The Army Corps brought some of its staff to take pictures. Engineer Cathy Crosset from Caltrans appeared before the supervisors to show slides of many bridges undermined along the Russian River by excessive mining. But Caltrans' pleas to cut back on instream mining were ignored by the county in the new mining plan of 1994.

Other newspapers began to take notice. There was a superb article in the *Sacramento Bee* in 1993 about the danger of river strip-mining statewide, and Harold Gilliam wrote an article for the Sunday *San Francisco Chronicle* called "Wrestling Over the Russian River" with full-page photos of the ruptured gravel pits. We circulated these articles to every state agency that was failing to manage the river.

Enter the Coastal Conservancy

In 1992, the California Coastal Conservancy became concerned with the sinking riverbed and the loss of public access to the river. Without realizing the political maelstrom they were entering, they decided to develop a Russian River Enhancement and Access Plan. Laurel Marcus, a river expert who had worked on the restoration of Audubon Canyon Ranch's Cypress Grove Marsh, Olema Marsh, and Walker Creek in Marin County, was appointed project coordinator. She hired Karen Gaffney of Circuit Riders, a non-profit river restoration group, to prepare aerial maps; these revealed that the river had lost about seventy percent of its riparian forest habitat. They then hired the renowned firm of Philip Williams and Associates, which had done the study for the restoration of Tomales Bay, to develop a plan to restore the Russian River. (This superb hydrological study is available from the Coastal Conservancy.) To review the plan, Laurel immediately formed a broad-based Technical Advisory Committee which included the mining firms—even a paid lobbyist, Nick Tibbits, who disputed much of the plan. Some meetings turned into shouting matches.

Laurel Marcus (right), head of the Coastal Conservancy's Russian River Enhancement Plan, leads a field trip through the Alexander Valley in 1995 to study endangered wells, eroding instream strip-mining sites, collapsing river banks, and dying riparian forests. To her right are advisors Jerry Waxman and Kim Cordell.

The Conservancy nevertheless completed an access and estuary study, and volunteers were enlisted to clean up a huge garbage dump in the river below the Water Agency wells to create a beautiful new access, Steelhead Beach County Park. Their enhancement plan incorporated all reaches of the river in Sonoma and Mendocino counties, but in particular focused on the deep pits of the Middle Reach with recommendations to restore the meanders and to prevent "pit capture." The Conservancy's study was bitterly opposed by mining firms and others, and the process was stalled. In 1996 Laurel resigned and the Conservancy decided not to continue the enhancement plan.

The Wastewater Threat—Mark West Creek

My dad once considered Mark West Creek and Santa Rosa Creek, which drain the Santa Rosa plain, among the finest steelhead tributaries of the Russian River. I'm grateful he never learned that the state now considers Mark West Creek one of their most polluted waterways. I have frequently stopped on the narrow bridge on Wohler Road and looked over, only to be sickened by the sight of the pea-green-to-black, frothy, lifeless water.

Mark West Creek and Santa Rosa Creek join two miles before entering the Russian River. From October through March, Mark West Creek carries up to twenty million gallons a day of highly treated wastewater, discharged from huge storage ponds at Santa Rosa's and Windsor's sewage treatment plants. Santa Rosa's tertiary effluent, treated at enormous cost, runs for miles through the Laguna de Santa Rosa, where it is again polluted by failing septic tanks, manure and farm-chemical runoff, and ever-increasing polluted urban runoff from these growing cities.

Manager Miles Ferris drinks tertiary treated sewage wastewater from a beaker at the huge Santa Rosa Sanitary District plant in the Laguna that serves Santa Rosa, Sebastopol, Rohnert Park, and Cotati. Unfortunately, the expensively treated wastewater is recontaminated as it flows for fifteen miles through the polluted Laguna and Mark West Creek into the Russian River. The treated wastewater is now in great demand for agriculture and Geysers recharge.

By 1985 Santa Rosa's urban growth had exceeded its sewage treatment capacity, and it illegally released 750 million gallons of stored wastewater down the Laguna, through Mark West Creek, and into the Russian River. In retaliation Tom Lynch of Guerneville, dubbed the "Manure Man," dumped a load of manure on Santa Rosa's courthouse steps, gaining national coverage for the illegal spill. But Santa Rosa's destructive growth continued.

On a tour of the Santa Rosa plant in 1993, river activist Brenda Adelman and I gasped as we watched manager Miles Ferris drink a cup of treated wastewater. I said, "Miles, now we don't have to monitor the river; we'll simply monitor you." But Miles or anyone else would be crazy to drink water from Mark West Creek at any time of the year: its waters may contain sewage nutrients, coliforms, viruses, and chemicals.

The use of Mark West Creek to carry both the wastewater and polluted stormwater ("non-point pollution") for 200,000 people is intolerable by any public health standards. Aerial photos show that it connects the regional sewage plant with the regional drinking water system. For example, during floods polluted wastewater and stormwater enter the turbulent Russian River directly opposite the Water Agency's wells and huge infiltration ponds, contaminating them with muddy water. A half-million people depend on

Mark West Creek

Flood Waters from Mark West Creek

Russian River

Well

Well

Flooded Infiltration Ponds

Well

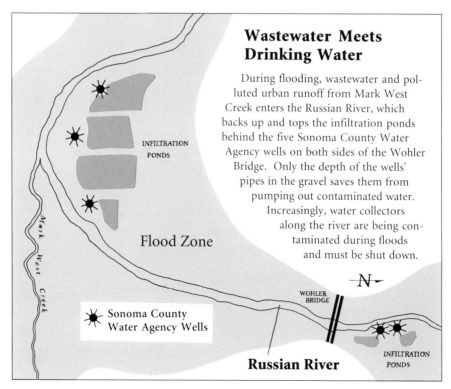

Wastewater Meets Drinking Water

During flooding, wastewater and polluted urban runoff from Mark West Creek enters the Russian River, which backs up and tops the infiltration ponds behind the five Sonoma County Water Agency wells on both sides of the Wohler Bridge. Only the depth of the wells' pipes in the gravel saves them from pumping out contaminated water. Increasingly, water collectors along the river are being contaminated during floods and must be shut down.

INFILTRATION PONDS

Mark West Creek

Flood Zone

-N-

WOHLER BRIDGE

★ Sonoma County Water Agency Wells

Russian River

INFILTRATION PONDS

In the photo above, floodwaters merge swollen Mark West Creek, entering from the left, with the Russian River in the center during 1997 flooding. On the right of the river bend are three giant Sonoma County Water Agency wells. Their vast drinking water infiltration ponds on the far right, usually protected by levees, are filled with muddy, polluted floodwaters. The ponds, forty acres across and fifteen feet deep, silt up each year and have to be bulldozed clean or else lose their filtration ability.

these wells and the vulnerable gravel aquifer for safe drinking water filtration. One of the huge water collectors (Number Five) is contaminated (turbid) during floods, according to Bruce Burton of the Office of Safe Drinking Water.

The cost of an artificial filtration and chemical treatment plant, if the Agency's drinking water supply is contaminated, has been estimated by Miles Ferris at $300 million, plus huge annual maintenance costs. This money would be better spent getting mining and wastewater out of the river and managing the watershed responsibly.

Downstream from the wells is the exclusive Bohemian Grove, where two thousand of the nation's leaders gather in the summer, a site where "the effluent meets the affluent." Huey Johnson wrote an opinion editorial in the *San Francisco Examiner* in 1993 asking them to help solve the river's woes, and a supportive group has formed.

Brenda Adelman's Army

Without persistent guardians like Brenda Adelman of Guerneville, the governor-appointed directors of the Regional Water Quality Control Board would continue to turn the Russian River into an open wastewater conduit to the ocean, sacrificing fisheries, wildlife, safe drinking water, and public recreation.

Santa Rosa's illegal spill, and others that followed, aroused the ire of Brenda Adelman, a tenacious, self-educated biologist who formed the Russian River Watershed Protection Committee, which now has more than two thousand members. She has educated the entire county on the recent findings of the dangers of drinking water contaminated even with minute doses of estrogenic chemicals known to interfere with reproduction. For the past decade Brenda has led the bitter struggle to keep wastewater out of the river, the ocean, and the estuaries along the coast. She was helped by Friends of the Estuary lawsuit led by Marin activist Tom Yarish and Richard Charter of Bodega Bay. Santa Rosa has spent $11 million on a draft Environmental Impact Review, completed in 1997, hoping to justify increasing the dumping of wastewater to equal up to twenty percent of the river flow. There are powerful public health and safety reasons why this must be opposed and why the only safe standard is zero discharge by every city along the river in order to protect the region's quality of drinking water.

At the harbor seal haulout at Jenner, Dian Hardy of the Stewards of Slavianka (the Russian name for the river) monitors the health of the seals and, through them, the health of the river. During the sewage spills the seals were smart—they fled, although some are now diseased.

Russian River Steelhead Trout— New Zealand's Choice

Russian River native steelhead trout are of international, national, and regional significance because of their superior qualities as game fish. In Auckland, New Zealand, a monument stands with a plaque inscribed:

> In 1883-1884 the Auckland Society obtained from the Russian River, California the first rainbow trout ova to reach New Zealand. They were hatched nearby using water from these springs and became the progenitors of all Rainbow Trout in the country. The present hatchery at Puketurua is one of the finest in the world and is capable of producing 1,000,000 fry and fingerlings a year.

Today, a century later, stock from Russian River steelhead still make up this world-famous fishery, and the New Zealand Tourist Bureau proclaims the fact in its published literature. Such strong, large, highly adaptable, hard-fighting fish are unique and deserving of the most painstaking efforts for preservation and enhancement in their native habitat.

While Russian River steelhead thrive in New Zealand, they have suffered terrible decimation in their home waters. Our steelhead have shown a 90% decline since 1940. While the exact number of adult steelhead is not known, it is probably about 10% of the historical figure of 62,000. We believe, however, that the potential remains to restore the Russian River to its former status as a blue ribbon steelhead producer and the west's greatest steelhead waterway.

— *Warm Springs Dam Environmental Impact Report*, 1973

Fishing for steelhead on the Elwa River in Washington State in 1907 before it was dammed could be rewarding. To restore the fishery, Washington is now in the process of removing the Elwa Dam.

Friends of the Russian River

In 1993 Joyce and I along with David Bolling, formerly head of Friends of the River, and Tom Roth, a former Congressional press secretary, founded the Friends of the Russian River, a non-profit coalition of eighteen river-protection groups in three counties, to present a united voice for the Russian River. First, we organized a Congressional Forum at Santa Rosa Junior College, conducted by Representatives Lynn Woolsey and Dan Hamburg, on the future of the Russian River. More than two hundred and fifty people attended, and many spoke against the mining and other abuses. *The Press Democrat* ran an editorial asking for a riverwide Master Plan, indicating wide public support.

Philip Williams, fluvial geomorphologist, conducted the Russian River Hydrology Study for the Coastal Conservancy, the Tomales Bay and Bolinas Lagoon Restoration Studies, and plans for restoring Sonoma baylands. He electrified a Guerneville meeting organized by the Russian River Environmental Forum after the 1997 flood with new concepts of flood management as opposed to flood control. He is president of Philip Williams Associates and the International Rivers Network.

In April 1994 Friends of the Russian River put on an educational conference entitled "The Russian River in Peril" at which river experts and agency chiefs promised to take strong action. It was attended by four hundred people, most of them enthusiastic river supporters, and included federal, state, county, and city officials. California Resources Secretary Doug Wheeler spoke, along with two former state secretaries who had helped me in the West Marin battles: Ike Livermore and Huey Johnson. The State Lands Commission handed out its superb report, *California's Rivers*, written by Sonoma County native Diana Jacobs, and David Bolling released his book, *How to Save a River*. State Senator Mike Thompson promised to hold statewide hearings "to save the rivers." Three hundred people signed a petition to the Governor requesting a Comprehensive Management Plan for the Russian River.

We chose the Villa Chanticleer in Healdsburg, where the Warm Springs Dam had been endorsed many years before and whose town politics were dominated by the gravel miners, for this high-powered conference. Not surprisingly, the supervisors advised their own planning department staff not to attend. We featured our supervisorial candidate, Pete Foppiano, as the celebrity chef who prepared the linguini for the luncheon. He lost in the November election by a narrow margin, but not because of his cooking.

To raise money for Friends of the Russian River, Hop Kiln Winery has been the site of annual Russian River Appreciation Festivals. Supervisor Esposti called the first festival "a threat to public safety," and we had to get a special permit costing four hundred dollars. However, the publicity was overwhelming; the picnic was oversubscribed and we raised enough money to employ public relations expert Tom Roth as executive director.

Meanwhile, Therese Shere and Eric Monrad of the Russian River Task

Bob Coey, tributary restoration specialist with State Fish and Game, leads a Russian River Environmental Forum field trip to see the planting of 1,500 willow sprigs to help restore Griffin Creek on the Bishop's Ranch.

Force monitored every mining hearing to make sure no permits were issued by our supervisors without our attorney's knowledge.

Training the Troops for Action

Friends of the Russian River realized that an educated public would be key to developing a new county General Plan that featured and protected the Russian River. With the help of the Marin Environmental Forum, educator Barbara Meyn, Joyce and I created the Russian River Environmental Forum in 1993 to educate Sonoma and Marin citizens about the Russian River. With Healdsburg planner Meg Alexander as coordinator, the Forum has used seminars and field trips to gravel pits, agency pumps, and politicians' offices to train over one hundred people to date in both counties as experts on river issues. Significantly, our classes have included supervisorial candidates and delegates from river regulatory agencies.

After the 1997 flood, the Forum held a seminar to educate Guerneville victims on "Upriver Causes of Downriver Flooding."

There is no reason why wealthy Sonoma shouldn't be among the slowest growing and greenest counties in California, a model of watershed planning. All it takes is an educated public and a three-two vote on the Board of Supervisors.

The Supervisors Hold Out

Gradually, saving the Russian River has become a major topic of political debate throughout the county. But in December 1994, after heavy lobbying by the mining firms, the supervisors approved a new mining Plan. We had only one substantial victory: they required a 450-foot setback from the river for new gravel pits. Tragically, the plan allows dredging of two hundred additional acres of vineyards overlying the crucial aquifer on the Middle Reach near Windsor's and the Sonoma County Water Agency's wells. Coming full circle, the plan also opened up the gravel bars along twenty magnificent miles of Digger Bend behind Fitch Mountain to strip-mining, the site I fondly remember as the place where our family camped and fished when I was a boy.

Leo Cronin, a director of the Marin Municipal Water District and President of Trout Unlimited, made up for the dams on Lagunitas Creek by leading the restoration of the lower creek for coho salmon spawning. Now tiny Lagunitas Creek has a higher coho count than the abused Russian River.

Nor was there any help from state legislators. A bill introduced by Assemblyman Byron Sher in early 1995 that prohibited mining in drinking water aquifers statewide was quickly squelched by the state mining lobby.

Since 1994, the only plan for the Russian River is this new single-purpose, twenty-year mining plan which has come under attack for its giveaway of public resources. This is Esposti's legacy. There are no significant penalties to the mining firms if they damage wells, undermine bridges, or contaminate the region's water supply, nor are the supervisors held accountable for the damages, as lawsuits against them are paid for by the mining firms.

What a dilemma. Having tried nearly everything, we were ready to sue the State of California itself.

Victory: A Watershed Management Program for All California Rivers

By 1996 Friends of the Russian River had formed a seasoned team: land-use planner Joan Vilms as president, Mike Swaney from Trout Unlimited and American Rivers, Mark Green, chair of Conservation Action, Krista Rector from the Sierra Club, Tom Roth on government agencies, Fred Euphrat on forestry, Therese Shere on mining, and me on fundraising and drinking water.

We decided that our best hope would be a Public Trust lawsuit similar to *Marks vs. Whitney* on Tomales Bay that protected the tidelands of the state

Can the Fisheries of the Russian River Be Restored?

In the early fifties, rancher Marty Hoffman and I explored the Russian River in a surplus raft before Coyote Dam was built. Late fall rains had brought thousands of steelhead and salmon up the main stem, and they were fanning out into the tributaries to spawn. There were rows of men lined at the mouth of each tributary with flashing fish touching their waders. The run was especially heavy up Pieta Creek, Big Sulfur Creek, Dry Creek, and Mark West Creek. Downriver fishermen were having a field day at the great holes from Steelhead Beach to Monte Rio. Large schools of fish were assembling to run up Austin Creek and Willow Creek.

There were probably a thousand or more fishermen along the river in December, January, and February. Schools were let out so children could admire the great run of fish ascending the falls near the mouth of Mill Creek. Fish equipment stores sold out; boat stores, motels, restaurants, and bars were crowded with excited, happy steelhead fishermen and their families.

Economists set the benefit value of each steelhead and coho salmon at $2,000 for the 60,000 fish that ascended the great river each year to spawn. This was one of the great miracles of nature, a gift to mankind, an ecological as well as economic treasure. But within a decade the fishery was decimated.

With the federal listing of coho salmon and steelhead as Threatened Species in 1996 and 1997, the Sonoma County Water Agency began pouring millions of dollars into tributary restoration, hoping to avoid an Endangered listing. This is an unparalleled opportunity for citizen activists to make sure the restoration succeeds.

Joan Vilms, president of Friends of the Russian River, is a fishery protection expert. She chairs Sonoma County's Fish and Wildlife Advisory Board and helped launch the County's Agricultural and Open Space District. Here she explores the unspoiled Digger Bend steelhead habitat which should be preserved as a county treasure.

Digger Bend, an S-shaped loop behind Fitch Mountain near Healdsburg, was my childhood paradise. Today it still has the highest canoe hours of any river in California. The county wants to spoil it by allowing strip-mining of its life-filled gravel bars. Instead, the Russian River should be permanently preserved under the state's Wild and Scenic Rivers program as are the Eel, Klamath, Trinity, and Smith rivers.

from abuse and the Mono Lake case that protected its tributaries. A lawsuit was needed that could establish for all time that California rivers belong to the public for navigation, ecological values, fisheries, drinking water, recreation, wildlife habitat protection, and open space.

Friends of the Russian River hired public trust attorney Richard Roos-Collins of the Natural Heritage Institute to develop a strategy to force the state agencies to coordinate and enforce their regulations of the Russian River. Early in 1996 we filed an "intent of lawsuit" against the powerful State Water Resources Control Board and other state agencies for failing to protect the Public Trust resources of the Russian River.

The strategy paid off. Rather than face litigation, the government agencies met with us in repeated negotiations in Sacramento. In May 1996, in an unrelated development, the Russian River watershed was singled out for a nationwide restoration project. A group of twenty officials led by Glenda Humiston of the Resource Conservation Districts met on my front porch with Jim Lyons, Undersecretary of the US Department of Agriculture, who pledged $100,000 to start the ball rolling. This helped our negotiations with the state. It also helped that the National Marine Fisheries had just listed the

Russian River coho salmon as a threatened species and required a recovery plan.

In September 1996, with a federal Endangered Species listing for coho salmon and steelhead trout looming, the California Environmental Protection Agency took serious note of our proposed suit. The response was a far-reaching "Watershed Management Initiative" that would apply to all watersheds in California. It outlined goals, funding, and timetables, and was sent to all regulatory agencies as well as to citizen groups. It called for a *Coordinated Watershed Management Program* for all the state's rivers, with selected rivers as models.

It had been thirty-four years since the strip-miners cut down Russian River riparian forests and its heron and osprey nests on Griffin Creek and other ranches, triggering the unprecedented waves of litigation by citizens that state agencies now refer to as "The Sonoma Experience" (*see Appendix*). Maybe now a watershed management program will truly begin to save the Russian River and other coastal California rivers in peril. But it will require continued citizen involvement to make sure the plans are developed and implemented.

A Plot to Save Sonoma County

DEFENDING THE COUNTY'S TREASURES FROM URBAN SPRAWL

It's time for Sonoma County to slow down its growth and think where it's going. The Russian River fishery crisis and water shortage present an historic opportunity for voters to change Sonoma from a developer-driven county to a citizen-controlled county.

One key to preserving the County's quality of life is preserving the $1.5 billion a year wine-grape and tourism industry, the County's largest, centered in the Russian River, Dry Creek, and Alexander Valleys near Healdsburg. Unfortunately, these prime vineyard regions are located close to Highway 101 and, by adding freeway lanes, could be lost to sprawl. Development in Cloverdale will squeeze the Alexander and Dry Creek Valleys, and an ever-expanding Windsor and Santa Rosa will become the cinch in the lower river wine-grape belt itself.

To save Sonoma County requires:

1. Electing slow-growth supervisors and city council members who will develop a City-County General Plan featuring mass rail transit to serve cities along the existing publicly-owned right-of-way, before adding new freeway lanes.

2. Passing legislation putting the Sonoma County Water Agency under direct public control by election, thereby removing the Sonoma County Board of Supervisors as its directors; enacting laws to prevent watershed deforestation and to preserve gravel aquifers and the regional drinking water supply; acquiring a Russian River Protection and Meander Corridor free of gravel mining, sewage wastewater, and polluted urban runoff; and restoring the steelhead and salmon fishery.

3. Returning part of the Eel River diversion water to Mendocino and Humboldt counties and making up for the loss by stopping illegal Russian River diversions, opposing new water appropriations, and requiring state-of-the-art water conservation and wastewater reuse by farmers and cities.

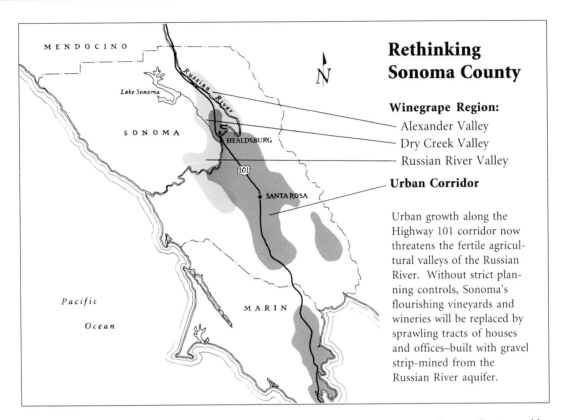

Rethinking Sonoma County

Winegrape Region:
— Alexander Valley
— Dry Creek Valley
— Russian River Valley

Urban Corridor

Urban growth along the Highway 101 corridor now threatens the fertile agricultural valleys of the Russian River. Without strict planning controls, Sonoma's flourishing vineyards and wineries will be replaced by sprawling tracts of houses and offices–built with gravel strip-mined from the Russian River aquifer.

Sonoma County could be on the cutting edge of sustaining its resources if it were zoned by watersheds—natural ecological units managed by scientists, visionary political leaders, and citizen watershed councils.

4. Adopting a Comprehensive Flood and Watershed Management Program with building restrictions on the overbuilt Windsor-Santa Rosa Plain to protect downriver communities.

5. Designating the Russian as a Wild and Scenic River, reinstating legislation to restore the Laguna de Santa Rosa as a National Park, and including the Russian River Estuary in the Gulf of the Farallones Marine Preserve.

Sonoma County urgently needs a new County Planning Department led by the nation's finest ecologically trained planning staff and backed by alert citizen planners. Few counties in California are blessed with such a superb climate, rich soils, separated coummunities, an undeveloped coast and wildlands, and a magnificent river. These are its vital resources—on the edge of the abyss—that we must protect and sustain for future generations.

CHAPTER SEVENTEEN

Coming Home: Saving Our Creeks and Rivers

Government cannot function alone. Watershed management works
best when local citizens band together to help protect their resources.

—Jane Forster, member State Water Resources Control Board,
Cal/EPA Report, September 1996

After years of fighting to preserve other waterways, I realized that I had been neglecting my own natural treasure, Griffin Creek, mauled by the gravel miners and degraded by poor land use practices. Symbolic of many degraded tributaries of the Russian River, this small creek is only five miles long and drains a watershed of just three square miles. Restoring it for steelhead and salmon spawning could inspire other tributary land owners to do the same.

I remember how a colony of egrets coming home each spring to Audubon Canyon Ranch on Bolinas Lagoon captured the hearts and vision of Marin County voters who recognized that they were superb indicators of the health of their watershed. Similarly, the return of the great migratory fish to the Russian River could awaken the public to a renewed sense of watershed stewardship.

The Tale of Griffin Creek

When I bought my ranch near Healdsburg in 1961, the gravel dredgers were soon at work near the creek's mouth, eventually sinking the creekbed as much as twenty feet, undermining bridges, and toppling towering cottonwoods. Up the creek in a park-like virgin canyon abounding with wildcat, deer, fox, coyote, nesting wood ducks, and an occasional mountain lion, a neighbor planned to construct a large dam and lake for a fancy resort just beyond my property line. Two-hundred-year-old oaks, bays, madrones, and

A crane opens up the levees during the dedication ceremony for the Petaluma River Marsh Restoration Project on August 24, 1994. This model Sonoma Land Trust project will allow the tidal action of San Francisco Bay to gradually reclaim the marsh and restore its intertidal wildlife habitat. Scientific restoration will be needed for the rivers of California after the gravel mining is eliminated.

We created the Griffin Russian River Riparian Preserve on both sides of the river by donating a forty-four acre conservation easement to the Sonoma Land Trust. This gives the river room to meander and to recharge the underlying aquifer, and it also protects our vineyards from erosion. The Sonoma County Water Agency is long overdue on acquiring a similar ninety-mile River Protection Corridor. At the upper left is Geyser Peak and the Mayacamas ridge.

Douglas fir were cut down. The trunks were bulldozed into piles in the creek bottom and set fire, but they were too green to burn. Then the project was abandoned, leaving a dry pitiful pasture.

The damage was done. The deep, cold canyon pools of Griffin Creek, backed with great moss- and fern-covered rocks and filled with newts and small steelhead trout, soon filled with silt. The trunks washed down the creek, plugging it, and ending the steelhead and salmon spawning runs for the next thirty years. This desecration made me mourn for Bugs Cain and the lost canyon of my boyhood, Camp Dimond in the Oakland foothills. It also made me appreciate all the more David Bouverie's gift of his wild canyon and its unspoiled creek to Audubon Canyon Ranch and a gift to all the children of Sonoma County.

Then, in 1985, Supervisor Nick Esposti proposed a huge county garbage dump—a "sanitary land fill"—hidden in the steep canyon up Griffin Creek. The creek was to be buried in a long culvert. Public Works officials were ecstatic and said the dump would serve the rapid growth of Sonoma County for the next fifty years. Using their police power, they intended to condemn for their use the Griffin Ranch, the Russell Ranch, and the Episcopal Bishop's Ranch next door, and bulldoze their rolling oak-studded hills overlooking the Russian River Valley for landfill to keep down the smells.

When this dump was designated "high priority" by the County, Westside Road neighbors arose in fierce opposition. The city of Healdsburg was also outraged because three hundred garbage trucks a day would whine past their Chamber of Commerce offices and down Westside Road to the dump. After a year of bitter struggle, with no help from the Water Agency, we won the battle by showing how the leachate from the dump could pollute the aquifer and the Water Agency's own drinking water wells at the Wohler Bridge on the Russian River.

Griffin Creek Is One of Many in Peril

These alarming land-use conflicts over just one small creek are symbolic of the plight of dozens of similar creeks damaged by the failure of the Supervisors to implement a watershed management plan during the forty-seven years they've controlled the Water Agency. These creeks are living arteries, essential to public health and to the health of the river and its salmonid fishery. What good was it, I thought, to hire attorneys to stop the gravel mining or the wastewater dumping by cities along the river if these crucial tributaries are ruined by the uninformed farmers or developers who own them?

Joyce and I received the Otto Teller Sonoma Land Trust Award in 1992 for our donation of the Griffin Riparian Preserve on the Russian River. The Russian River Corridor provides habitat for over 270 species of plants, 108 species of birds, 20 species of mammals, 8 species of amphibians and reptiles, and 15 species of butterflies. However, many species are in serious decline due to habitat loss.

Aerial photos of the watershed taken by the Coastal Conservancy showed there were numerous creeks stripped of vegetation, sprayed and riprapped, and many small stockdams blocking spawning tributaries. Life-filled meanders had been bulldozed and farmed, and vineyards had been planted too close to the river's edge and on steep slopes causing severe erosion.

The erosion, which some say is as bad as the Yangtze River, was measured at Hacienda Bridge by the US Geological Survey at 1.2 million tons of suspended silt per average winter, and probably three times that in the floods of 1995. This enormous so-called "non-point pollution" smothers spawning grounds, clogs water intakes, and sends huge plumes of mud out in the blue Pacific, some of it ending up in Bodega and Tomales Bays. The North Coast Regional Water Quality Control Board has for years stonewalled, through what the courts refer to as *deliberate silent inaction*, remedies to this apocalyptic erosion problem. As a result, "inaction" could eventually destroy the viability of the salmon fishery and the wine-grape industry and, all the while, continue endangering regional drinking water supplies.

Creating a Russian River Riparian Preserve

The Griffin Russian River Riparian Preserve and Greenway Project was born during the struggle to save the Russian River from the mining barons. In 1990, Joyce and I donated forty-four acres of second growth riparian forests and gravel bars to the Sonoma Land Trust as a conservation easement stretching for half a mile on each side of the Middle Reach channel. Griffin Creek runs through it.

Our intent is to use this Preserve as one anchor in a ninety mile long wilderness river Greenway—in planners lingo a "River Protection and Meander Corridor." The Greenway would extend from Coyote Dam through the eroding, barren Alexander Valley Reach, wild Digger Bend, and the Middle Reach to the harbor seal haulout at the estuary near Jenner. Currently this navigable stretch is one of the most heavily canoed rivers in America. Just thirty years ago it was considered the finest accessible steelhead fishing river in the state.

Included in the Greenway, and therefore preserved from further harm, are about 1,400 gravel-dependent municipal, domestic, and farm wells that 500,000 people depend on for pure naturally filtered drinking water. This Greenway would become a county and regional treasure, celebrating its most valuable, irreplaceable natural resource.

Enter the Episcopal Bishop of California

Shortly after I started practice in Marin in 1950, Dr. Bloomfield, the Chief, phoned me, "Marty, I want you to look in on a delightful patient of mine who is recuperating from a heart condition. He's staying with friends in Ross. He's a fantastic cook so you'll have to watch his diet, and yours. By the way," he added, "your new patient is Bishop Karl Block, the Episcopal Bishop of California."

Bishop Block and I became friends and, later, after he recovered, he told me that the church had bought sixty-four hilltop acres on Westside Road as a retreat. I visited it and fell in love with the area.

The Bishop's new ranch was part of the former giant White-O Ranch of some ten-thousand acres that included groves of redwoods and fir, and creeks abundant with steelhead and coho salmon. The Bishop and his successors refurbished the rambling early California mansion built with redwood timbers milled at the ranch. A small shining chapel overlooks Mt. St. Helena, and in springtime one can enjoy the sight of the mustard-covered

vineyards of the Russian River Valley wine district. Even the gravel pit ponds look inviting—from a distance. The retreat floundered along for some years after Bishop Block died and there was talk of selling it, which broke my heart.

In 1991, the Rt. Reverend Bishop William Swing set out to revitalize the ranch, and he purchased one hundred and eighty acres bordering two miles of Griffin Creek which he called the "new territory." I was thrilled; finally there was a chance to restore the creek and its healthy steelhead habitat.

Together, Bishop Swing and I plan to establish a Russian River Greenway Education Center at the Bishop's Ranch. Land stewards Sean and Carolyn Swift have begun a program to restore the creek and its watershed, with supervision and financial help from the Resource Conservation District, the Sonoma County Water Agency, and California State Fish and Game.

In 1995 led by Bob Coey of State Fish and Game, and Sean White, Water Agency fishery biologist, young women and men from President Clinton's Americorps were assigned to start work making the stream habitable for steelhead and salmon. Hundreds of red and yellow native willow sprouts were successfully planted on barren stretches to shade the water and provide insect food for fish.

Bishop Swing wrote an inspiring letter about the "coming home" of the wondrous steelhead, and helped bring the concept of *watershed stewardship*

The Episcopal Diocese of California owns the ranch retreat with the white chapel next to my ranch (left), bordering two miles of Griffin Creek. Together we are planning to restore the entire creek and its steelhead habitat. The Episcopal Board embraced the concept of watershed stewardship and celebrated the "coming home of the wondrous steelhead trout." Most of the two ranches are wildlife preserves.

Hop Kiln: A Landmark on the Greenway

The Griffin Russian River Riparian Preserve adjoins and is part of the Hop Kiln Winery and the Griffin Ranch Vineyards. The Winery, with the old hop drying barn we restored, is one of many historic landmarks along the proposed Russian River Greenway.

The three-towered structure was built in 1905 in just thirty-five days by "Skinny" Sodini, an Italian stonemason. For nearly forty years, its large wood-fired kilns dried the light seed pods used for making premium beer, but they also consumed the valley oaks for miles around. At one time there were about one hundred similar hop kilns between the Wohler Bridge and Hopland, upriver. Sonoma hops were famous and were shipped to other continents, commanding high prices. But they were overcropped, became diseased, and were abandoned during World War II when some factory workers were content to switch to lighter brews.

The restored Hop Kiln Winery overlooks the Griffin Russian River Riparian Preserve. The barn is a relic of the years when hop growing for premium beers was Sonoma's largest agricultural enterprise.

Since 1974 the Winery has been registered as a County, State, and National Historic Trust Landmark. The antique Zinfandel vineyards were designated a National Historic Trust Agricultural District, having been in continuous production since 1880. When the Winery was bonded in 1975, Davis Bynum was the only other winery on Westside Road; in 1997 there were sixteen, many with tasting rooms and superlative wines.

The well-drained valleys of the Russian River, radiating like spokes from the river at Healdsburg, are blessed with rich topsoil and hot summer days tempered with coastal fog. Here, growers can bring nearly every grape variety to full maturity. What a tragedy if these three great productive valleys that depend on the Russian River were lost to the same kind of sprawl that destroyed the rich vineyards of Windsor next door in just twenty years.

Drawing by George Rockrise

to the attention of the thousands of Bay Area members of the church.

With high water in 1996, a handful of endangered coho salmon fought their way up the small waterfalls of Griffin Creek and spawned in the gravel. Seeing these fish return after 30 years reminded me of the exaltation I felt when we knew we had rescued the great American egrets on Bolinas Lagoon so many years ago.

This hands-on, pool-by-pool restoration of a once-productive fishery is an example of how ranchers, land owners, schools, and others can unite with government agencies to adopt and restore a damaged tributary.

The Russian—A Wild and Scenic River?

In 1972 Senator Peter Behr sought to include the Russian River in his Wild and Scenic Rivers bill along with the Eel, Trinity, and Klamath but the Warm Springs Dam forces made it impossible. Now, with growing public awareness that the river is as precious to Sonoma County as Tomales Bay is to Marin, it's time to renew the effort.

A canoe trip from the Coyote Dam to the estuary at Jenner should convince any skeptic that this river is similar to the incomparable Point Reyes Peninsula—a "wilderness next door," a local and national treasure crying out for preservation. The only urban aspects of the Russian River are the mining, wastewater, and channeling. Once these are remedied, the river will heal itself.

Professor Robert Curry (center) visited the Russian River gravel pits in 1994 with his class from the School of Geology at UC Santa Cruz. Curry is a renowned fluvial geomorphologist—an expert on all aspects of rivers—who helped us win our Sonoma County lawsuits between 1990 and 1996.

At the Jenner estuary the Wild and Scenic Russian River could connect with an expanded Gulf of the Farallones National Marine Sanctuary, ensuring permanent preservation of the Marin-Sonoma Coast. The cost of acquiring conservation easements and restoring the meanders and the riparian forests along the Wild and Scenic River should be borne by the Sonoma County Water Agency, which has profited by wholesaling its water and can now use their gains to protect the long-abused source of that water.

Greed, Gravel, and Growth Are Driving California's Counties

Richard Charter of Bodega Bay is former director of the Sonoma Land Trust. For years he led the fight against oil drilling rigs off the coast. He also spear-headed the legal battle to keep Santa Rosa's wastewater out of the esteros of Bodega Bay.

During our battles against gravel mining on the Russian River, I began hearing from river mining foes all over the state who told me horror stories about their broken rivers. Janet Levers, a fiery Yolo County walnut grower, was also battling Syar Industries; Mike Morford of Ukiah, head of Salmon Unlimited, was trying to save twenty miles of the gorgeous Gualala River from being strip-mined; and John Hooper had established FROG, Friends of the Garcia, to save this sparkling gem on the Mendocino coast. In 1990 we held a joint meeting with people from Cache Creek and the Eel, Mad, Merced, Tuolomne, and Ventura rivers. In the group was Avery Tindall, a Cache Creek farmer whom I'd known as a Boy Scout at Camp Dimond in Oakland. Avery was irate because a state bridge over Cache Creek in Yolo County had been undermined and had later collapsed in a flood.

Avery knew the murky inner workings of the State Department of Mines and Geology in Sacramento where, with Healdsburg engineer Ed Gustely, we researched why the regulation of river gravel mining statewide was such a failure. This advisory agency administers the Surface Mining and Reclama-tion Act (SMARA) of 1975.

We found that State Mines had two standards which, if followed, could cut river mining statewide and save the state's fisheries, drinking water, and bridges. One was simply to paint a red line on each bridge pier marking the level below which gravel could not be extracted for a predetermined distance upriver or downriver. The other was to prohibit mining in gravel aquifers that the public depends on to filter its drinking water. They said the problem lies with Caltrans, which doesn't insist on the red line to protect its bridges, and the county supervisors, who regulate their county's land and river use and can enforce these standards—but don't.

Astoundingly, the amount of gravel, sand, and quarry rock (aggregate) used in California each year is equivalent to about six tons per person as their share of building the state's freeways, roads, houses, office buildings, malls, and other structures. Of the total, seventy-five percent is strip-mined from our rivers, and about fifteen percent of that is being used by Caltrans. The rocks in the rivers of California gather no moss: Caltrans and the mining industry won't give them a chance.

The tonnage of gravel and sand mined from the instream beds and flood plains of our rivers has risen to about 135 million tons a year. And where does the sand and gravel go? According to State Mines and Geology, to accommodate its thirty-two million and growing population, the state is being urbanized with concrete at the rate of 48,000 acres per year.

About ten times more instream gravel is being extracted than is being replenished, estimates hydrologist Matt Kondolf, meaning that many of the state's riverbeds are steadily sinking, permanently changing the structure of our rivers. What will happen when the state population grows to sixty million? The *Sacramento Bee* stated in a 1993 report: "Rock mining pits the state's economy against the state's rivers."

The State Mining Board says there are eight hundred active aggregate mines in the state's fifty-eight counties. Sonoma County, one of the state's largest producers of river gravel, supplies five counties including Marin from about thirty mining sites on the Russian and Gualala rivers. Two of these counties, Solano and Sonoma, are among the fastest-growing in the state with seemingly insatiable demands for rock. About four million tons are extracted along the Russian River some years when mining hasn't been temporarily stalled by lawsuits. Officials we spoke with openly admitted that river mining in Sonoma County was out of control.

Sonoma's policy is to phase out river mining in the next ten to twenty years, meaning whenever the gravel is gone or the miners give up. Of course, by then it will be too late to save our rivers and creeks.

In the fire-prone foothills of the Sierra and the Central Valley, the state's finest forests and farmlands are being gobbled up by housing tracts and paved over with tons of gravel mined from our state's broken rivers. Just as damaging, the Auburn Dam is being proposed on the American River as a flood control measure, but its real purpose is to supply the burgeoning sprawl.

Barbara Salzman of Marin is a longtime defender and restorer of Bay Area tidal bays and salt marshes. She is currently working on the 7,000 acre San Pablo Baylands Protection Corridor.

A Circular System

Unfortunately, the beautiful smooth gravel from our rivers is largely wasted; much of it ends up buried in trenches. Possibly half is crushed to give it sharp edges to match specifications similar to quarried rock. Absurdly, as late as 1998 Caltrans still allowed its contractors to use river gravel for the concrete used to replace bridges undermined by gravel mining in the river. To the north, ecologist Aldaron Laird says that Arcata wells are endangered by excessive Mad River mining. Prodigious amounts of gravel are being pit-mined from the rivers that drain the length of the Sierra. On these rivers, deep gravel pits similar to those of the Russian River have captured and changed the course of the riverbeds. State Mines has photos of pits on the Tujunga River in San Diego County, for example, that captured the riverbed in a flood and took out two state highway bridges which had been undermined.

Laird notes that one can correlate the destruction of these rivers with the enormous demand for gravel to construct each section of the state's freeways and bridges by Caltrans. In other words, Caltrans is essentially undermining their own bridges by buying river gravel from mining firms—a circular, looped welfare system.

The Federal Highway Commission issued a policy statement in 1995 that may force Caltrans to collect from the mining firms any mining-related damages to the state's undermined bridges. Damages amounted to more

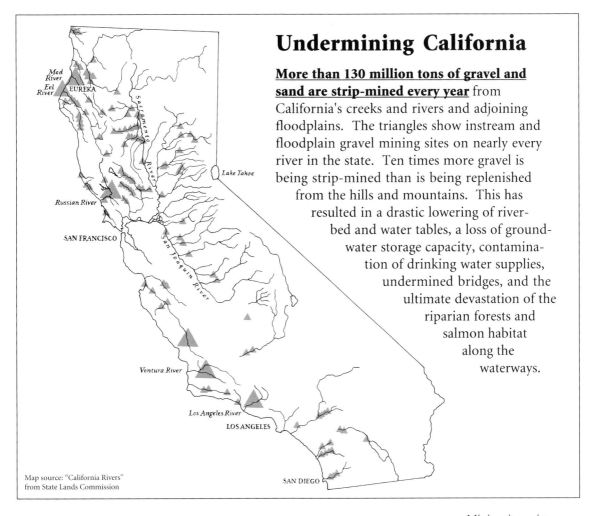

Undermining California

<u>More than 130 million tons of gravel and sand are strip-mined every year</u> from California's creeks and rivers and adjoining floodplains. The triangles show instream and floodplain gravel mining sites on nearly every river in the state. Ten times more gravel is being strip-mined than is being replenished from the hills and mountains. This has resulted in a drastic lowering of river-bed and water tables, a loss of ground-water storage capacity, contamina-tion of drinking water supplies, undermined bridges, and the ultimate devastation of the riparian forests and salmon habitat along the waterways.

Map source: "California Rivers"
from State Lands Commission

than $130 million in the 1995 floods alone, they said. If this policy was enforced, it could stop instream gravel mining statewide. But Caltrans shows no intention of collecting from the mining firms that undermined the mighty Highway 101 bridge at Healdsburg that Al Regina and I reported, claiming it is being replaced as an "earthquake retrofit." The taxpayers and the river lose again.

Throughout the nation, unlike California, most of the construction aggregate comes from blasting and crushing rock in quarries, which inciden-tally provides more jobs. Also there's plenty of it; the entire state and nation is underlain with rock. There is also a growing market for recycled concrete. We calculated that it only costs about one dollar more per ton to produce quarried rock in California, a small price to pay to save the rivers of the state. Some mining firms oppose the opening of hardrock quarries in order to

Mining sites exist on nearly every river in the state. Three quarters of all aggregate (sand, gravel, and crushed rock) used for construc-tion in California is strip-mined from the state's dying rivers and creeks.

In California, Gravel is More Valuable Than Gold

California's biggest dollar-value non-fuel mineral is not gold but gravel and stone.

Last year, 192 million tons of "construction aggregate"—gravel, sand, and crushed stone—were mined in California, carrying a value of $913 million. That figure represents nearly one-third of the total value of all non-fuel minerals extracted in the state in 1989—$2.839 billion.

Despite a new gold rush in the state, gold has a long way to go to catch aggregate: The 700,000 ounces of gold mined in 1989 were worth only about $250 million. Other big-dollar California minerals include limestone and borax.

According to the state Division of Mines and Geology, which compiles mineral statistics, each Californian's share of construction aggregate mined in 1989 was 5.5 tons. The industry itself says that figure is closer to 6.5 tons.

"That's an incredible amount," said David Beeby, senior geologist with the division. "[Construction aggregate] is probably the thing you see most often that you don't recognize as a mined product," said Beeby, noting its use in all infrastructure and concrete foundation construction.

In Sonoma County, gravel-mining operators and wine growers are at loggerheads. Statewide, the dollar value of wine grapes is nearly as high as construction aggregate. The 1989 wine-grape crop was worth $852 million in cash receipts to growers, according to the California Department of Food and Agriculture. Wine sales were significantly higher.

—Stephen Kulieke, *San Francisco Daily Journal,*
Monday, October 5, 1990

Thousands of tons of cheap-to-mine gravel and sand are hauled by truck from Russian River mining sites every working day. Along some county roads there are hundreds of truck-loads per day. A road damage mitigation fee is charged.

keep the easier, cheaper, and hence more profitable terrace and river mining going until our rivers are depleted.

Death of the Nile River

Broken, dying rivers are a worldwide tragedy. I saw this first-hand in 1995 when Joyce and I floated down the Nile River on a barge not quite as luxurious as Cleopatra's. It had been thirty-three years since the Russian engineers had built the Aswan Dam, the second-largest in Africa. Wherever we went I was reminded of the Russian River. At Abu Simbel the enormous statues of Ramses II reminded me of the arrogant lieutenant colonels from the US Army Corps of Engineers who had built the Warm Springs Dam.

The damming of the Nile has created a crisis for Egypt, the Earth's cradle of civilization. Temples were moved and temples were lost as the water rose, and now a huge block of Egypt is said to be sinking from the weight of Lake Nassar and its trapped silt. Below the dam, farmers were evicted as the annual floods no longer enriched their lands. Countless families of fishermen and farmers all along the river and the coast were displaced to Cairo to live in its slums, cemeteries, and garbage dumps. The relocated population increased Cairo to eighteen million, creating more poverty and political instability, and hurting tourism. The wealthy began buying up the riverbank farms for villas.

Highways, roads, shopping centers, parking lots, office buildings, and much more depend on an enormous supply of construction aggregate. The smooth river gravel of the rivers of California, however, is often crushed to meet industry needs when abundant, crushed quarry rock could be used instead.

All along the river we saw damage similar to that below the dams on the Russian River. Sediment-starved "hungry water" released from the dam was eroding and downcutting the bed and banks of the Nile. Undermined giant palm trees, still erect, were slowly sliding into the riverbed. The river was turning into a canyon requiring costly locks to handle the river traffic. The great flocks of waterfowl we had seen depicted on the tomb walls in the Valley of the Kings were decimated and the native fish population faces extinction.

The great Nile Delta, the product of rich silted floodwaters for eons, is losing the papyrus that was once used for scrolls in the ancient University of Alexandria. People who swim or dangle their feet in the canals along the river find a new threat from schistosomiasis, tiny worms that lodge in the liver and bladder. The rich fisheries of the Mediterranean that supplied abundant food to dynasties for thousands of years are being wiped out in

Watershed Campaigns

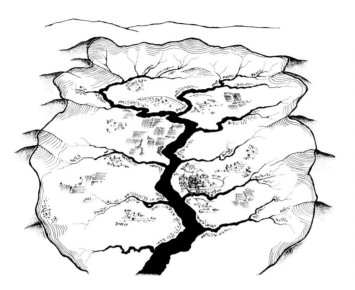

The American Heritage Dictionary *defines* **watershed** *as: 1. a ridge or stretch of high land dividing the areas drained by different rivers or systems, 2. the area drained by a river or system, 3. a crucial turning point affecting action, opinion, etc. To defend and restore the ecological quality of our watershed home should be the highest priority of physicians — and their patients.*

Illustration by Sarah B. Lauterbach/ Watershed 2000.

River Network, a national organization based in Portland, Oregon, is spearheading a nationwide movement to protect rivers and watersheds. The thrust of their five-year plan, Watershed 2000, is to establish vigilant and effective citizens' organizations in each of America's two thousand major watersheds. They see these watershed councils as the first line of defense for rivers, tackling issues such as dams, polluted farm and urban runoff, logging, mining, floodplain development, and development of streamside lands.

Huey Johnson, head of San Francisco's Resource Renewal Institute and founder of the Trust for Public Lands, introduced world-wide watershed sustainability in his 1995 book, *Green Plans.* New Zealand is on the forefront of watershed management, having reorganized its political boundaries into seventeen watershed districts.

Ecologists are gaining insights into workable methods for restoring health to streams using the watershed approach. They tell us that we must look at the whole watershed, the entire land area that contributes waters to the stream, in order to protect any part of it.

Learning about the watersheds we live and work in helps us understand our relationship to those resources that are at the core of our quality of life — and our very survival. California's hard-won "wild and scenic" rivers need watershed councils to ensure permanent protection.

one generation.

Throughout developing nations, the same scenario is being played out by international construction and engineering firms competing for work, often financed by the World Bank.

Mortgaging Health

The economic growth of sprawling California, made possible by the construction of its large dams, is being touted in other countries to entice the poorest nations to mortgage their futures to build dams. Yet it is likely that these dams will bankrupt these countries and displace millions of indigenous people who depend on the natural cycles of their rivers for their survival.

The International Rivers Network based in San Francisco is one grassroots organization set up to combat dams in Third World countries. It is led by Philip Williams, who was chief hydrologist for the Russian River Enhancement Plan. These rivers around the globe include China's Yangtze, Nepal's Arun, Africa's Zambezi, Asia's Mekong, and India's Ganges. The Network has already had some notable successes, but they are up against powerful political and economic forces, not the least of which are water lobbies in league with local politicians—just as in California.

My granddaughters Kira (left) and Gina look to the future: What will it be like for their generation? What will it be like for California? Will the rivers run clear and cold with abundant salmon and steelhead? Will they gaze in awe at fields of blue lupine, golden mules ear, and green gentian? Will the purple mountains' majesty be visible above the fruited plain?

Professor of Epidemiology at UC Berkeley, Dr. Warren Winklestein, used to tell our class, "The environment is a primary determinant of the health status of the population, rather than the quality or quantity of medical care."

Cleverness and technology keep us alive (for awhile). If wells are contaminated, we build costly, chemically-treated drinking water filtration plants or drink bottled water. We import seafood and grow poultry, beef, and vegetables around our cities using large doses of chemicals. Those who can afford it fly to Alaska to fish. Suburban children live sedentary lives cut off from nature. What will happen when the population doubles? Will even the gated communities survive?

In Third World countries if fisheries die from dammed rivers, the people could be swept by starvation, disease, war. The US has been lucky so far. But how much more time do we have to stabilize our population and repair the vital aquatic ecosystem of watersheds that maintains our health, our prosperity, and our lives on this beautiful Earth?

Changing California's Land Ethic

What better way to fight the destruction of Nature than to place in the hearts of the young this powerful plea for a land ethic.

—Aldo Leopold, *A Sand County Almanac*

California stands today on the slippery brink of an environmental and social cataclysm as its unplanned population growth soars by another eighteen million by 2025. That's the equivalent of adding two new counties the size of Los Angeles! In his remarkable book, *Reluctant Metropolis,* urban planner William B. Fulton traces the collapse of unmanageable, congested Los Angeles to imported water and a cartel of development interests he calls the "growth machine." This "machine" depends on the constant subdivision of new lands for enormous profits without regard for the consequences.

My training in public health emphasized ecological factors that may put people at risk of disease, for example, air pollution and lung disease, rapid urban growth and heart disease, water pollution and malignant disease. Yet it stopped short of that crucial link—how to change the political landscape in order to minimize these risk factors. We must learn to "bell the cat"–to identify and replace the elected officials in each city or county who conspire with the land speculators, developers, water agencies, promoters, bankers, and the like to create the "growth machine."

Each wave of developer-driven growth in county after county has left a horrendous ecological price to be paid by our children. For their sake each county must create its own land ethic revolution (as Marin did), in which their land and water, fauna and flora are treated as sacred allies, not adversaries. This can best be accomplished at the county level, where voters can gain political control of their county government and establish effective land-use and slow-growth population strategies. It took Marin's grassroots

Someday we hope to again share this river swimming hole with abundant steelhead, coho salmon, turtles, osprey, cottonwood giants, wild grapevines, and Dutchmen pipe. My grandson, Steve, is studying the tracks of a rarely seen river otter.

organizations about fifteen years to defeat the same insatiable growth machine that overwhelmed Los Angeles, but that victory included achieving a stabilized population growth, a sound economy, and superb long-range land use planning. (See the Appendix for a partial list of environmental organizations in Marin and Sonoma counties.)

Furthermore, to truly save our counties requires a vast expansion of outdoor classroom teaching. I would like to see the hands-on methods of Mrs. Terwilliger, "Bugs" Cain, Zumie, and our Audubon Canyon Ranch naturalists used in every school. We've found that inspired students will work to restore their creeks and watersheds.

Young people soon learn that their own health is closely linked to the quality of the watershed in which they live. They also grasp Leopold's simple truth that flora is the engine that pumps life into the great organ fauna, and that these are found on no other planet that we know of except Earth, with its fertility provided by water, sun, soil, and air. Like the late country singer John Denver, our children should cry with delight when they see the sun rise in a smogless sky.

Voters must learn to select their state governor, their county supervisors, and their city council members with the same care they use to select their dentist or physician. Developers know that the easiest way to obtain permits to pave farmland, drain wetlands, fill estuaries, or mine rivers is to control county government. We learned this yet again just as we drew close to winning the battle for gravel mining controls. Suddenly we had to start an entirely new battle with county supervisors to prevent the clear-cutting of thousands of acres of steep, forested Russian River watershed lands for conversion to vineyards by syndicated investors and huge agri-businesses. As its population grows beyond its carrying capacity, each county faces the destruction of its most vital resources.

Noted ecologist and naturalist Aldo Leopold (progenitor of the noted University of California family of river scientists) said it best in his 1948 *Sand County Almanac*:

> *Quit thinking of land-use as solely an economic problem. Examine each question in terms of what is ethically and esthetically right. A thing is right when it tends to preserve the integrity, stability and beauty of the biotic community. It is wrong when it does otherwise.*

Think what a boon it would be for California's health if the state and the counties developed a coordinated land-use plan that managed and restored our lands based on Aldo Leopold's standards. To ecologists, the loss of biodiversity is the greatest challenge facing California and the planet. We have seen how civilizations have quickly turned their land into barren wastelands. In my lifetime, for example, the delta marshes of the Colorado River, a "wilderness of milk and honey" as Leopold called it, have been dried up by dams to provide water for the desert cities of Las Vegas and Southern California.

Unless we face the challenge squarely and recognize that the cumulative impact of mediocre water- and land-use planning forced on our counties by land speculators, co-opted politicians, and the like is blighting our land and our economic future, we will continue to see a steady decline in the health of our families and communities, and in the quality of our lives. The world of wildlife—egrets and salmon, songbirds and frogs—is a reliable indicator. We must heed its warnings.

On looking back, it is the vision of those majestic steelhead trout charging their gills in that wild coastal river seventy years ago that has charged and recharged my entire life. Many wonderful friends, family members, and colleagues have also recharged my life in the great battles to save California.

Finally, I salute Miss Olin, my fourth-grade teacher in Oakland who inspired her students in 1929 to sing truthfully, "I love you, California, you're the grandest state of all," Caroline Livermore, Peter Behr, Brenda Adelman, and Bill Kortum, who showed the power of one person to turn first their county and then their state around.

Timeline: Diverting Rivers for Development

1908	The Potter Valley Power Project: 160,000 acre feet of Eel River water diverted by tunnel into the Russian River each year, giving Sonoma County a huge new source of free water called "abandoned water." System purchased by PG&E in 1929.
1949	Sonoma County Water Agency chartered by the state to sell water to Marin, Sonoma, and Mendocino, with Sonoma County Supervisors in charge.
1955	Metropolitan Water District of Southern California makes plans to dam North Coast rivers for diversion south.
1957	Sonoma County Water Agency begins to channelize miles of tributaries and drain 57,000 acres of land on the Santa Rosa Plain in anticipation of development for more than 200,000 people.
1959	Army Corps builds Coyote Dam on the Russian River (in Mendocino County) with the Sonoma County Water Agency to regulate the Eel River diversion.
	Freeway hearings begin for massive Marin-Sonoma Coast development utilizing diverted Russian and Eel River water.
	Marin Audubon Society created to fight building 2,000 houses by filling Richardson Bay (San Francisco Bay).
1961	Marin Supervisors adopt the Bolinas Basin Master Plan for 50,000 people on the Southern Marin coast.
	Creation of Audubon Canyon Ranch Sanctuary on Bolinas Lagoon and Highway 1 helps heighten opposition to coastal freeways and aqueducts.
1962	Point Reyes National Seashore authorized, but underfunded.
	PG&E commences the nation's largest nuclear power plant on Bodega Bay—without public hearings.
	Warm Springs Dam on the Russian River authorized.
1965	Eel River Water Council created by eight North Coast counties to dam the Eel River—largely to supply Southern California—with the Sonoma County Water Agency at its center.
1967	Bolinas Harbor District Master Plan defeated by the "Kent Island Coup."
	West Marin General Plan for 150,000 people adopted by Supervisors for the east shore of Tomales Bay.
	Plan proposed to extend Russian River aqueduct to new Tomales Bay cities.
1968	Marin voters reject freeways and sprawl in crucial election, putting slow-growth Supervisors in the majority for the first time.
1969	Governor Reagan kills the enormous Dos Rios Dam on Eel River.
	Audubon Canyon Ranch sanctuaries created along Tomales Bay and Highway 1 to block development and to help save the Point Reyes National Seashore.

"SOS Campaign" (Save Our Seashore) led by Peter Behr succeeds.

1971   Russian River-Marin aqueduct defeated by Marin voters 9-1.

West Marin Master Plan and coastal freeways withdrawn by Supervisors.

1972   Purchase of Point Reyes National Seashore and Golden Gate National Recreation Area completed.

"Wild and Scenic River Act" by State Senator Peter Behr protects Eel, Trinity, Klamath, and Smith rivers from dams.

Marks vs. Whitney Supreme Court Public Trust decision protects Tomales Bay and other California tidelands from land-fill.

California Coastal initiative (State Proposition 20), originated by COAAST in Sonoma County, passes.

1973   Water moratorium on new hookups by Marin Municipal Water District slows county growth; EIR and initiatives delay Warm Springs Dam.

Land Investors Research gives up on subdividing of 7,805 acres on Tomales Bay.

Final "slow growth" Marin Countywide Plan and 60-acre agricultural zones adopted by Supervisors.

1976   California Coastal Act creates permanent Coastal Commission to regulate development along 1,100 miles of coast.

1980   Marin Agricultural Land Trust created to preserve agriculture.

1983   Warm Springs Dam completed on Russian River by Army Corps for Sonoma County Water Agency—the last large dam in California.

1989   Russian River Task Force files first lawsuit to protect Middle Reach wells and drinking water aquifers from gravel mining.

1992   Having established growth controls, Southern Marin voters approve bond issue to import Russian River water, but implementation is unlikely.

1994   Federal legislation proposed to protect agriculture on the boundaries of Point Reyes National Seashore.

Sonoma Supervisors adopt twenty-year Mining Plan allowing dredging of 200 more acres of the Russian River Aquifer.

1995-1997   American Rivers lists Russian River "one of the nation's most threatened."

Repetitive Russian River flood damages total $130 million.

1996   Friends of the Russian River threatens to sue the state for failing to protect the public trust resources of California rivers. Cal/EPA adopts Watershed Management Initiative for all California rivers.

Hearings to increase Russian River drinking water appropriations postponed. River is declared over-appropriated and in need of management.

Russian River coho salmon listed as threatened species (steelhead listed in 1997).

1997   Sonoma County Water Agency's attempt to buy the Potter Valley Power Project from PG&E put on hold pending scientific studies of the decline of the salmonid species in the Eel and Russian Rivers.

1998   Gravel mining in the Russian River Aquifer continues.

"The Sonoma Experience"

MANAGING THE RUSSIAN RIVER BY LAWSUITS

This long list of legal actions related to gravel mining is unprecedented in California counties and results largely from mismanagement of the Russian River by the Sonoma County Supervisors–Directors of the Sonoma County Water Agency, who also control gravel. None of the suits were frivolous; all sought to correct serious environmental wrongs, with litigation a tragic last resort.

I. Dry Creek Farmers, Sierra Club, and Russian River Task Force (wineries and growers)

1976	Successful litigation by twenty Dry Creek and Middle Reach farmers against Sonoma County and ten mining firms for allowing excessive mining, which resulted in the riverbed dropping about twenty feet and the loss of wells and property. All mining stopped; the litigation resulted in the 1981 Aggregate Resources Management (ARM) Plan, soon ignored.
1990	Successful litigation by the Sierra Club and Russian River Task Force against Sonoma County challenging rezoning of a designated agricultural and groundwater preservation area to accommodate Syar Industries' 30-acre Phase II terrace mining project in the Middle Reach. The case resulted in a published opinion in the Court of Appeal, *Sierra Club et al. v. County of Sonoma, (Syar)* (1st Dist. 1992) 6 Cal.App.4th 1307. The County was required to prepare an Environmental Impact Report (EIR) prior to consideration of mining. The case exposed the lack of feasible reclamation in terrace mining, affecting Syar's Phase I and Phase II pits, and resulted in preparation of an EIR and also the new 1994 ARM Plan.
1992	Litigation by the Sierra Club and the Russian River Task Force against Syar Industries and Sonoma County for expanded dredging of Syar's Phase I, fifty-acre gravel pit without an amended permit. This pit is adjacent to Healdsburg's wastewater gravel pit that ruptured into the river during floods of 1995 and 1997.
1993	Litigation by the Sierra Club and the Russian River Task Force against Sonoma County and Syar Industries for dredging the 35-acre Phase II gravel pit deeper than the riverbed without a study of levee stability and pit capture. A supplemental EIR was ordered by the Superior Court in April 1994, but levees ruptured in the floods of 1995 and 1997 before the EIR was completed.
1994	Supervisors adopt ARM Plan that allows dredging 200 more acres in the aquifer without repairing old pits to prevent pit capture. Litigation anticipated.
1997	Pending litigation by the Russian River Task Force against Sonoma County for issuing a ten year instream mining permit to Dewitt Sand and Gravel without first completing its critical pending environmental studies of ARM Plan inadequacies relative to the cumulative impacts of instream mining on flooding, erosion, fisheries (including recent "threatened" listing of coho salmon), and water supply.

II. Fishery Groups

1985-1996   Successful litigation by Trout Unlimited against Sonoma County requiring a fish ladder over the Healdsburg Dam, checkpoint in the sinking river bed from excessive mining (adjacent to undermined Highway 101 bridge). Cost of fish ladder one million dollars not built by 1997.

III. Former Mining Employees and Aggregate Contractor

1991   Two lawsuits. A former employee and a contractor against Kaiser Sand and Gravel and Syar Industries for alleged price fixing and bid rigging in the sale of aggregate. Federal investigation. Settled out of court in 1995.

IV. Cities, State Attorney General, District Attorney, Grand Jury

1980   Unsuccessful litigation by the City of Ukiah against Mendocino County for allowing excessive mining adjacent to its wells. Ukiah ordered to construct the first drinking water treatment plant on the Russian River by State Office of Drinking Water because of contaminated wells. Cloverdale received the same order in 1995. The Sonoma County Water Agency may be next because of contamination of drinking water infiltration ponds and one well during floods.

1990   Year-long County Grand Jury investigation of Sonoma County Supervisors and planning department for failure to regulate gravel mining. Ninety-six-page report and Task Force litigation resulted in new ARM Plan.

1991   Litigation by the Sonoma County Environmental District Attorney against Kaiser Sand & Gravel for dredging the 72-acre Benoist pit near The Sonoma County Water Agency wells for three years without a valid permit. This pit ruptures in each flood.

1992   Two suits by the State Attorney General on behalf of the State Lands Commission against Syar Industries for obstructing the river, silting public water intakes, creating a public nuisance, and mining on state property at the Doyle pit. Only the latter issue remains unsettled.

1993   Litigation by the City of Healdsburg against Sonoma County over impact of the Healdsburg Dam on its wells.

1997   Caltrans replaces the undermined Highway 101 bridge at Healdsburg at a cost to taxpayers of eleven million dollars. It is not known if the state will litigate. The Federal Highway Department ruled in 1995 that miners pay for mining-related bridge damages.

V. Friends Of the Russian River

1995   Successful litigation by Friends of the Russian River against City of Healdsburg to stop use of Syar's gravel pit for wastewater dumping after it ruptured into the river during floods. Such use abated by the Regional Water Quality Board in 1995, but they gave six more years.

1996   Friends of the Russian River and Natural Heritage Institute filed notice of intended litigation against state agencies for failing to protect the Public Trust Resources of the Russian River. Negotiated outcome: a Watershed Management Program ordered by CAL/EPA for each river in California.

VI. Other

1985-1998   Lawsuits by Russian River Watershed Protection Committee against Santa Rosa Sanitary District for repeated excessive wastewater discharges.

Environmental Organizations and Officers

Audubon Canyon Ranch

Sponsoring Audubon Chapters
Madrone, Marin, Golden Gate, and Sequoia

Executive Director
Maurice A. Schwartz

Presidents

L. Martin Griffin Jr., M.D.*	1961-1962, 1966-1967, 1968-1970
William S. Picher*	1962-1966, 1977-1979
George Peyton Jr.	1967-1968
Howard Allen	1970-1972
Dudley Hubbard	1972-1974
Edward P. McElhany	1975-1977
Thomas S. Price	1979-1981
Bruce Howard	1981-1983
Robert Conrath	1983-1984
Flora Maclise	1984-1986
Richard Baird	1986-1988
Jack Harper	1988-1990
Gary Holloway	1990-1992
Robert Hahn	1992-1994
Steve Thal	1994-1995
Len Blumin, M.D.	1995-1997
Jack Harper	1997-

*Founders, with Aileen Pierson

Docent Council Presidents

Mary Belle Van Voorhees	1969-1970
Joyce Henshaw	1971
Lani Valentine	1972
Jo McLeod	1973
Nadine Hastings	1974
Barbara Chase	1975
Nancy Barbour	1976
Jane Ferguson	1977
Beverly Sarjeant	1978
Debbie Ablin	1979
Mary Ann Sadler	1980
Gerry Snedaker	1981
Elizabeth Harsook	1982
Mildie Whedon	1983-1984
Kit Lee	1985-1986
Katie Beacock	1987-1988
Fran Korb	1989-1990
Barbara Beck	1991
Cia Donahue	1992-1993
Jeni Jackson	1994-1995
Betsy Stafford	1996
Patti Blumin	1997-1998

Ranch Guides
Coordinators: Eileen Libby, Ray Peterson

Audubon Canyon Ranch
  Bolinas Lagoon Preserve
  Bouverie Preserve
  Cypress Grove Preserve
4900 Shoreline Highway
Stinson Beach, CA 94970
(415) 868-9244

Bouverie Audubon Preserve

Docent Council Presidents

Suzanne Weis	1984-1985
Ginny Fletcher	1985-1986
Eleanor Decker/ Kate Henderson	1986-1987
Gwen Dhesi	1987-1988

Faylene Roth	1988-1989
Phyllis Ellman	1989-1990
Maxine Hall	1990-1991
Anita Stelling	1991-1992
Sara Cleg	1992-1993
Mary Engebreth	1993-1995
Shel Bernstein	1995-1996
Noelle Bon	1996-1997
Pat McLorie	1997-1998

Bouverie Audubon Preserve
A Branch of Audubon Canyon Ranch
P.O. Box 1195
Glen Ellen, CA 95442
(707) 938-4554

The Environmental Forum of Marin

*Founded by Audubon Canyon Ranch in 1972,
Independent since 1975*

Presidents

Polly Smith	1972, 1982
Barbara Violich Bouchke	1973
Karin Urquhart	1974
Nancy Wise	1975, 1979
Gloria Duncan	1976
Phyllis Faber	1977
Judy Alstrom	1978
Ruth Solomon	1979
Ginny Havel	1980
Eleanor Siperstein	1981
Barbara Salzman	1983, 1985
Shirley Bogardus	1984
Virginia Souders-Mason	1986, 1987, 1990
Barbara Perlman-Wyman	1988, 1989
Dorothy Walters	1991
Kathy Lowrey	1992, 1993
Karol Raymer	1994, 1995
Julie Grantz	1996, 1997

Founders and Instructors, 1972

Howard B. Allen*
Mary Jane Baker
David Cavagnaro
Kathy Cuneo
Nona Dennis
Phyllis Faber
Martin Griffin, M.D.*
Remmy Kingsley
Pam Lloyd
Ray Peterson
William S. Picher*
Mary Belle Van Voorhees*
Clerin Zumwalt*

*ACR Board Members, 1972

The Environmental Forum of Marin
P.O. Box 74
Larkspur, CA 94977

National Audubon Society– California and the Richardson Bay Audubon Center

Director
Beth Huning

**National Audubon Society–California
and the Richardson Bay Audubon Center**
370 Greenwood Beach Road
Tiburon, CA 94920
(415) 388-2524

Marin Conservation League

Marin Conservation League
55 Mitchell Blvd., Suite 21
San Rafael, CA 94903

Griffin Russian River Riparian Preserve

Griffin Russian River Riparian Preserve
c/o Sonoma Land Trust
1122 Sonoma Avenue
Santa Rosa, CA 95405

Friends of the Russian River

President
Joan Vilms

Founders, 1993

Martin & Joyce Griffin, David Bolling,
Tom Roth

Coalition Members, 1998

California Native Plant Society,
  Milo Baker Chapter
Citizens for Cloverdale
Forestville Chamber of Commerce
Friends of the Esteros
Healdsburg Alliance for Responsible Citizens
Madrone Audubon Society
Marin Conservation League
Mendocino Environmental Center
Russian River Alliance
Russian River Chamber of Commerce
Russian River Unlimited (Hopland)
Sequoia Paddling Club
Sierra Club, Sonoma County Group
Sonoma County Conservation Action
Sonoma Ecology Center
Sonoma Watershed Council
Stewards of Slavianka
Trout Unlimited
Western Sonoma County Rural Alliance
Russian River Task Force

Friends of the Russian River (FORR)
1217 14th Street
Santa Rosa, CA 95404

Russian River Environmental Forum

Coordinators
Meg Alexander, Tam Fraser, Pam Netzow

Russian River Environmental Forum
538 Tucker
Healdsburg, CA 95448

Russian River Task Force

Coordinators
Therese Shere, Martin Griffin

Legal Counsel
Susan Brandt-Hawley

Russian River Task Force
P.O. Box 309
Glen Ellen, CA 95442

Russian River Watershed Protection Committee

Founder/Coordinator
Brenda Adelman

Russian River Watershed Protection Committee
P.O. Box 501
Guerneville, CA 95446

Sonoma County Conservation Action

Sonoma County Conservation Action
540 Pacific Ave.
Santa Rosa, CA 95404

Army Corps of Engineers. *Final Environmental Impact Statement, Part II. Warm Springs Dam and Lake Sonoma Project, Russian River Basin, Sonoma County, California.* Washington, DC: Department of the Army, November 1973.

Arrigoni, Patricia. *Making the Most of Marin.* Fairfax, Calif.: Traveler Publishers International, 1990.

Ashley, Beth. "Kent Name Solidly Imprinted on Face of Marin." *Marin Independent Journal,* August 1, 1993.

_____. *Marin.* San Francisco: Chronicle Books, 1993.

Audubon Canyon Ranch Natural History Handbook. Stinson Beach, Calif.: Audubon Canyon Ranch, 1996.

Barbour, Michael, et al. *California's Changing Landscapes: Diversity and Conservation of California Vegetation.* Sacramento: California Native Plant Society, 1993.

Bastian, Beverly and Barbara Gnoss. *A Pictorial History of Belvedere 1890-1990.* Tiburon, Calif.: The Landmark Society, 1990.

Behr, Peter. *Oral History Interview.* Conducted 1988 and 1989 by Ann Lage, Regional Oral History Office. Berkeley: University of California for the State Government Oral History Program.

Bolling, David M. *How To Save A River: A Handbook for Citizen Action.* Covleo, Calif.: Island Press, 1994.

Bowen, Michael, ed. *Streamkeepers Log, Special Steelhead Edition.* San Francisco: California Trout, March 1995.

Brickson, Betty. "Drinking at the Water Table; Ground Water: Our Hidden Resource." *Pacific Discovery,* Winter 1993: 32.

Brower, David. *The Life and Times of David Brower.* Salt Lake City: Peregrine Smith, 1990.

California's Rivers and Streams, Working Toward Solutions. Prepared by Division of Water Quality, Sacramento: January 1995.

California Water Atlas. Sacramento: State of California, 1976.

Caughman, Madge and Joanne S. Ginsberg, eds. *California Coastal Resource Guide.* Berkeley: University of California Press, 1987.

Chatham, Russel. *Angler's Coast.* Livingston, Montana: Clark City Press, 1990.

Collins, Brian and Thomas Dunne. *Fluvial Geomorphology and River-Gravel Mining: A Guide for Planners, Case Studies Included.* Sacramento: California Department of Conservation, Division of Mines and Geology, 1990.

Conradson, Diane R. *Exploring Our Baylands.* Palo Alto, Calif.: Palo Alto Chamber of Commerce, 1966.

Corwin, Ruthann, Martin Griffin, et al. *Tomales Bay Study, Compendium of Reports.* Prepared for The Conservation Foundation, Washington DC, 1972.

Covel, Paul F. *Beacons Along a Naturalist's Trail: California Naturalists and Innovators.* Oakland: Western Interpretive Press, 1988. (on "Bugs" Cain)

Curry, Robert R. "Russian River Middle Reach—Aggregate or Aquifer?" Friends of the Russian River Conference Report. Healdsburg, Calif., March 31, 1994.

Davis, Margaret Leslie. *Rivers in the Desert: William Mulholland and the Inventing of Los Angeles.* New York: Harper Perennial, 1993.

Dunn, James. "Goodbye, Agricultural Preserves, Owners of thousands of acres of Sonoma County farmland are swapping tax breaks for the opportunity to develop." *Sonoma Business.* Santa Rosa, Calif., April 1989.

EIP Associates prepared for State Mining and Geology Board, US Army Corps of Engineers, City of Healdsburg. "EIR/EIS Russian River Instream Mining." *Syar Industries, Inc. Mining Use Permit Application.* June 1997.

Evens, Jules G. *The Natural History of the Point Reyes Peninsula, Rev. Ed.* Point Reyes, Calif.: Point Reyes National Seashore Association 1993.

Faber, Phyllis. *Common Riparian Plants of California, A Field Guide for the Layman.* Mill Valley, Calif.: Pickleweed Press, 1989.

Fairley, Lincoln. *Mount Tamalpais: A History.* San Francisco: Scottwall Associates, 1987.

Fellmeth, Robert C. Ed., *Power And Land In California, The Ralph Nader Task Force Report on Land Use in the State of California.* Vol. 1. Preliminary Draft. Washington DC: Center for Study of Responsive Law, 1971.

Florsheim, Joan, and Philip Williams. "Observations from the January 1995 Flood on the Russian River." Prepared for the California State Coastal Conservancy, March 1995.

_____. "Geomorphic and Hydrologic Conditions in the Russian River, California." Discussion Document prepared for the California Coastal Conservancy and the Mendocino County Water Agency, December 1993.

Flosi, Gary, Forrest L. Reynolds and others. *California Salmonid Stream Habitat Restoration Manual.* Sacramento: California Department of Fish and Game, October 1994.

Friends of the Russian River. *Russian River in Peril, An Educational Conference.* Program Report. Healdsburg, Calif.: FORR, March 1994.

Galloway, Allan J. *Geology of the Point Reyes Peninsula, Marin County, California.* Bulletin 202. Sacramento: Division of Mines and Geology, 1977.

Gilliam, Harold. *Island In Time.* New York: Charles Scribners 1962.

_____. *Between the Devil & the Deep Blue Bay: The Struggle to Save San Francisco Bay.* San Francisco: Chronicle Books, 1969.

_____. "Wrestling Over the River, Are agriculture and recreation losing out to gravel mining in a battle for the Russian River?" *This World, San Francisco Chronicle.* San Francisco: July 4, 1993.

_____ and Ann Gilliam. *Marin Headlands: Portals of Time.* San Francisco: Golden Gate National Park Association, 1993.

Griffin, Martin. "Nepal." *Sierra Club Bulletin,* October 1970.

_____, ed. *Landmarks in the History of Audubon Canyon Ranch.* Stinson Beach, Calif.: Audubon Canyon Ranch, 1961-1973.

_____. "Gravel Mining vs. Clean Drinking Water." *E.I.R. Environmental Impact Reporter.* Sebastopol, Calif., April 1992.

Gustafson, Joel F. *Ecological Studies, Bolinas Lagoon, Marin County, California.* Stinson Beach, Calif.: Audubon Canyon Ranch, June 1, 1969.

Hart, John. *San Francisco's Wilderness Next Door.* San Rafael, Calif.; Presidio Press, 1979.

_____. *Farming on the Edge: Saving Family Farms in Marin County, California.* Berkeley: University of California Press, 1991.

_____. *Storm Over Mono, The Mono Lake Battle and the California Water Future.* Berkeley: University of California Press, 1996.

Heig, James, ed. *Pictorial History of Tiburon, A California Railroad Town.* Sponsored by the Landmarks Society of Tiburon and Belvedere. San Francisco: Scottwall Associates, 1984.

Heller, Alfred, ed. "The California Tomorrow Plan, Revised Edition" *Cry California, The Journal of California Tomorrow.* Summer 1972.

Hurd, Edith Thacher. *The Blue Heron Tree.* Mill Valley, Calif.: Pickleweed Press, 1991.

Jacobs, Diana, Principal Contributor, State Lands Commission. *California's Rivers: A Public Trust Report.* Sacramento: California State Lands Commission, 1993.

Johnson, Huey D. *Green Plans: Greenprint for Sustainability.* Lincoln: Univ. of Nebraska, 1995.

Kondolf, G. Mathias and W. V. Graham. "Geomorphic and Environmental Effects of Instream Gravel Mining." *Journal of Landscape and Urban Planning.* Berkeley, University of California Dept. of Landscape Architecture, June 16, 1993.

LeBaron, Gaye. "Gaye LeBaron's Notebook," *The Press Democrat,* 1962-1998. "What's Hiding Out There on Bodega Head?" December 17, 1995. "How in the World Did This Happen to Our Creeks?" October 22, 1995.

_____ and Joann Mitchell. *Santa Rosa, a Twentieth Century Town.* Santa Rosa, Calif.: Historia Ltd., 1993.

Leopold, Aldo. *A Sand County Almanac, and Sketches Here and There.* New York: Oxford University Press, 1949, 1968.

Leys, John, with Robert Curry, (advisor). *Sustainable Development of the Middle Reach Aquifer.* Senior Thesis for Environmental Studies, University of California at Santa Cruz, March 22, 1996.

Livermore, Norman B. *Oral History Interview.* Conducted by Anne Lage and Gabrielle Morris, Regional Oral History Office. Berkeley: University of California for the State Government Oral History Program, 1981, 1982.

Livingston, D. S. (Dewey). *"A Good Life," Dairy Farming in the Olema Valley: A History of Dairy and Beef Ranches of the Olema Valley and Lagunitas Canyon.* San Francisco: National Park Service, Department of the Interior, 1995.

Madrone Associates and Arthur D. Little, Inc. *The Russian River Water Supply Project*, Environmental Impact Report, Draft. San Rafael, Calif.: Marin Municipal Water District, September 1973.

Marcus, Laurel. *Russian River Resource Enhancement Plan*, Status Reports. Oakland, Calif.: California State Coastal Conservancy, 1991-1995.

_____. *Scientific Data, Russian River Enhancement Plan, Referral and Submitted Background Documentation*, Oakland, Calif.: California State Coastal Conservancy, March 1995

Marin Countywide Plan. San Rafael, Calif.: Marin County Planning Department, 1973. Revised 1995.

Marin Municipal Water District. *An Historical Summary of the Marin Municipal Water District.* Marin County, Calif., November 1972.

_____. *Environmental Planning Study.* Report Prepared by Thomas G. Dickert & Robert H. Twiss. Marin County, Calif., November 1972.

Marin Women's Hall of Fame. Annual Honorees. Anne T. Kent Room. San Rafael, Calif.: Marin County Library.

Mason, Jack. *Earthquake Bay: A History of Tomales Bay, California.* Inverness, Calif.: North Shore Books, 1976.

McHarg, Ian L. *Design With Nature.* New York: John Wiley & Sons, Inc., 1992.

Mount, Jeffrey F. *California Rivers and Streams: The Conflict Between Fluvial Process and Land Use.* Berkeley: University of California Press, 1995.

North Coast Regional Water Quality Control Board Staff. *Public Report On A Watershed Planning Framework For The Russian/Bodega Watershed Management Area.* Santa Rosa, Calif.: NCRWQCB, March 7, 1996.

Oregon Water Resources Research Institute. *Gravel Disturbance Impacts on Salmon Habitat and Stream Health.* Vol. II: Technical Background Report. Salem: Oregon State University, April 1995.

Pacific Rivers Council, Inc. *The Decline of Coho Salmon and the Need for Protection Under the Endangered Species Act.* Eugene, Oregon: Pacific Rivers Council, Inc., August 31, 1993.

Palmer, Tim, *California's Threatened Environment: Restoring the Dream.* Covelo, Calif.: Island Press, 1993.

Paul, Joseph. "Fight for the Eel, Klamath, Trinity, Wild Rivers Bill Reaches Congress." *Wild Rivers Reporter*, Summer 1970. (Available from California Trout)

Poten, Constance. "Canaries of the Biosphere," *Montanan.* Fall 1995:12. (on life in river aquifers)

Pratt, Helen. *Herons & Egrets of Audubon Canyon Ranch.* Stinson Beach, Calif.: Helen Pratt, 1993.

Rector, Krista. *Sonoma County Water Agency Russian River Watershed, Mendocino, Sonoma and Marin Counties, California.* Santa Rosa, Calif.: Friends of the Russian River (FORR), April 1996.

Reisner, Marc. *Cadillac Desert: The American West and Its Disappearing Water.* New York: Penguin, 1986.

Rivers, Trails and Conservation Assistance, National Park Service (RTCA). *Economic Impacts of Protecting Rivers, Trails and Greenway Corridors, A Resource Book*, 3d ed. Washington, DC: National Park Service, 1992.

Rowntree, Rowan A. *Biological Considerations in Bolinas Lagoon Planning: A Summary and Analysis.* Prepared for The Conservation Foundation, Washington, DC and Berkeley, January 1971.

Scarborough, Katie and Scot Stegeman. *Farmland Worth Saving: The Present Value, Potential And Preservation Of Sonoma County Agriculture.* Santa Rosa, Calif.: Sonoma County Farmlands Group, October 1989.

Scott, Mel. *The Future of San Francisco Bay.* Institute of Governmental Studies. Berkeley: University of California Press, September 1963.

Schell, Orville. *The Town That Fought To Save Itself.* New York: Pantheon 1976. (on Bolinas)

Slade, David C. Esq. "The Public Trust Doctrine, A Primer for Friends of America's Rivers." Portland, Oregon: River Network, Summer 1993.

Smith, Edmund H. and Johnson, Ralph G. *The Environmental Study of Tomales Bay.* Report for the Water Quality Office, Environmental Protection Agency, Project #18050DFP, August 1971.

Snyder, Gary. *A Place in Space: Ethics, Aesthetics and Watersheds.* Washington, DC: Counterpoint, 1995.

Sonoma County. *Aggregate Resources Management Plan and EIR*, Santa Rosa, Calif., November 1994. (Hydrology by Philip Williams Associates)

Sonoma County Water Agency. *Environmental Impact Report. Russian River to Cotati Intertie Project.* Santa Rosa, Calif.: Sonoma County Water Agency, July 1974.

_____. *The Russian River Water Plan, Section A, Russian River Project, Section B, Sonoma-Marin Water Transmission System.* Santa Rosa, Calif.: Sonoma County Water Agency, 1969.

_____. *Wohler Aquifer Acquisition and Pumping Capacity Restoration, Russian River-Cotati Intertie Project. Expanded Initial Study and Negative Declaration of Environmental Impact.* Santa Rosa, Calif.: Sonoma County Water Agency, May 6, 1991.

_____. *Russian River Well Field Development.* Santa Rosa, Calif.: Sonoma County Water Agency, April 22, 1994.

_____. *The Russian River: An Assessment of Its Condition and Governmental Oversight.* Prepared by Bob Beach, Sonoma County Water Agency, August 1996.

_____. *Sonoma County Water Agency Russian River Activities Workshop.* Santa Rosa, Calif.: Sonoma County Water Agency, March 1995.

_____. *Water Supply and Transmission System Project.* Draft, Environmental Impact Report. Vol. I. Santa Rosa, Calif.: Sonoma County Water Agency, September 1996.

_____. *Russian River Action Plan, A Regional Assessment of Resource Needs and Restoration Opportunities.* Santa Rosa, Calif.: Sonoma County Water Agency, March 1997.

Specter, Rosanne. "Doctor for the Environment, Dr. Marty Griffin" *Stanford MD,* Winter 1994/95.

State of California Water Resources Control Board. *Russian River Project. Decision 1610.* Staff Report. Sacramento: State of California, State Water Resources Control Board, April 1986.

_____. *Russian River Watershed.* Staff Report. Sacramento: State of California, State Water Resources Control Board, August 15, 1997.

Steiner Environmental Consulting. *A History of the Salmonid Decline in the Russian River.* Sponsored by Sonoma County Water Agency and California State Coastal Conservancy. Potter Valley, Calif.: Steiner Environmental Consulting, August 1996.

Steinhardt, David. "The Story of Richardson Bay, the Lyford House, the Founding of Richardson Bay Audubon Center and Marin Audubon Society." *Richardson Bay Journal,* Tiburon, Calif.: National Audubon Center, 1996.

Terwilliger, Elizabeth. *A Naturalist's Guide to the National Audubon Society's Richardson Bay Wildlife Sanctuary and Education Center.* Tiburon, Calif.: Elizabeth Terwilliger Nature Education Foundation, 1980.

The Economic Imperative of Protecting Riverine Habitat in the Pacific Northwest. Oregon Rivers Council, Research Report No. V, January 1992.

Walker, David W. *Bolinas Lagoon, An Environmental Management Program for Bolinas Lagoon, California.* Washington, DC: The Conservation Foundation, February 1971.

Wallin, Phillip and Rita R. Haberman. *People Protecting Rivers: A Collection of Lessons from Successful Grassroots Activists.* Prepared for River Network. Portland, Oregon: April 1992.

Philip Williams Associates and Avocet Research Associates, *Draft, Bolinas Lagoon Management Update.* San Rafael, Calif.: Marin County Dept. of Parks, Open Space and Cultural Services, August 1995.

Whitaker, Scott (Anil Verma, Thesis Director). *Griffin Riparian Preserve: Design for Restoration, Preservation.* Final Thesis Project. UCLA Extension Landscape Architecture Program, Spring 1992. (Available at Preserve, Healdsburg)

Wyatt, Bruce and others. *The Third Biennial State of Tomales Bay Conference.* Point Reyes, Calif.: Environmental Action Committee, October 24, 1992.

Zimmerman, Joy. "Russian Roulette, Longtime Activist Marty Griffin warns of a river in peril." *Pacific Sun.* March 16-22, 1994.

Zumwalt, Clerin W. *The History of Audubon Canyon Ranch.* Draft Manuscript. Stinson Beach, Calif.: Audubon Canyon Ranch, 1996.

References to illustrations are printed in italics.

Marin County Board of Supervisors, 107, 108, 109, 110
  and Pt. Reyes National Seashore, 129
  and Warm Springs Dam, 107
Marin County Open Space District, xviii, 68, 108, 111
Marin Countywide Plan, xvii, 89, 107-108, 110, 137, 255
Marin Master Plan, Mary Summer's, 71
Marin Medical Society, 47, *51*
Marin Municipal Water District, 10, 18, *30,* 139-141, *143,* 255
Mark West Creek, 220, *213, 221*
Marks vs. Whitney, 133, 134, 255
Marks, Larry, 134
Marshall, Harry, 25, 78
Marshlands, x, 213, 233
  filling of, *9-10*
  freshwater, 102, 127
  importance of to birds, 9, 17
  permanent protection of California's, 134
  as real estate, 18
  saltwater, 17
Martinelli, Jordan, 146, *147*
Martinelli, Leroy, 83-84
Mason, Jack, 51
Matthews Walker Timber Company, 85
May, Richard, *171*
McDaniel, Gene, 35-36, 58
McGuire, Warren, 148
McNamara, Steve, 50
McPhail, Jack, 146, *147*
Media, 67, 77, 219. *See also* Strategy, media; *Independent Journal*; *Pacific Sun*
Metropolitan Water District of Southern California, 163, 172, 254
Meyer, Amy, 128, 132
Meyn, Barbara, 225
Middle Reach gravel aquifer, *153,* 177, 195, 205, *216, 226,* 236. *See also* Sonoma-Marin Aquifer
  description, 179
  effect of mining on, 209
  mining of, *178, 179,* 256
  plan to restore, 220
Miller, Alden, 6
Miller, Congressman Clem, 31
Miller, Frank, *85*
Miller, Gordon, 164, *187,* 191, 196
  promoter of dams, 186
  and state water lobby, 187

Millerton Point Ranch, 117
Mining, xii, 177, 206, *218,* 226, 240-242, 246
  destructive effects of, *179,* 180, 198, 218, 233, 242
  destruction of natural water filter, 192
  and drinking water quality, 193, 195, 256-257
  effects on tidelands, 18
  erosion, *198,* 217, 256
  firms, 220, 242-243, 256-257
  and flood damage, 216
  instream, 219, 256
  interests, 205
  pits, *217,* 256-257
  quarry, 206
  vs. river, 243, 245
  sites, *243*
  and threat to water quality, 198, *211-216,* 217, 256-257
Mono Lake, 134, 163
Monrad, Eric, 225
Moore, Harry and Callita, 93
Morford, Mike, 240
Morgan, Angela, 159
Morrison, Bob, 195, 199, 211, 219
Morro Bay, 61
Mt. Livermore, *13*
Mt. Tamalpais, 15, 17
Muir Beach Butterfly Preserve, 132
Murphy, George, 132

National Audubon Society, 20, 25, 39, 78-79, 134, 259
National Audubon Society Chapters, xviii. *See also* Marin Audubon Society; Golden Gate Audubon Chapter
Nature Conservancy, The, xviii, 63, 65, 66, 67, 107, 155
Navarro River, 7
Newell, Paul, 63, 65, 76
Nicasio Creek, 95
Nicholas, Janet, 202
Nichols, Richard, 182
Nile River, 245
Nixon, President Richard, 129, 132
North Coast Regional Water Quality Control Board, 235
North Marin Water District, 114

Oceana Marin, xii, 109
Oko, Captain Adolph, 119
Olema Freshwater Marsh, xix, 127, 130
Olin, Miss, 6, 251

Open space, xiv, 111, 119, 142. *See also* Marin County Open Space District
Oswald, William J., 69
Otis, Webster, 114, 116
Owens Valley, 163
Oysters, 102, 119

Pacific Flyway, 17, 61, 103
Pacific Sun, 50, *60,* 85, *168*
Parcher, Loren, 83
Paul, Joseph, 169, 170, 171
Penny Island, 181
Petaluma River Marsh Restoration Project, *232,* 233
Peterson, John, 158, *159*
Peterson, Ray, *88,* 89, *93,* 258, 259
Peyton, George, 63, 76, 115, 124, 258
  biography, *135*
PG&E, 180-181, 254
Philip Williams and Associates, 219
Picher, Stan, 21, 34, 41-42, 50, 52, 76, 77, 92, 115, 120, 158, 258-259
  biography, *48, 53*
  fundraising, 49, 53, 77, 89, 127, 135
  Galloway Ranch, 73
  Kent Island purchase, 66
  Picher Canyon, 43, 53
  purchase of Audubon Canyon Ranch, 39, 40
Picher, William Stanton. *See* Picher, Stan
Pierce Point, 114
Pierce Point Ranch, 113, 116
Pierson, Aileen, 41
Pikes Gulch. *See* Galloway Ranch
Pit-mining. *See* Mining
Planning, land use, xvii, 108, 110, 250, 251
Pleydell-Bouverie, David. *See* Bouverie, David
"The Plot to Save Marin", 106, 139, 140, 162
Point Reyes Bird Observatory, 74, 128
Point Reyes National Seashore, xii, xviii, *28,* 31, 71, *94,* 95, 129, 135, 255
  authorized, 254
  funding of, 132
  and Land Investors Research, *115,* 116
Point Reyes Peninsula, xii-xiv
Poole, Randy, 199
Population growth, xvii, 4, 110, 202, 249

Aero Photographers, Inc.: 14, 30, 70, 116.

Michael Amsler: 227.

Peter Arrigoni: 105.

Audubon Canyon Ranch Archives: 48 (BRY), 51 *right,* 53, 56 (Walter Goodman), 57, 75 (John M. King), 83 (Tori Hafer), 86 (BRY), 87 (BRY), 88 (Bob Stendel), 90, 91, 92, 93, 157, 158, 169 (BRY).

Robert Bastian, *San Francisco Chronicle:* 18, 67.

Sally Behr: 129.

Belvedere-Tiburon Landmark Society: 19 *upper,* 20, 22, 23 (Philip Planert).

Bolinas Museum: 69.

The Buffalo News/United Press Syndicate, Cartoon by Tom Toles: 242.

California State Highway Commission: 35, 72, 73.

Robert Campbell: *ii, iii,* 190.

Richard Charter: 240 (Martin L. Nelson).

County of Sonoma: 192.

Martin Griffin Archives: 4, 5 (Ken Rice), 6 (Ken Rice), 7, 8, 10, 16, 17, 21, 24 *lower,* 25, 32, 36, 37, 38, 41, 42, 43, 46, 52, 65 (Les Walsh), 76, 77, 78, 80, 102, 109, 110, 113, 114, 119, 120, 122, 124, 125, 126, 129, 132, 133, 136, 138, 141, 142, 144, 163 (Richard Erskine), 165, 167 *lower,* 170, 172 *upper right,* 177, 179, 188, 195, 201, 206, 207, 208, 209, 211, 216, 218, 219, 221, 222, 224, 225, 228, 234, 239, 241, 244, 247, 248.

Robert Griffin: 189.

Healdsburg Historical Museum: 160, 174, 186.

Bettylou Hutton: 154.

Independent Journal: 49, 64, 84, 142, 147 (Jim Kean).

Robert Janover: 191.

Steve Kearsley, *San Francisco Chronicle:* 214, 215.

John Kelly: 33, 96, 98, 112, 118, 133.

Martye Kent: 166, 167 *upper* (Clifford S. Lawrence).

Bill Kortum: 181.

Gaye LeBaron: 180.

George Livermore: 26.

Dewey Livingston: 178 *lower.*

Laurel Marcus: 203, 218, 245.

Marin Conservation League: 100, 101.

Marin County Library, Anne T. Kent Room: 107.

Marin Medical Society: 51 *left.*

Marin Municipal Water District: 143.

North Marin County Water District: 117.

Pacific Sun: 60, 168.

John Peterson: 156, 159.

George Peyton: 135.

Planning and Conservation League: 171.

Art Poulin: 199.

Jeanne Price: 24 *upper,* 127.

Pt. Reyes Light: 137.

Anne Ransome: 196.

Bill Ring: 183.

River Network: 223 (Washington State Historical Society).

George Rockrise: 238.

Santa Rosa Public Utilities District: 220.

Save San Francisco Bay Association: 9.

Charles Schulz, United Media: 79.

Sonoma County Water Agency: 194.

Sonoma Land Trust: 232, 235.

Stanford M.D. Magazine: 62, 85, 111.

Christina Taccone, *San Francisco Daily Journal:* 176, 178, 204.

Tom Thorner: 140.

Trout Unlimited: 226 (Brian Hines).

US Army Corp of Engineers: 184, 187.

Edgar Wayburn: 128.

Clerin Zumwalt: 2, 34, 39, 45, 54, 59, 63, 82, 134, 237.

Loyal Martin Griffin, Jr., MD, MPH, was born in Ogden, Utah, on July 23, 1920. He has had a distinguished medical and wildlife preservation career spanning forty years and including a major role in creating some of the most magnificent wildlife sanctuaries in North America.

Educated in the Oakland, California, public schools, he graduated from the University of California in Berkeley in 1942 with a degree in zoology. After working in the Richmond shipyards on night shifts, he made enough money to enroll at Stanford Medical School, where he received his medical degree in 1946. He served as a Captain in the US Army Medical Corps at the end of World War II.

Dr. Griffin interned at Stanford Hospital in San Francisco, and practiced in Marin County for seventeen years. There he helped start the Ross Valley Clinic, Ross General Hospital, Kentfield Psychiatric Hospital, and The Tamalpais retirement center. He served as chief of medicine at both Marin General and Ross Hospitals, and was certified as a diplomate of the American Board of Internal Medicine in 1953.

In 1961, under Griffin's leadership, Audubon Canyon Ranch was created, and grew to include large wildlife sanctuaries on Bolinas Lagoon, Tomales Bay, and Sonoma Creek. Ranch purchases of key parcels helped to protect the area surrounding the Point Reyes National Seashore from development. Griffin was a co-founder of The Environmental Forum of Marin and also helped establish a wildlife preserve as part of the Haleakala National Park at Kipahulu, Maui. In 1973 he was elected a director of the Marin Municipal Water District.

Wildlife work in Nepal whetted his interest in public health, and he returned to UC School of Public Health for a Master's Degree in 1972. Dr. Griffin served for fifteen years as Public Health Director at the Sonoma State Hospital for developmental disorders in Glen Ellen. In 1980 he was appointed Chief of the Hepatitis B, and later AIDS, Task Force for the eleven State Hospitals. On his retirement, he was given the Governor's Award for his successful Hepatitis B Immunization Program.

In 1975, Dr. Griffin founded Hop Kiln Winery on the Russian River near Healdsburg. To protect the river and to encourage watershed management plans for all of California's rivers, he founded the Russian River Task Force in 1990, the Russian River Environmental Forum, and co-founded Friends of the Russian River. He and his wife Joyce established the Griffin Russian River Riparian Preserve in 1990.

Dr. "Marty" Griffin has long combined his passion for steelhead fly fishing, wildlife, and the environment with his skills in medicine and epidemiology. In numerous articles about his career, he has been called the "environmental physician," "the nature doctor," and "the doctor with mud on his shoes." He has four daughters and six grandchildren.